FINANCIAL

INTELLIGENCE

VOLUME ONE

WORTH MAGAZINE · ESTABLISHED 1992

About the Worth Leading Wealth & Legal Advisors
Every firm and individual featured here has been vetted by *Worth* researchers and analysts at PaladinRegistry.com, a leading information services company founded by Jack Waymire, author of *Who's Watching Your Money: The 17 Paladin Principles for Selecting a Financial Advisor*. To be considered for the *Worth* program, these professionals allow our analysts to screen and evaluate their credentials and ethics. **The participating advisors help to underwrite the production cost of the magazine.**

The Worth Leading Wealth & Legal Advisor admittance process is based on, but not limited to, the Advisor's experience, education, certifications, fiduciary status, compliance record, wealth management services, methods of compensation and scope of current business, with all information and data provided to *Worth* and Paladin Registry by each Advisor. All information and data are not independently verified by Paladin Registry and all relevant background checks, due diligence and investigation into any such claims, information and data must be solely and exclusively done by the Investor or Potential Investor. The Investor or Potential Investor, and all members of the General Public, agree to hold *Worth* and Paladin Registry harmless and to indemnify *Worth* and Paladin Registry against any losses or civil claims of any nature regarding reliance on any claim, information or data provided by any Advisor located via this book, the magazine or on www.worth.com. While the data, information and claims provided by any Advisor and published are potential characteristics that may assist an Investor or Potential Investor to make an intelligent, careful and knowing decision regarding the selection of such Advisor, all such data and information must be independently investigated by the Investors or Potential Investors. While a certain percentage of Advisors who apply for admittance to the program voluntarily withdraw or are declined for various reasons, all Investors and Potential Investors must still complete an independent investigation of the Advisor prior to placing any assets with Advisor, buying the sales recommendations of Advisor, or following Advisor's advice. *Worth* and Paladin Registry do not represent that the financial professionals profiled in this book will produce superior results compared to professionals who are not profiled in the book. Financial professionals profiled in the book are not endorsed or recommended by *Worth* or Paladin Registry. Investors and Potential Investors use the information to screen and contact the advisors and are solely responsible for the decision to select particular advisors.

Library of Congress Control Number: 2010939687
ISBN-13: 978-0-9800398-4-9
ISBN-10: 0-9800398-4-3

THE EVOLUTION OF FINANCIAL INTELLIGENCE

From the publishers of Worth Magazine
www.worth.com

Sandow Media LLC
Corporate Headquarters
3731 NW 8th Avenue
Boca Raton, FL 33431
www.sandowmedia.com

Printed in the United States of America
10 9 8 7 6 5 4 3 2 1

FINANCIAL INTELLIGENCE

VOLUME ONE

ADVICE, INSIGHT AND COUNSEL FROM WORTH MAGAZINE'S LEADING WEALTH ADVISORS AND ATTORNEYS

More than 60 essays written exclusively for Worth Magazine
on wealth management topics relating to:

FAMILY ISSUES

INSURANCE

INVESTING & THE ECONOMY

PHILANTHROPY

RETIREMENT PLANNING

TAX PLANNING

WEALTH TRANSFERENCE & SUCCESSION PLANNING

PLUS:

WHAT TYPE OF ADVISOR IS RIGHT FOR YOU

HOW TO INTERVIEW A FINANCIAL ADVISOR

HOW TO VET YOUR WEALTH ADVISOR

{ FROM THE PUBLISHERS OF WORTH MAGAZINE }

TABLE OF CONTENTS

ABOUT THE WORTH LEADING WEALTH & LEGAL ADVISORS

Every firm and individual featured here has been vetted by *Worth* researchers and analysts at PaladinRegistry.com, a leading information services company founded by Jack Waymire, author of *Who's Watching Your Money: The 17 Paladin Principles for Selecting a Financial Advisor*. To be considered for the *Worth* program, these professionals allow our analysts to screen and evaluate their credentials and ethics. **The participating advisors help to underwrite the production cost of the magazine.**

The Worth Leading Wealth & Legal Advisor admittance process is based on, but not limited to, the Advisor's experience, education, certifications, fiduciary status, compliance record, wealth management services, methods of compensation and scope of current business, with all information and data provided to Worth and Paladin Registry by each Advisor. All information and data are not independently verified by Paladin Registry and all relevant background checks, due diligence and investigation into any such claims, information and data must be solely and exclusively done by the Investor or Potential Investor. The Investor or Potential Investor, and all members of the General Public, agree to hold *Worth* and Paladin Registry harmless and to indemnify *Worth* and Paladin Registry against any losses or civil claims of any nature regarding reliance on any claim, information or data provided by any Advisor located via this book, the magazine or on www.worth.com. While the data, information and claims provided by any Advisor and published are potential characteristics that may assist an Investor or Potential Investor to make an intelligent, careful and knowing decision regarding the selection of such Advisor, all such data and information must be independently investigated by the Investors or Potential Investors. While a certain percentage of Advisors who apply for admittance to the program voluntarily withdraw or are declined for various reasons, all Investors and Potential Investors must still complete an independent investigation of the Advisor prior to placing any assets with Advisor, buying the sales recommendations of Advisor, or following Advisor's advice. *Worth* and Paladin Registry do not represent that the financial professionals profiled in this book will produce superior results compared to professionals who are not profiled in the book. Financial professionals profiled in the book are not endorsed or recommended by *Worth* or Paladin Registry. Investors and Potential Investors use the information to screen and contact the Advisors and are solely responsible for the decision to select particular Advisors.

FOREWORD

BY RICHARD BRADLEY

WORTH EDITOR IN CHIEF

Welcome to Financial Intelligence. We hope you find the information inside explanatory, insightful and useful. Those are the goals that all of us at *Worth* have for the magazine, and the same is true here.

What's this book about? Simple. In part, it's a guide to issues that high net worth investors confront—or should confront—as they look for the right person to manage and protect their wealth. For many people, finding the right advisor is a matter of asking a friend for a recommendation. And while this method can work—sometimes—your wealth is too important, not only to you but to future generations of your family, not to employ a more rigorous and thoughtful process. What are the different types of advisors and what does each type really do? What questions should you ask an advisor before signing on with him or her? How do you know that your advisor is ethical? Why is it a mistake to become friends with your advisor?

Questions like these are essential to the growth of your wealth, but many highly intelligent people fail to ask them. The reasons are certainly understandable. Sometimes they find the questions difficult to articulate; sometimes they just don't know what to ask. But a relationship with an advisor should not be lightly entered into, because it involves something very important (financial security) and because it is not easily severed. On the other hand, if you

> **QUESTIONS LIKE THESE ARE ESSENTIAL TO THE GROWTH OF YOUR WEALTH, BUT MANY HIGHLY INTELLIGENT PEOPLE FAIL TO ASK THEM.**

find the right advisor, that relationship can last for fruitful decades and serve as a source of security and peace of mind throughout your life. Much of the material contained herein will help you take that crucial first step: Finding the advisor who's right for you.

This book is also a discussion about some of the many issues and options in wealth management, presented by advisors featured in The Worth Leading Wealth & Legal Advisors program, a special section in each issue of *Worth*. Some of these issues are probably familiar to you, and in the pages ahead you may find different and constructive ways of thinking about them. Some issues presented here may be new to you—but unexpectedly relevant or even urgent. One important caveat: every person's financial situation is different, and there are no one-size-fits all rules. It is our sincere hope that *Financial Intelligence* will invigorate your search for a new advisor or foster a more intelligent and informed dialogue with your current advisor.

Who are they and what exactly do they do?
What you've always wanted to know about financial advisors.

In his book *In Defense of Food: An Eater's Manifesto*, author Michael Pollan sums up the secret to a healthy diet in seven simple words: "Eat food. Not too much. Mostly plants." When it comes to protecting and growing wealth, the adage goes something like this: "Invest. Not too aggressively. With the right kind of advisor." The quest to find the right advisor begins with making sure the business model fits, but financial advice, like food packaging, isn't always properly labeled. Here's a field guide to the professionals clamoring to be your financial advisor.

ACCOUNTANTS: Certified public accountants (CPAs) are regulated by state authorities and have expertise in tax planning, filing income tax returns, and preparing personal and corporate financial statements. In recent years, CPAs have begun expanding into other areas of financial planning, including investments. The American Institute of Certified Public Accountants (AICPA) offers a Personal Financial Specialist (PFS) designation to the growing number of CPAs wishing to demonstrate specialized proficiency in financial planning. To qualify, CPAs must be members in good standing of AICPA and complete educational and testing requirements.

Find an accountant with a PFS designation online at www.aicpa.org/credentialsrefweb/PFSCredentialSearchPage.aspx.

ATTORNEYS: Lawyers must pass a bar examination in the state where they practice and, in the context of financial advice, typically specialize in trust, estate or tax planning. Often attorneys partner with investment advisors, brokerage firms and financial planners to refer business to each other. Trust and estate lawyers draft trusts, handle trust disputes, and write wills and powers of attorney as well as comprehensive estate plans. Many attorneys who specialize in tax and estate planning work are solo practitioners or part of a larger firm with many specialties. Still, there are several well-known national and international private client law firms focused exclusively on the personal, business and even charitable needs of wealthy individuals and families. Private client law firms may also handle transactions that involve a family business or family office, as well as litigation, family and employment law.

The American College of Trust and Estate Counsel has a website featuring attorneys who have made substantial contributions to the field of trust and estate law. Visit www.actec.org/public/roster/FindFellow.asp.

BROKERS: Like "investment advisor," "broker" is a legal term that refers to a professional who buys and sells securities on behalf of a client. (The term "broker/dealer" describes firms that also sell securities they own.) In addition to being regulated by state securities commissioners and the SEC, brokers are subject to oversight by the Financial Industry Regulatory Authority (FINRA), a self-regulatory body. Brokers are generally not considered to owe a fiduciary duty to their clients. Instead, they must recommend "suitable" investments, a generally weaker standard. The lines are blurry, however; some brokers may also be investment advisors, and the advice they provide on certain products and services may be held to the higher fiduciary standard. Brokers are legally called "registered representatives," but may also call themselves "financial advisors," "financial consultants" or "investment consultants." The term "wirehouse broker" refers to the large, national firms. Independent broker/dealers, by contrast, are stand-alone operations that affiliate with a national broker/dealer for infrastructure and investment support. Discount brokers tend to charge lower commissions than do full-service rivals, but the trade-off can be no-frills service.

To vet a broker online, go to www.finra.org/Investors/ToolsCalculators/BrokerCheck/index.htm

FINANCIAL PLANNERS: Although it's not a term defined in any law or regulation, "financial planner" commonly refers to advisors who develop and implement comprehensive financial plans based on an analysis of long-term goals, including investments, estate planning, tax planning, insurance and even debt management. Caveat emptor: Some 90 different professional designations in existence today are designed by various entities to convey expertise in some or all aspects of financial planning. Not all of them are credible; still fewer may be relevant to your situation. The most widely respected designation is Certified Financial Planner (CFP). These advisors must pass a comprehensive financial planning exam; abide by a code of ethics, which includes adhering to a fiduciary standard; and comply with certain practice standards. Most financial planners are investment advisors, but the reverse is not necessarily true. Some financial planners also call themselves "wealth managers," especially those aiming for higher net worth clients. Financial planners may be fee-based, meaning they charge both commissions and fees, or fee-only.

You can find an advisor with a CFP designation at **www.cfp.net/search**

INSURANCE AGENTS: Insurance agents—many of whom are also financial planners—are licensed and regulated at the state level and tend to work on commission. Independent insurance agents sell policies for more than one insurance company; exclusive agents represent a single company. Some large national and international insurers coordinate their services to high net worth individuals and families through dedicated private client groups, which offer advice and underwriting for property, casualty, life and long-term care polices, and can advise on the integration of insurance into estate planning.

INVESTMENT ADVISORS: This legal term describes advisors who provide advice on investments and are registered with state securities regulators or with the SEC if they have more than $25 million under management. Investment advisors are typically paid based on a percentage of assets under management, not commissions on transactions, and must provide certain up-front disclosures to investors. Most importantly, investment advisors owe a "fiduciary duty" to their clients and are thus legally bound to put clients' interests first. In practice, this means investment advisors must have a reasonable basis for the investment decisions they make and ensure that those decisions are consistent with a client's strategy and objectives. Most investment advisors are small businesses that operate independently of big financial services firms. They may also call themselves financial advisors, money managers, asset managers, investment managers, investment counselors, portfolio managers or registered investment advisors (RIAs).

To research basic information about an advisor, visit **www.adviserinfo.sec.gov**

INVESTMENT CONSULTANTS: These advisors specialize in evaluating, selecting and managing other investment advisors rather than the underlying securities. Some earn a percentage of the assets under advisement; others charge an hourly or project fee. Consultants typically serve institutional investors, but some also cater to ultra-wealthy individuals and families with sizeable portfolios.

MULTIFAMILY OFFICES: For individuals and families with more than $20 million to invest, multifamily offices provide wealth management services with a focus on the protection and growth of financial assets and the preservation of family heritage. Traditional services such as investment, tax and financial management are often supplemented with asset protection, financial education and philanthropic services. Multifamily offices have typically evolved from a single-family office that added new clients to exploit economies of scale. Clients benefit from cost savings, group purchasing, an alignment of interests and the advantages of being a client rather than the manager of what is essentially a financial services business. A single-family office may require as much as $50 million to $100 million in assets in order to be viable.

PHILANTHROPIC ADVISORS: If your commitment to philanthropy has grown beyond your ability to manage it, a philanthropic advisor can help. Philanthropic advisors can coordinate the start-up activities of a family foundation with your legal, tax and financial advisors to ensure that your charitable efforts are integrated with your overall financial plan. They can also provide assistance with everything from developing a family philanthropy mission statement and goals, to researching and recommending specific grants, to helping manage the nuts and bolts of a charitable foundation, including advice on bylaws, governance and board and grantee communications.

PRIVATE BANKERS: Private banking dates back to 2000 BC, when the first private banking system recorded was established in Babylon. In Switzerland, where most private bankers can trace their origins back to the 18th century, when King Louis XVI of France appointed the Genevese private banker Jacques Necker head of the royal treasury, the term has legal significance: It refers exclusively to firms structured as private partnerships in which at least one partner has unlimited liability for the bank's obligations. Outside of Switzerland, all manner of firms, from commercial bankers to trust bankers to wirehouse brokers, refer to themselves as private bankers or as providers of private banking services. The common thread: All are aiming to serve high net worth and ultra high net worth investors. Another common thread among firms that call themselves private banks is the service model. Typically, a relationship manager serves as the point of contact and coordinates advice from various parts of the bank or firm, including investments, trusts, philanthropic services, insurance and tax planning.

What to Ask when hiring a financial advisor

Entrusting your hard-earned assets to a financial advisor may always be in part an act of faith. But doing so blindly—as Bernie Madoff's clients will attest—can have disastrous consequences. With more than 650,000 registered advisors in the United States alone, avoiding the crooks, the incompetents or even just the mediocre takes serious research. Finding an advisor who provides the unbiased advice you need requires a significant investment of time, some introspection and a willingness to ask tough questions. Advisors who are serious about your business won't hesitate to provide complete answers—in writing.

What to Ask Yourself …

1 What level of financial and investment advice do I need? Am I looking for investment ideas alone— or sophisticated financial planning services that might include wealth forecasting, estate planning or creating a charitable trust?

2 What kind of relationship am I seeking? Am I comfortable delegating discretionary authority so that an advisor can manage my money directly, or would I prefer to retain ultimate control of trading decisions?

3 What type and frequency of communications with my advisor do I need to be comfortable? Am I content to speak with somebody by phone, or would I prefer regular face-to-face meetings with my primary advisor to review overall progress?

What to Ask Potential Advisors …

1 Are you a broker or a registered investment advisor or both? When managing my account(s), are you required by law to put my interests first? If so, will you acknowledge your fiduciary duty to me in writing? If not, how will you acknowledge your conflicts of interest when providing me with investment recommendations?

2 How are you and your staff paid to advise me— fees, commissions or both? How, if at all, do money managers or other service providers compensate you for any products you might recommend to me?

3 What is your investment philosophy? How is it different from other firms or advisors?

4 What is your past performance? What are the drivers of this performance?

5 What benchmarks will we use to evaluate the performance of my accounts? What other qualitative and quantitative measures will we employ to review the quality of your advice?

6 How many clients do you work with and what level of attention can I expect? How often will we meet to review my accounts? How frequently will I receive written reports on my portfolio?

7 What is your educational background? What professional designations, if any, do you hold and what do they mean?

8 How many years of financial experience do you have and how long have you worked as a financial advisor?

9 Describe your typical client. Please provide me with three current clients whom I may contact for a reference.

10 Do you keep your clients' assets at a reputable, independent custodian? Does an independent, licensed, brand-name accounting firm audit your financial statements? Whom may I contact at these institutions to verify your relationship?

11 Have you ever been sued by a client? If so, what was the outcome?

12 Have you ever been disciplined by an industry or government regulator? If so, why? If you are an investment advisor, can you provide Parts 1 and 2 of your Form ADV*?

Asking tough questions like these isn't easy. But even if you plan to delegate complete authority to a financial advisor, you can never abdicate responsibility for ensuring that the relationship remains productive. Schedule quarterly check-ins with your advisor—and be willing to make changes as circumstances warrant. After all, it's your money. Ⓦ

*Investment advisors must file Form ADV with the U.S. Securities and Exchange Commission and/or state securities regulators. Part 1 includes information about an advisor's education, business and disciplinary history within the last 10 years and is available online at adviserinfo.sec.gov. Part 2 details information on services, fees and investment strategies, and should be obtained directly from any advisor with whom you are considering working.

A former wealth manager, Jack Waymire is the author of *Who's Watching Your Money? The 17 Paladin Principles for Selecting a Financial Advisor* and the founder of paladinregistry.com, an advisor evaluation and documentation website for high net worth investors.

WHY YOU
SHOULDN'T LIKE
YOUR FINANCIAL ADVISOR

Because friendship and money don't mix.

You've probably read more than you ever expected to about Bernie Madoff, Ponzi schemes and investment rip-offs targeting affluent investors. You probably noticed that the victims shared a common lament about the swindler: "I thought we were friends." Even after the con men have been arrested, many investors remain in denial and shock. They simply can't believe that their "friends" stole from them.

Madoff may be the most infamous of such perpetrators, but he's hardly the only one. In 2009, Daniel Hawke, director of the SEC's Philadelphia office, charged Joseph S. Forte, a Pennsylvania investment advisor, with operating a $50 million Ponzi scheme. "Forte engaged in lies and deception at the expense of innocent investors, many of whom considered themselves to be friends and close acquaintances," Hawke said. "Forte promised outrageous returns and, because of his relationships with investors, he was able to lull them into trusting him with their assets." (In June 2009 Forte pleaded guilty to several related charges.)

A friendship with a financial advisor can be a blessing: Advisors often know intimate details of your life and can help you navigate through difficult transitions. But liking your advisor can also cause you to act in ways contrary to your financial interest. Here's how.

Likeability

It's natural: People prefer to work with professionals they like. Personal relationships make it easier to talk about private financial matters. Consequently, a business relationship evolves into a personal one. (Or, sometimes, the other way around.)

Trust

We want to like our advisors because we have to disclose personal information to them. But advisors also want us to like them. Why? Because liking fosters trust, and trust makes it easier to sell clients investment products. We tend to be less skeptical about recommendations from people we trust. That may work if the trust is based on a track record of positive results. But affection is no substitute for due diligence.

Vigilance

Just because you like an advisor doesn't mean that the person is competent and ethical. You may like the person for the wrong reasons—charm, a sense of humor, an easygoing style—when what counts is his ability to make money for you.

Results

If you like your advisor, you're more likely to tolerate bad results—and don't think your advisor doesn't know that.

Let's say that your advisor delivered two years of bad performance. He knows your patience is wearing thin and you may fire him any day. Most advisors will use their relationship with you to buy time. "Give me another quarter," your advisor might say. "Give me till the end of the year."

You have to weigh the value of the relationship against results that may undermine your long-term financial security.

The Quant

If you care too much about the personal relationship, you'll miss out on high-quality advisors who happen to lack sparkling personalities. Some of the best advisors are quantitative, intellectual and analytical—nerdy, even. These qualities won't help their owners win personality contests, but they're great for helping you achieve financial goals.

Minimize Your Risk

Let's face it: You can't help having a relationship with your advisor. You're only human. Besides, a personal connection promotes discussion of sensitive issues—marriage, divorce, children, death—and their financial consequences. Just be careful a personal relationship should never supersede your business relationship: Business comes first. As they say in Washington, if you want a friend, get a dog. Ⓦ

PRIVATE

INVESTIGATIONS

Want to know if a financial advisor has been the subject of investor complaints? (You should.) Here's how.

One way to assess advisors' ethics is to visit the website of the organization responsible for licensing and regulating them (*finra.org*). The industry-funded Financial Industry Regulatory Authority maintains a database of hundreds of thousands of advisors it calls brokers and tens of thousands of broker-dealers who employ or license the brokers.

You can use the BrokerCheck system on finra.org to check out advisors and see if complaints have been filed against them. Unfortunately, BrokerCheck isn't easy to use, and as a result most investors

derive little benefit from it. The best way to access the system is to enter the advisor's CRD (Central Registry Depository) number. But most investors don't know that this number exists and most advisors aren't about to volunteer it. You can also enter the advisor's name, but good luck if your advisor has a common one.

If you do find the advisor you're looking for, the FINRA database provides basic information about previous employers and current licensing. There may be compliance disclosures on the FINRA

record. Some disclosures are extremely important and some should be disregarded. Here's how to tell which is which:

The biggest sign of trouble is if an advisor has made financial restitution to an investor. Knowing that settlement is a permanent blemish on their record, advisors rarely settle unless they have to. A slightly lesser blemish occurs when the advisor's company, but not the advisor, makes a payment to an investor. The company may have approved a product, the advisor sold the product to clients, and later the product proved deficient.

The next most important disclosure comes when a regulatory organization such as FINRA suspends the advisor's licenses and registrations. These advisors can be reinstated in fewer than 12 months, after which it is business as usual. Advisors will never volunteer that they've been suspended.

Some disclosures are frivolous and shouldn't reflect badly on the advisor. Such complaints rarely produce information for investors because advisors and their firms are protected by the service agreements that clients sign.

Finra.org may not be as easy to use as it should be, but it remains an essential resource. Ⓦ

» **Obtain the advisor's CRD number** or full legal name.

» **Go to finra.org** and click on Investors / Broker Check / Start Search.

» **Accept FINRA's terms and conditions** and click the Continue button.

» **Enter the advisor's CRD number,** legal name or the name you know. Click the advisor's name to open the file. Read the content on this page.

» **Click "Get Detailed Report"** to obtain additional information.

» **Click on a second "Get Detailed Report"** under the box that shows if the advisor has one or more disclosures.

» **Read every complaint in the advisor's file.** Who filed the complaint (investor, company, regulatory agency)? How was the complaint resolved? Did the advisor pay restitution to investors or fines to a regulatory agency? Was the advisor suspended for any period of time?

If you think the allegations are serious, discuss them with your current or potential advisor before making any decisions.

THE FINE PRINT

The agreement you sign with a financial advisor is long and tedious.
But not reading it carefully can cost you.

Before becoming a client of a financial advisor, you must sign what's known as a "financial advisory service agreement" provided to you by the advisor. If you're like 90 percent of investors, you don't bother to read the agreement before signing it and turning over your assets. Most likely, your rationale for not reading is, "If I trust the advisor enough to invest, why waste my time reading an endless service agreement?" But that's a dangerous way of thinking.

The term "financial service agreement" is a euphemism for "contract"—in other words, the kind of thing your attorney should review. And if you had an attorney review this legal, binding document, there's a good chance he'd recommend changes before you sign it. Why? Because most agreements aren't written to protect your financial interests, but those of the company that holds the licenses and registrations of your advisor.

Look for the following warning signs before signing your advisor's service agreement.

1 It's Incomprehensible
Many if not most service agreements are several pages long, printed in a tiny font and loaded with legalese. Financial services firms make the task of reading their agreements onerous so you won't read them.

2 Hedge Words
Watch out for hedge words that limit the responsibility of the financial firm and advisor. Examples include: "may," "best efforts," "attempt" and "not responsible." An agreement stocked with hedge words may mean that the firm has no binding responsibility for its advice, products, actions or results.

3 Total Expense
By far the most important information in a service agreement is the total expense to be deducted from your assets. Possible fees include management fees, advisor fees, custodial fees, trading costs, marketing expenses and administrative fees. Make sure this information is clearly delineated.

4 Financial Services
Investors pay fees to advisors for expert advice, planning and investment services. Make sure the services you expect to receive are itemized.

5 Compensation
Another important feature is full disclosure of advisor compensation. This information is more than just a fee schedule. You want to know the source and amount of every dollar the advisor or advisor's firm will earn from investing your assets.

6 Billing Arrangement
Financial firms do not want to bill you because you may not pay the bills. So their agreements give them the power to deduct fees, commissions and expenses from your accounts. Make sure that they do not deduct fees from tax-deferred accounts. Also ensure that the billing frequency is monthly or quarterly and not annually in advance.

7 Discretion
Some agreements give advisors discretionary authority over your assets. This means they can buy and sell investments without your advance approval. Giving discretion to an advisor should be a calculated risk. Will the advisor churn your account? Will smart decisions be made about your assets? Are you comfortable giving up control?

8 Custody
Make sure the agreement names the organization that will have physical possession of your assets. Ideally, the custodian is a third party not owned by the financial firm that is giving you advice or selling you products.

9 Indemnification
Some agreements require you to indemnify your advisor and the firm from any future legal action stemming from their advice, services or results. An indemnification clause may not be legal in your state and SEC regulations prohibit them if your advisor's firm is a registered investment advisor.

End Result: Giving this level of scrutiny to a financial services agreement may take time, but remember, this is the beginning of a long and important relationship. Ⓦ

Advisors are listed here alphabetically by first name.

TABLE OF CONTENTS

INVESTING & THE ECONOMY

PHILANTHROPY

WORKING WITH A FINANCIAL ADVISOR

Note: Advisors are listed here alphabetically by topic and first name.

Fairfield County, CT   **Leading Wealth Advisor**

LLBH Private Wealth Management
Kevin Burns, Partner, Bill Loftus, Partner,
Bill Lomas, CFP®, Partner,
Jim Pratt-Heaney, CIMA®, Partner

" Why is it a good time to use intra-family loans and sales in estate planning? "

By Bill Loftus

Historically low interest rates and asset valuations make this possibly the best opportunity we will see in a generation to employ intra-family loans and sales. In fact, we consider them one of the last great gains in estate planning.

To illustrate just how effectively intra-family loans and sales can preserve your legacy, I am going to create a scenario for a family of five: Mom, Dad, three married children. We will present this family with a pair of challenges:

1. If the parents own a home worth, say, around $3 million, how can they use the home to create wealth for their children, to minimize taxes, and to preserve family relationships?

2. Let us also say the mother has a dynasty trust. How can this family use that trust to create a legacy for the family's grandchildren?

For starters, we will also assume the parents have exhausted their gift tax exemptions. With that option off the table, an LLC would be created that would hold the property. Next, 50 percent of the property would be sold to the three children within the LLC, and then the parents would take back a note.

To meet federal requirements, a strategy like this would have to operate like a real sale or real loan, and here is where the historically low interest rate comes in. In March 2010, the applicable federal rate, calculated monthly by the IRS, had a rate of 0.64 percent for three years, 2.69 percent for three to nine years, and 4.35 percent for nine-plus years. Additionally, over time, these parents can forgive some principal or interest on the loan as long as it is done under the gift tax laws.

The LLC must be treated as a separate business entity. Accordingly, a separate bank account must be established for the LLC and the parents would have to pay fair market value rent to continue to use the property.

Over time Mom and Dad could make partial sales or grants of their LLC interest or shares to the children, so they would have a minority interest in the property at the time of their subsequent deaths. As they sold an interest in the LLC (as opposed to interest in the underlying property), they would be able to discount the $3 million prop-

erty value by as much as 20 percent. And let us say they made improvements in the property and increased its market value to $5 million. The bottom line in this scenario is that this family's tax savings could exceed $2 million on the $5 million value of the home.

To meet challenge number two for this family of five and to create a separate nest egg for the grandchildren, a multigenerational irrevocable life insurance trust (ILIT) would acquire an $11 million life insurance policy on the mom by borrowing a certain amount a year from her dynasty trust. When the mom passes, an $11 million net death benefit would be paid to the ILIT. **Any death benefit remaining, after repayment of the loan to the dynasty trust, would be held in the ILIT and eventually pass to the grandchildren tax free.**

So, the proverbial bottom line in this scenario is that the plan saved just over $2 million in taxes by not gifting the house outright and it created a tax-free benefit to the grandchildren—all for the cost of some minor legal expenses. Ⓦ

"The bottom line in this scenario is that this family's tax savings could exceed $2 million on the $5 million value of the home."
– Bill Loftus

How to reach Bill Loftus

I look forward to discussing how I can help you reach your financial goals. I can be reached directly at 800.700.5524.

Left to right: Jim Pratt-Heaney, Bill Lomas, Kevin Burns, Bill Loftus

About LLBH Private Wealth Management

After 15 years teaching, Jim Pratt-Heaney joined EF Hutton in 1986. He became a vice president at Smith Barney before moving to Merrill Lynch in 1998. He is a certified investment manager analyst and leads LLBH's asset management. Bill Lomas started with Paine Webber in 1981, spent 18 years as a senior vice president at Prudential Securities and Smith Barney and joined Merrill Lynch in 1998. Mr. Lomas, a Certified Financial Planner and chartered retirement planning specialist, leads LLBH's holistic investment planning process. Kevin Burns, whose career began at PaineWebber in 1981, became a senior vice president at Oppenheimer & Co. and Smith Barney before joining Merrill Lynch in 2000. He leads LLBH's new client asset acquisition and client service and contact operation. In 1986, Bill Loftus joined Merrill Lynch then spent 10 years as a senior vice president at Smith Barney before returning to Merrill Lynch in 1998. He leads LLBH's corporate executive advanced wealth planning, lending and alternative investments.

Assets Under Management $600 million (team)	**Compensation Method** Asset-based
Minimum Fee for Initial Meeting None required	**Primary Custodian for Investor Assets** Pershing
Minimum Net Worth Requirement $10 million (for investment services)	**Professional Services Provided** Planning, investment advisory, money management, advanced wealth transfer planning and corporate services
Largest Client Net Worth $100 million	**Association Memberships** Investment Management Consultants Association
Financial Services Experience 120 years (combined)	**Website** LLBHpwm.com **Email** bloftus@llbhpwm.com

LLBH Private Wealth Management   33 Riverside Drive, 5th Floor, Westport, CT 06880   800.700.5524

Los Angeles, CA   **Leading Wealth Advisor**

Charles W. Mason & Associates
Charles W. Mason, CFP®, CLU®, Founder, President
Brent Mason, Vice President

"Would you share with me what goes into the crafting of a strong family mission statement?"

By Charles W. Mason

Planning for a family's successful financial future remains a priority with high net worth individuals, especially for baby boomers, the eldest now reaching 63. Some worry that heirs may waste their inherited good fortune. To limit that possibility, high net worth individuals, as part of their life planning process, should create a personalized family mission statement that functions as a playbook for the family's estate plan.

In the past, traditional wealth managers were reluctant to delve into the personal family dynamics of estate planning, leaving most of that work to attorneys or other counsel. Today times have changed, and well-experienced, independent managers do not just manage a family's investable net worth but help create a well-executed plan and corresponding family mission statement. Some hire psychologists or other professionals to draft this creed, but most wealth managers have educated themselves on the intricacies of drafting and implementing a statement.

The team of planners at Charles W. Mason & Associates educates clients on the need for a mission statement as part of the life planning process. Each new client has a heart-to-heart discussion with the planning team, and central to that discussion is a family's relational estate. Understanding a client's goals for financial as well as nonfinancial assets, such as a horse or an art collection, is key to developing a successful mission statement. The relational estate rests on three fundamental building blocks: genetics, family history and family heritage. The goal is to connect each of these elements and build off their inner workings to develop a client's initial mission statement. Once those values are defined and understood, a high net worth family can expound on those core values and fully adopt a mission statement that adheres to the family's basic set of principles and values.

Developing the mission statement often rests on the shoulders of the eldest family benefactors, but younger family members should not be ignored or kept from planning and implementation discussions. They are often involved in the planning of a statement without being made aware of specific assets of an estate or gifting bequests. Your family's implemented mission plan should be reviewed with advisors and family members at least every few years. In reviewing the mission, a family's goals and aspirations are reaffirmed and may be retooled or refocused. However, the overall core values of the mission statement are never altered.

A well-written family mission statement should focus on healthy family relationships and honor the past in order to better the future generations. The goal of wealth managers should be to develop a mission statement for clients that will be key in implementing a successful long-term life plan. A well-crafted mission statement can significantly affect how a client's estate plan eventually plays out in the lives of inheritors. A successful statement gives a role and importance to all family members and influences how they wish to operate as part of the family. ⓦ

> ## "The relational estate rests on three fundamental building blocks: genetics, family history and family heritage."
> – Charles W. Mason

We prefer our initial consultation with prospective clients to be held face-to-face. Please schedule a complimentary appointment by calling our offices at 888-988-401k.

I NEVER LEAVE HOME WITHOUT...

Charles: Wedding ring, wallet and humility
Brent: Wedding ring, BlackBerry and a positive attitude

WHAT'S ON MY DESK...

Charles: Inspirational books
Brent: Family photos and inspirational quotes

MY HOBBIES ARE...

Charles: Golf, watercolor painting, educational reading and community volunteering
Brent: Skiing, golf, U.S. history and travel

Charles W. Mason

Brent Mason

About Charles W. Mason & Associates

A wealth management and financial planning firm with over 70 years of experience, Charles W. Mason & Associates specializes in unique life planning strategies. Clientele include businesses, multigenerational families and high net worth individuals. Its life planning process ensures each area of a client's life matches stated goals and financial objectives. CWM & Associates advises on a much broader scale than traditional planners and advisors, providing planning solutions based on one's financial and emotional future. CWM & Associates' meticulous planning and exceptional follow-through make a positive difference in the lives of its clients.

Assets Under Management **$300 million**	Compensation Method **Asset-based and hourly fees**
Minimum Fee for Initial Meeting **None required**	Primary Custodian for Investor Assets **Pershing, National Financial Services and Fidelity**
Minimum Net Worth Requirement **$500,000**	Professional Services Provided **Planning, investment advisory and money management services**
Largest Client Net Worth **$150 million**	Association Memberships **FPA, NAIFA**
Financial Services Experience **70+ years**	Website **www.cwmason.com** Email **cwmason@cwmason.com** **brentmason@cwmason.com**

Charles W. Mason & Associates   7474 North Figueroa, Los Angeles, CA 90041   323.254.3072

New York, NY **Leading Wealth Advisor**

Gerson, Guarino & Meisel Group at Morgan Stanley Smith Barney
Jeffrey S. Gerson, Director–Wealth Management, Senior Portfolio
Management Director

" How can the family of a special needs individual effectively plan for that person's future? "

By Jeffrey S. Gerson

Planning for the future of an individual with special needs requires preparation, careful research and experienced professional guidance. Special needs can include physical, mental and emotional conditions caused by accidents, injuries or birth.

Choosing professional advisors may be one of the most important steps you will take in planning for the future of an individual with special needs. The right advisors take the time to understand your situation and help you define your vision for your child. They should also help you understand what to expect during the course of your child's life, and introduce you to resources that can provide you with useful, ongoing assistance. Three advisors you should consider engaging are:

Life Care Planners There are organizations, sometimes referred to as "Life Care Planners," which can help evaluate your individual needs. We have relationships with several of these organizations and assist our clients in arranging for the services of a Life Care Planner.

Trust and Estate Attorneys It is also important to deal with a legal professional who has an expertise in helping individuals with special needs so they can establish the appropriate trusts to meet your family's unique needs. Your attorney's knowledge of methods of obtaining additional benefits, state-specific requirements and special needs

law updates are all critical to the planning process.

Financial Advisors A competent financial advisor should be at the core of your special needs planning process. Among a financial advisor's responsibilities are helping to evaluate available resources, coordinating efforts with other advisors, analyzing strategies, developing a plan, providing trust services and offering funding and investing options.

Three sources of funding to consider for a special needs individual are:

Supplemental Security Income Supplemental Security Income (SSI) and/or Medicaid are often the primary sources of funds for individuals with special needs. In most cases, losing these government resources could be devastating, making protection of benefits an important component of any financial or estate plan.

Outright Bequests and Gifts Many people make direct gifts to disabled individuals during their lifetime, or include provisions for the transfer of assets to the individual in their wills or trusts. Since these assets must be spent for the individual's care, use of the assets by the beneficiary may be minimal and short-lived.

Trusts In many instances, a preferable way to proceed is to create a Special Needs Trust (SNT). As mentioned, an attorney who has an expertise in helping individuals with special needs can establish these trusts. (See sidebar.) Ⓦ

BENEFICIARY NEEDS DETERMINE THE CHOICE OF A SPECIAL NEEDS TRUST (SNT)

A Special Needs Trust (SNT) is created for beneficiaries with special needs. Supplementing government benefits such as SSI and Medicaid, an SNT may be funded with proceeds obtained by beneficiaries through a court proceeding, inheritance, life insurance claim, settlement of a medical malpractice or personal injury case, or a gift. There are two types of SNTs:

A "Third-Party" Special Needs Trust is established for an individual with special needs with funds from someone other than the special needs individual, his or her spouse, or someone legally responsible for the expenses of caring for the individual with special needs.

A "Self-Settled" Special Needs Trust allows an individual with special needs to protect his/her own property received either from a personal injury settlement or other source. There are three types of "self-settled" trusts: a Pay Back Trust, a Qualified Income Trust and a Pooled Trust. When establishing a self-settled SNT, plan early to avoid transfer penalty problems.

"A competent financial advisor should be at the core of your special needs planning process."

– Jeffrey S. Gerson

How to reach the Gerson, Guarino & Meisel Group at Morgan Stanley Smith Barney

The GGM Group can be reached at 212.643.5757.

Left to right: front row–Jeffrey S. Gerson; back row–Shawn P. Landau, Christopher Guarino, Gregory Meisel and Richard DiVenuto

About the Gerson, Guarino & Meisel Group

The Gerson, Guarino & Meisel Group (GGM) is a wealth management team at Morgan Stanley Smith Barney, one of the largest wealth advisory firms in the world. With their 100-plus years of combined advisory and investment experience, the team's partners—Jeffrey S. Gerson, director–wealth management (24 years of experience); Christopher Guarino, senior portfolio management director (19 years); Gregory Meisel, senior vice president–wealth management (15 years); Richard DiVenuto, senior vice president–wealth management (15 years); and Shawn P. Landau, first vice president–wealth management (9 years)—help their clients achieve their most meaningful financial goals. Through an uncompromising commitment to delivering intellectual strength, quality advice and personalized attention, the GGM Group provides an intensely personal experience to high net worth individuals, their families, corporations and charitable institutions.

Assets Under Management
$1.5 billion (as of 03/31/2010)

Minimum Fee for Initial Meeting
None required

Minimum Net Worth Requirement
$3 million

Largest Client Net Worth
$400 million (as of 11/16/09)

Financial Services Experience
100+ years (combined)

Compensation Method
Asset-based fees and commissions (insurance products)

Primary Custodian for Investor Assets
Morgan Stanley Smith Barney

Professional Services Provided
Planning, portfolio management and money management services

Association Memberships **Portfolio Management Institute**

Website **fa.smithbarney.com/ggmgroupsb**

Email **jeffrey.s.gerson@mssb.com**

Gerson, Guarino & Meisel Group at Morgan Stanley Smith Barney | One Penn Plaza, New York, NY 10119 | 212.643.5757

" How does a couple guarantee that a prenuptial agreement is not only fair, but that it will be upheld in a court of law? "

By Judith R. Forman

The notion of putting binding financial arrangements in place before marriage resonates strongly in many situations. Perhaps prospective spouses have already established a business or profession. Maybe they have created or will be inheriting significant assets, or have children from previous marriages. There may even be a concern about protection from debts of the spouse-to-be.

In any of those circumstances, prenuptial agreements can serve as an effective financial planning tool in recognition of the reality that, in every state in the U.S., marriage carries with it certain legal rights and responsibilities which, in the absence of an enforceable agreement to the contrary, will substantially impact income, assets, property rights and liabilities in the event of a divorce. The key to understanding the efficacy of "prenups" resides in understanding their context.

First, they are contracts, which will be governed by state law. This means you need to know whether your state has passed the Uniform Premarital Agreement Act (UPAA), a comprehensive set of laws enacted by more than half of the states in this country, prescribing how property rights may be altered by agreement prior to marriage, or whether non-UPAA statutes and case law will govern

the prenup. You also need to know you may have options for choosing governing law.

Next, you need to understand that to have a prenup upheld, the agreement must have been voluntary and generally must have been negotiated well before the wedding, with both parties represented by independent counsel and with both parties making full disclosure of all facts bearing on income, assets, and liabilities.

Generally the purpose of the prenup is to have one or both spouses give up what otherwise would have been his or her legal rights, so there must be reasonable and fair provisions in return. That said, fairness is always subjective, so be cognizant that the ultimate arbiter of fairness may end up being a court. Public policy and legal precedent in your state should always play an implicit if not express role in guiding negotiations and setting parameters for the agreement.

And finally, the psychological impact of pre-wedding financial negotiations on an intimate personal relationship needs to be understood in all its complexity. Whether the relationship survives and is strengthened or undermined will depend on many factors, including how the entire prenup process is handled, and may serve as a bellwether for the marriage itself. **ⓦ**

SEVEN THINGS YOU NEED TO KNOW ABOUT PRENUPS

01 Among the Uniform Premarital Agreement Act (UPAA) states are CA, IL, TX, NJ and VA.

02 Among statute/case law states are NY, FL, PA, MD and MI.

03 The UPAA can govern a prenup if you live or intend to live in a UPAA state, or will be married in a UPAA state.

04 Child support cannot be waived in a prenup.

05 Some, but not all, states enforce alimony waivers.

06 Prenups can only be modified or revoked by subsequent written agreement, but "sunset" clauses in the agreement can limit the prenup's duration.

07 In some states, a minor legally able to marry can enter into a prenup.

Certified as a Family Law Specialist State Bar of California Board of Legal Specialization

"Marriage carries with it certain legal rights and responsibilities which, in the absence of a contrary enforceable agreement, will substantially impact income, assets, property rights and liabilities in the event of a divorce."

– Judith R. Forman

How to reach Judy Forman

I prefer an initial telephone conversation with prospective clients, followed by a meeting. My assistant will happily schedule a convenient time for both. You can reach her at 310.444.8840.

WHAT'S ON MY DESK...

Coffee mug saying "Things could be worse...we could be trying on SWIMSUITS"; family pix; voodoo doll and pins to help clients remember the curative power of laughter

I NEVER LEAVE HOME WITHOUT...

My BlackBerry, iPod, and black cashmere shawl for the plane

MY HOBBIES ARE...

Travel, travel, travel

About Judith R. Forman

Judith Forman heads a Los Angeles firm representing clients in family law matters that involve complex multi-asset estates, high-income support awards, custody and paternity. Born and raised in Philadelphia, Ms. Forman became an "Angeleno" in 1978 and maintains homes in Los Angeles and her Philly hometown. She is listed annually in the Bar Register of Pre-Eminent Lawyers, Best Lawyers in America, Southern California Super Lawyers and Top 50 Women Lawyers. Ms. Forman has written and lectured extensively on family law topics, including child custody, division of intellectual property, and trial advocacy.

Professional Services Provided
Negotiation, mediation and litigation of family law matters

Education **JD, Villanova University; MA, University of Pennsylvania; BA, University of Pennsylvania; certificate, Sorbonne, Paris**

Legal Experience **34 years**

Email **jrf@familylawcounsel.com**

Bar Admissions
Pennsylvania, 1975; California, 1978; U.S. District Court, Eastern District of Pennsylvania; U.S. District Court, Central District of California; U.S. Court of Federal Claims

Certifications
Certified Family Law Specialist (CFLS), as governed by the State Bar of California Board of Legal Specialization, since 1986

Association Memberships
Association of Certified Family Law Specialists; Beverly Hills Bar Association, Family Law Section; Los Angeles County Bar Association, Family Law Section

The Law Offices of Judith R. Forman P.C.   11355 W. Olympic Boulevard, Los Angeles, CA 90064   310.444.8840

San Francisco Peninsula—
Silicon Valley, CA

**Leading
Legal Advisor**

White Law P.C.   Mary White, JD, EPLS

" How should I make loans to my children to lock in current low interest rates? "

By Mary White

Does this question sound familiar? Your advisors are telling you that this is the perfect environment to pass wealth to your children: Interest rates are low and appreciation is likely. Your children concur. You do not want to set up a trust or other expensive tax structure right now and, quite frankly, do not want to make a gift. You also want to keep open the possibility of getting the money back. What can you do? Show them the promissory note.

THE PROMISSORY NOTE

Yes, these are your kids, but when cash changes hands between parents and children, there should be no confusion about the nature of the transaction: Use a formal written promissory note signed by the child. If you purchase a blank form of a promissory note, be sure to fill in all the blanks: date, principal amount, borrower (debtor) and lender (beneficiary), and, most importantly, the terms. The note terms for repayment trigger the tax consequences and, in 2010, make the intrafamily promissory note an irresistible planning opportunity.

THE NOTE TERMS

The IRS classifies notes as short term (fewer than three years), midterm (three years to less than nine years), and long term (nine years or more). Each month, the IRS publishes allowable (Section 7872) rates in the Applicable Federal Rate table. This past year the rates have hovered around historic lows, making this an ideal time to lock in low rates.

Here is an example: Using May 2010 rates, a parent could loan a child $100,000 at 0.79 percent interest or $790 payable within three years (or $7,900 on a $1 million loan). If the May 2010 loan is a midterm loan, the rates fluctuate slightly depending on the frequency of required interest payments (2.87 percent annually or 2.84 percent quarterly), so the child makes annual interest payments of $2,870 on a $100,000 loan (or $28,700 on a $1 million loan).

LIFE WITH THE NOTE

Even though the IRS is willing to allow interest on intrafamily loans far below commercial rates, debts to children should be treated like third-party obligations. Parents should keep records showing that interest payments are being made in a timely way and properly reported for income tax purposes. Records should also show that the loan principal is likely to be repaid (securing the loan against the child's property is even better).

Although a parent can use the current $13,000 annual gift tax exclusion (or $1 million lifetime gift tax exemption) to forgive principal, the child should keep up the interest payments. Otherwise, you risk the IRS characterizing the transaction as a disguised gift. With interest rates this low, there is really no excuse for a child to miss a payment. In fact, you might consider making interest payments due on your birthday. So, my advice is to lock in these low interest rates now.🕊

"Even though the IRS is willing to allow interest on intrafamily loans far below commercial rates, debts to children should be treated like third-party obligations."

– Mary White

How to reach Mary White

I prefer an initial conversation by phone. Please contact my assistant at 650.854.7950 to schedule a telephone appointment.

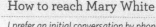

MY FAVORITE ACCESSORY...

My orange briefcase

WHAT MAKES A GOOD CLIENT...

The willingness to become engaged in the process and appreciate the benefits of professional advice

WHAT MAKES A GOOD WEALTH ADVISOR...

The ability to listen, simplify the complex, maintain integrity and inspire confidence... all without judging others

About Mary White

Mary White is known throughout the Peninsula and San Francisco as a favorite trust attorney among sophisticated accountants, investment managers, trust departments and charitable organizations. She is celebrating her 15th year of private practice as the only estate planner on Sand Hill Road. Gaining from her experience of 13 years at historic Pillsbury Madison & Sutro, and as a mother of four children, she offers technical, yet practical, advice. "After 25 years, I still love my work...listening to clients' wishes, applying complexities of trust and tax law to their objectives and then presenting a plan—intricately drafted, simply explained and exceeding expectations."

Professional Services Provided **Estate and gift tax planning; charitable planning; generation skipping tax planning; estate and trust administration and family succession planning**

Education **JD, University of Santa Clara, School of Law; BS, business administration, Menlo College**

Legal Experience **30 years**

Bar Admissions
California State Bar, 1979

Certifications
California Certified Specialist in Estate Planning, Trust and Probate Law

Association Memberships
San Mateo County Bar Association, Silicon Valley Bar Association, Los Angeles County Bar Association

Website
www.orangebriefcase.com

Email
mary@orangebriefcase.com

White Law P.C. | 2200 Sand Hill Road, Suite 220, Menlo Park, CA 94025 | 650.854.7950

"What can be done when dementia strikes?"

By Patricia C. Brennan, CFP®

DOLLARS AND DEMENTIA

Her husband seemed fine—most of the time. He was a CPA by profession, the CFO of a midsize company, known for his quick wit and brilliant mind. She noticed his periods of confusion; tasks that were so routine just a few months ago became challenging, but she did not want the kids to worry. It was one thing when his memory was not the same—easy to write off by saying, "We're at that age now." But when the bank called to alert them that checks were bouncing because he had sent more than $100,000 to an arbitrary charity, she knew she could not ignore the signs anymore.

Dementia support groups are filled with stories like this.

Dollars and dementia: This is the financial equivalent to the perfect storm. Dementia is one of the hardest health issues to detect, primarily because early lapses are just momentary, and family members do not see it or recognize what is going on. According to the Alzheimer's Association,

one in eight persons age 65 and older have one of the variations of dementia. This is not something that happens overnight; Alzheimer's has seven stages, five of which are varying degrees of diminished capacity. It is these middle stages that can be so damaging personally and financially, and they need to be addressed while full capacity is still intact.

Even before a diagnosis is made, it is critical to gather and organize all financial documents. Like any progressive disease, the lapses will occur more frequently, going from moments to hours, then days. The individual can be functional one day, then out of touch the next. Those closest will often miss the cues, sometimes until it is too late and irrevocable financial damage has been done. Another family went into panic mode when they found out their very intelligent father had already seen an attorney to have his will changed. While he appeared quite coherent to the attentive attorney, his afflicted brain had decided that his children were trying to

steal his money. Already a generous member of the community, he decided to leave his entire estate to a small charity to benefit the children of Haiti. When individuals develop dementia, they often become paranoid and irrational. Early contingency planning is essential to seamless care and ongoing financial solvency.

Much has been written about the importance of a living trust and a durable power of attorney, but the practical aspects must be considered even before they come into play. Paramount are the relationships you have with your attorney, CPA and financial advisor. These advisors know you, understand your wishes, and would question a request that seemed out of the ordinary. Like any relationship, it takes some work and commitment, but these persons can protect you—if you let them. Sometimes, one questions the fees paid for financial advice, but trusting the judgment of an advisor who knows you at full capacity can help prevent financial ruin when you are not. ⓦ

ABOUT PATRICIA C. BRENNAN
*Candidates for the Philadelphia Business Journal and Barron's were determined by The Winner's Circle. Candidates were valued on criteria such as assets under management, revenues, experience and record of regulatory compliance and complaints. Candidates were further vetted based on in-depth interviews and discussions with management, peers and customers, as well as professional achievements and community involvement. The Winner's Circle does not receive compensation from participating firms or their affiliates, financial advisors or the media in exchange for rankings. In addition to the criteria used for the Barron's article and the Philadelphia Business Journal, Wealth Manager magazine takes into consideration service to industry organizations and mentoring to others. Presented to 7 percent of wealth managers with five years of experience in the financial services industry, all professions within a market area. Each wealth manager was reviewed for regulatory actions, civil judicial actions and customer complaints. http://www.fivestarprofessional.com/fiveStarAssets/pdfs/GenericResearchWM.pdf
Third-party rankings from rating services or publications are no guarantee of future investment success.
    Working with a highly ranked advisor does not ensure that a client or prospective client will experience a certain level of performance or results. These rankings should not be construed as an endorsement of the advisor by any client nor are they representative of any one client's evaluation.
    The views expressed are not necessarily the views of Royal Alliance Associates Inc., and this material should not be relied upon as investment advice. There are risks inherent in all investments. Investors should seek counsel of their tax professional and investment advisor prior to making any changes.

The Delaware Valley region is defined as the following counties: Pennsylvania—Berks, Bucks, Chester, Delaware, Montgomery, Philadelphia; Delaware—New Castle; Maryland—Cecil; and New Jersey—Atlantic, Burlington, Camden, Cape May, Cumberland, Gloucester, Mercer, Ocean, Salem.

"When individuals develop dementia, they often become paranoid and irrational. Early contingency planning is essential."

– Patricia C. Brennan, CFP®

How to reach Patricia C. Brennan

New clients may contact me at 610.429.9050 to schedule an initial consultation.

MY MOST INFLUENTIAL TEACHER...

William Byrne at Georgetown University

IF I WERE NOT A WEALTH ADVISOR, I'D BE...

An ICU nurse

WHAT MAKES A GOOD WEALTH ADVISOR...

Great listening and influencing with integrity

About Patricia C. Brennan

A graduate of Georgetown University and a Certified Financial Planner, Patricia C. Brennan strives to communicate complex financial concepts in understandable terms. She has frequently been named one of *Barron's* top 100 women financial advisors, as well as one of its top 1,000 financial advisors in America (February 2009)*. Other accolades include: one of America's top 100 independent advisors, *Registered Rep* magazine, November 2007; one of the 50 most influential women in wealth management, *Wealth Manager* magazine, April 2008; number two in the Greater Philadelphia Area, *Philadelphia Business Journal*, October 2008; and five-star wealth manager, *Philadelphia* magazine, November 2009.

Assets Under Management **$300 million**	Compensation Method **Asset-based and fixed fees; commissions (investment and insurance products)**
Minimum Fee for Initial Meeting **None required**	Primary Custodian for Investor Assets **Pershing**
Minimum Net Worth Requirement **$500,000**	Professional Services Provided **Planning and investment advisory services**
Largest Client Net Worth **$70 million**	Association Memberships **Financial Planning Association**
Financial Services Experience **24 years**	Website **www.keyfinancialinc.com** Email **pbrennan@keyfinancialinc.com**

Securities and advisory services offered through Royal Alliance Associates, member FINRA/SIPC. Advisory services offered through Key Financial Inc., a registered investment advisor not affiliated with Royal Alliance Associates.

Key Financial Inc. | 1560 McDaniel Drive, West Chester, PA 19380 | 610.429.9050

Los Angeles, CA   **Leading Wealth Advisor**

**The Zamani Esmailbeigi Zamani Wealth Management
Team at Morgan Stanley Smith Barney**
Reza Zamani, Senior Vice President
Maziar Esmailbeigi, Vice President
Ali Zamani, Financial Advisor

" How can I teach my children to be responsible with money? "

By Morgan Stanley Smith Barney LLC
Courtesy of Reza Zamani, Maziar Esmailbeigi and Ali Zamani

By default, parents are usually the primary source of a financial education. However, many young people may receive allowances—or even sizable inheritances—without a sound base of knowledge in saving, budgeting, investing and financial planning. To help the children in your life develop a responsible attitude about money, it might help to consider these points:

Be a role model. A significant relationship exists between the way children view money and your own spending habits. Instead of viewing money and personal finance as a forbidden topic, discuss your own financial goals and plans. The level and amount of information shared is up to you, but bring the younger generation into at least a portion of your plans. How you deal with money issues—from the monthly bills to planning the family vacation of a lifetime—is important and offers long-lasting lessons about money management and the value of money.

Encourage savings and investments. One of the simplest ways to encourage a responsible attitude about money is to encourage children to save. This could include designating a portion of a child's allowance to a savings account or making gifts of cash directly to an account in the child's name. Discuss account statements together, and stress the concept of paying yourself first with dedicated, regular deposits. For younger children, set modest, attainable savings goals. For older children, encourage the development of a long-term savings plan for the purchase of a large-ticket item such as a computer or a car. Consider an occasional matching grant to encourage regular deposits and to help keep goals visible. Take the time to explain basic investment types such as cash instruments, stocks and bonds. Make investing interesting by engaging in conversation about companies that provide popular children's products such as toys or clothing.

Develop a sense of financial empowerment. Developing responsible spending habits means encouraging well-thought-out choices. Guide and advise rather than dictate how money should be saved and spent. Keep goals visible with pictures, or create charts that plot the growth of funds needed. Take children on window-shopping trips to compare prices and products, and adopt the mind-set that every trip to a store is an exercise leading to a potential purchase. To limit impulse buying, consider instituting a rule that prices and products must be compared at a minimum of three locations.

Give unto others. Involve children in your financial decisions regarding philanthropy. Discuss the merits of gift applications you may have received, and weigh the advantages and limits of each. Explain the tax advantages of charitable giving but, at the same time, stress the altruistic goals of giving. Even a contribution to a canned food drive or the creation of a holiday basket for a needy family can grow into a familywide event. By helping children contribute time or money to a charitable cause, you can teach them that money is important in ways other than personal consumption.

Developing a sound knowledge of basic financial practices can often go a long way toward helping the children in your life achieve lifelong financial security. Ⓦ

> **"Teamwork is the ability to work together toward a common vision. It is the fuel that allows common people to attain uncommon results."**
>
> – Andrew Carnegie

How to reach The Zamani Esmailbeigi Zamani Wealth Management Team

You can reach any member of our team at 888.826.6002.

THE LAST BOOK I READ WAS...

Reza: Outliers: The Story of Success, *by Malcolm Gladwell*
Maziar: Freakonomics, *by Steven D. Levitt and Stephen J. Dubner*
Ali: The Tipping Point, *by Malcolm Gladwell*

WHAT'S ON MY DESK...

Reza: *Pictures of my family*
Maziar: *Pictures of my family*
Ali: *A lot of work, my cup of coffee and a TV tuned to CNBC*

WHAT MAKES A GOOD WEALTH ADVISOR...

Reza: *Someone who listens. God gave us two ears and one mouth; listen first, talk second*
Maziar: *Someone who listens, interprets and helps clients implement a solid financial plan*
Ali: *Being able to listen to clients' goals and help them navigate the road to reaching them*

Left to right: Maziar Esmailbeigi,
Reza Zamani, Ali Zamani

About The Zamani Esmailbeigi Zamani Wealth Management Team

The Zamani Esmailbeigi Zamani Wealth Management Team was formed in 1999. They create life plans and utilize a tactical method of managing assets. Reza Zamani focuses on options strategies to manage portfolio risk and cash flow. He received his BA in business economics from UCSB and is a graduate of UCLA Anderson. Mr. Zamani and his wife, Lauren, reside in Calabasas, Calif., with their two children. Maziar Esmailbeigi focuses on fixed income and implementing structured strategies for risk management. He received his BA in biology from CSUN and lives in Woodland Hills, Calif., with his wife, Michelle, and their two children. Ali Zamani specializes in due diligence of institutional funds and ETFs. He received a BA in Business Economics from UCSB and lives in Brentwood, Calif.

Assets Under Management $250 million	**Financial Services Experience** 25 years (combined)
Minimum Fee for Initial Meeting None required	**Compensation Method** Asset-based fees
Minimum Net Worth Requirement $1 million	**Primary Custodian for Investor Assets** Morgan Stanley Smith Barney
Largest Client Net Worth $250 million	**Association Memberships** Financial Planning Association, Investment Management Consultants Association
	Website http://fa.smithbarney.com/zez **Email** TheZamaniTeam@mssb.com

The Zamani Esmailbeigi Zamani Wealth Management Team
at Morgan Stanley Smith Barney

21600 Oxnard St., Suite 2000   888.826.6002
Woodland Hills, CA 91367

"How serious is the threat of a multimillion-dollar lawsuit, and how do I protect myself?"

By Bob Courtemanche

The wealthier you are, the more attractive you are as a lawsuit target. Protect yourself by knowing both the reasons you could be sued and the insurance available for absorbing the risk.

Most individuals recognize the prospect of someone slipping and falling on their property as a liability risk, but suits can also arise when:

- **Your dog bites someone**
- **A guest is injured in an accident in your swimming pool**
- **A guest at your party becomes inebriated and causes an accident driving home**
- **Someone views your comment at a community meeting as character defamation**
- **You serve on the board of a charity, and the organization and board are sued**
- **A nanny you let go claims discrimination**

Even if the claims are frivolous, you could spend hundreds of thousands of dollars defending yourself. Successful plaintiffs could cost you millions. The 2007 data from Jury Verdict Research shows that 16 percent of personal injury awards exceeded $1 million; 6 percent exceeded $5 million.

Do not assume the liability coverage in your homeowners and auto insurance will fully protect you. Those policies typically do not offer options higher than $500,000. If you are hit with a multi-million-dollar settlement, you will have to pay the difference. In some cases, such as a nanny who sues for discrimination, the policies offer no coverage at all.

Adequate protection often requires an umbrella policy, which provides liability coverage over and above your homeowners and auto policies. Coverage limits from $1 million up to $100 million are available from carriers that specialize in serving individuals with substantial assets. Consult with your insurance or financial advisor to determine the appropriate amount for you. Be sure to consider your real estate equity, value of personal possessions and savings and investments, as well as future income stream from employment, because lawsuits can jeopardize all sources of your net worth. Because some lawsuits can threaten your reputation, too, the best umbrella policies will also cover the cost of a public relations firm for crisis management.

Ask about specialized coverage if you employ domestic staff or serve on the board of a nonprofit organization. These activities bring special risks. Disgruntled current and former domestic employees may file baseless suits alleging discrimination, sexual harassment or other wrongful employment practices with the hope that you will settle to avoid legal expenses. Employment-practices liability insurance will cover such cases, including defense costs. Volunteering on the board of a charitable, cultural or community organization can expose you to similar suits brought by paid staff. Because board members can be held personally liable when the insurance carried by the organization is inadequate, consider directors and officers liability coverage to acquire proper protection.

If you are lucky, you will find one carrier that can underwrite all the policies I have mentioned as part of a coordinated package—an approach that minimizes coverage gaps and wasteful duplications across policies. ⓦ

TAKING SMALL RISKS CAN HELP YOU MINIMIZE THE BIG RISKS

Will paying $1,000 to repair your car change your lifestyle? Will $5,000? Many affluent people carry deductibles of $500 or less for their auto or homeowners insurance when they could save hundreds, perhaps thousands, of dollars in annual premiums by choosing a higher amount—an amount they can easily pay. They are overinsuring at the low end of risk.

Meanwhile, there is a good chance that their insurance will not cover the full cost of rebuilding their home if it burns down. And they may not have the right level and types of liability coverage to withstand financially ruinous lawsuits. They are underinsuring at the high end of risk.

A savvy approach to optimize your insurance program is to absorb as much risk as you can tolerate on the low end so that you can offset the cost of sufficient protection on the high end.

"Protecting your net worth from catastrophic loss must involve an understanding of personal liability risk as well as investment risk."

– Bob Courtemanche

How to reach Bob Courtemanche

Please feel free to contact me at *BobC@acegroup.com*.

MY HOBBIES ARE...

Sailing, hiking and collecting sports memorabilia

MY FAVORITE CAUSE...

I am a trustee at the Bonnie Brae School for Boys in Liberty Corner, N.J.; it is a residential treatment center that prepares at-risk boys to become responsible citizens

WHAT'S ON MY DESK...

Pictures of my wife, two sons and a colleague lost on 9/11

About Bob Courtemanche

Bob Courtemanche, CEO of ACE Private Risk Services, has 30 years of personal lines insurance industry experience, with a focus on leading businesses that insure the assets of high net worth clients. Prior to joining ACE, he served in leadership positions for several global carriers, where he was instrumental in establishing insurance practices for clients with substantial wealth. He has been featured in *Worth* magazine's "Expert Forum," *Fox Business News*, *Fortune* magazine and numerous insurance industry publications. He was the keynote speaker at the American Society of Appraisers meeting in 2007.

ACE Private Risk Services provides flexible insurance solutions that can be tailored to the unique needs of high net worth individuals and families. Sold through independent agents and brokers, its products and services can enhance family security and protect wealth by handling a wide range of needs for homeowners, automobile, valuable collections, pleasure boat and yacht, and umbrella liability insurance—often within an easy-to-manage package policy. ACE Private Risk Services is part of the ACE Group. Headed by ACE Ltd. (NYSE: ACE), the ACE Group's core operating insurance companies are rated A+ (superior) by A.M. Best Comp. and A+ (strong) by Standard & Poor's. To learn more, go to www.aceprivateriskservices.com.

Insurance Services Experience	Website	Email
30 years	www.aceprivateriskservices.com	BobC@acegroup.com

ACE Private Risk Services | 7 Giralda Farms, Madison, NJ 07940 | 973.443.2800

Chicago, IL | **Leading Wealth/Insurance Advisor**

Lane McVicker LLC
Brett Woodward, Senior Vice President and Member
Kelley Danis, Assistant Vice President
Christopher Shanks, Account Executive
Julie Lovall, Associate Manager

"Why is my home insured for more than its market value?"

By Brett Woodward

It is no secret that the market value of nearly all real estate, including that of luxury residences, suffered in the economic meltdown. In fact, according to the Federal Housing Finance Agency (FHFA), in 2008 the average resale value for homes in the United States dropped 11 percent.

But here is yet another irony of our new economic paradigm, one you may have encountered if you reviewed your homeowners insurance recently: While the market value of your home has most likely decreased, the cost of your insurance to replace that home has increased. Logic would dictate that anything that has lost value would cost less to insure. So why the disparity?

While there has long been little correlation between market value and replacement cost, over the past 20 years the gap has become larger than ever. The reason can be explained in two words: construction costs.

For example, home values dropped 11 percent in 2008, but the FHFA reports the cost to repair a property after a loss increased by 5.8 percent. In 2009, according to the Chartis Private Client Group, building trends fluctuated, and by year's end home building costs were up less than 1 percent. However, home values in 2009 remained flat to down, so the value/replacement disparity continued to widen.

All of that said, you may still ask, "OK, I get that, but if I have one of my houses on the market for $4.4 million, why does my insurance policy show its replacement cost to be nearly double that amount?"

Before actually seeing your home, I might ask you a couple questions to confirm the validity of that replacement cost.

Was the home built more than 50 years ago?

If the home were totally or partially destroyed, would you want it rebuilt exactly as it was before the catastrophe?

If you said yes to both questions, then comparable materials, that is, those manufactured currently, are most likely not an option. Think of it this way: You cannot match hardwood floors installed in the 1920s, except with hardwood from the 1920s.

For example, a client of ours had his home insured for $1.2 million. We put it through an online estimator, and it was shown to be worth $1.9 million. Then the insurance company determined replacement cost would be $2.5 million. What was driving the cost? It was an older home with solid brick, a tile roof and many other details and materials from the period when it was built. It was originally insured as if being rebuilt with today's materials.

Knowing this, you may still say, "I do not care about all of that. I want the amount of my policy to match the market value of my house."

First off, top insurance companies would not allow you to underinsure your house. And if you decide to take the money and not rebuild, the company will not give you full value. It might give you a cash-out option if you insure the house for full value.

As your insurance advisor, here is another question, perhaps the most important of all, that I would ask: What is the value of your house to you? If you treasure its most beautiful details and qualities, would you want to replace them with anything less if it suffered a total or partial catastrophic loss? ⑩

"While the market value of your home has most likely decreased, the cost of your insurance to replace that home has increased."

– Brett Woodward

WHAT MAKES A GOOD INSURANCE ADVISOR...

A team focused on the needs of the individual, delivering product with compassion and competency

WHAT MAKES A GOOD CLIENT...

Someone who appreciates above-average product delivery and service

Left to right: Brett Woodward, Kelley Danis, Julie Lovall, Christopher Shanks

About the Lane McVicker Team

Lane McVicker is a personal-lines insurance agency headquartered in New York City, with offices across the country. The agency specializes in personal insurance, ranging from homeowners and automobile insurance to specialty lines, such as coverage for yachts, aircraft, fine art and antique cars. Lane McVicker has agency appointments with a number of leading insurance markets, including ACE, Chartis, Chubb, Fireman's Fund and PURE. Brett Woodward, who began his career at Chubb in appraisal management, is a senior vice president at Lane McVicker and leads a four-person team that combines sales and service. He has management experience with PLI Brokerage and holds a BS from the University of Scranton. Mr. Woodward has appeared frequently before wealth planning professionals. Kelley Danis, assistant vice president, holds a BS from Vanderbilt University and began her career at AON. Christopher Shanks, account executive, earned a BS from Illinois State University, has worked at PLI Brokerage and is completing the certified insurance counselor designation. Julie Lovall, associate manager, has a BS from Missouri State University, and holds the designation of certified insurance service representative.

Largest Client Net Worth	Insurance Services Experience	Website	Email
$500 million	50 years (combined)	www.lanemcvicker.com	brett.woodward@lanemcvicker.com

Lane McVicker LLC | 222 South Riverside Plaza, Suite 825, Chicago, IL 60606 | 312.704.7000

" How can I properly build my property and casualty insurance program with the right broker? "

By Bruce Gendelman, JD, Chairman, and Joseph Gendelman, President and CEO

You, your family and the assets you hold are targets for lawsuits and safety issues. You need a program in which you have absolute trust; one that will provide your family with choices, control, convenience and confidentiality. A recent Russ Prince survey stated what very wealthy families are most concerned about when dealing with lawsuits and safety:

- Theft of property 78%
- Lawsuits because of
  their wealth 54%
- Lawsuits from people
  injured on their property . . .53%
- Being kidnapped 35%

Look past the insurance buzz words to get to what really matters. For example, "service orientated"—how is that really defined? "Gaps in coverage"—how do you know? "Value-based coverage"—can you really trust a broker to give you this? **Here are the tangible ways to track your broker's service, risk-management skills and competitive pricing:**

Proven client track record. Ask the broker to provide comparable references, including comparable clients who have left the agent.

Education and experience excellence. Your broker must accept responsibility for your risk identification, assessment, analysis and mitigation.

Stable executive and support staff. You should be working with an extensive and highly proficient technical and service staff—not a service center or agency with high turnover.

Concierge approach to service. Your account commands 24/7 access, 365 days a year, with a fast and flexible response.

Highly rated insurance company choices. Your broker should make agnostic carrier choices based on a full market analysis with financially stable insurance companies.

Documentation. Insist on detailed, written proposals and annual service plans.

No conflict of interest with clients. The emphasis should be placed on your insurance program, and the broker's expertise in that niche area. Avoid brokers who offer additional services outside of the property and casualty insurance arena.

Full compensation disclosure policy. Ask for it in writing.

If your broker can demonstrate the above, you have found someone experienced and independent, with a laser focus on his or her clients' individualized needs.

Only a handful of personal insurance companies—ACE Private Risk Services, Chartis Private Client Group, Chubb and Fireman's Fund—truly specialize in all major aspects of the high and ultra high net worth insurance markets on a large-scale national and international basis (other insurance companies may have some of this business in various ways). From unique coverage options (insuring multiple homes located across the country, policies for collections that travel on exhibit, etc.) to service enhancements (complimentary background checks for private staff, assistance with hurricane pre-planning protection and post-event assistance, etc.), your insurance advisor (and the insurance company you choose) must be dedicated to doing everything possible to safeguard your family and protect your fortune.

An insurance broker's focus should be helping individuals, families, their organizations and their interests protect their wealth. It is important to develop risk-management strategies that can succeed in both hard and soft insurance markets. Privately owned and operated brokers can provide clients with stability and sophisticated risk-management advice, uncompromised by the demands of a public broker. Our personal approach is distinctive and backed by a thorough knowledge of the ultra high net worth insurance market. In addition, our carrier partners utilize their management teams to provide valuable advice on loss-prevention services, exposures and claims mitigation. Ⓦ

> ## "The client's interests are paramount. The focus of the business is in protecting the assets of the clients with total confidentiality and privacy."
> – Bruce Gendelman

How to reach Bruce Gendelman
Please contact me at 800.845.4145, ext. 11 for an initial consultation.

THE LAST BOOK I READ WAS...

The Fishbowl Principle: Building the Ark for the 21st Century, *by Bruce Gendelman, Robert Miller and David Taus (available at Amazon.com and on Kindle)*

MY MOST INFLUENTIAL PROFESSOR...

The late Dr. James Grasskamp, University of Wisconsin Graduate School of Business, PhD, risk management. He helped me integrate finance, risk management and law.

WHAT MAKES A GOOD CLIENT...

Families that ask questions and either understand the values of their assets or have an interest in understanding how the assets are valued. The more complex the risk, the better.

Bruce Gendelman

Joseph Gendelman

About Bruce Gendelman

Bruce Gendelman formed the Bruce Gendelman Company in 1982 to provide cutting-edge insurance solutions for affluent families and clients. The client's interests are paramount. The focus of the business is in protecting the assets of the clients with total confidentiality and privacy. He has a BA in economics and a JD from the University of Wisconsin. Active in the community, Mr. Gendelman is on the board of trustees for the United Way of the Town of Palm Beach and is involved with various charities. He divides his time between Palm Beach and Aspen. Mr. Gendelman and his wife, Lori, have been married 34 years and have four children. Their eldest son, Joseph, is the current president and CEO of the Bruce Gendelman Company.

Minimum Fee for Initial Meeting
None required

Minimum Net Worth Requirement
$10 million

Largest Client Net Worth
High-level Forbes 400

Insurance Services Experience
30 years

Compensation Method **Fixed fees and commissions**

Education **JD and BS, economics, University of Wisconsin**

Professional Services Provided
Ultra high net worth personal and property casualty insurance

Association Memberships
Florida Bar and the State Bar of Wisconsin

Website
www.gendelman.com

Email
bgendelman@gendelman.com

Los Angeles, CA | **Leading Wealth/Insurance Advisor**

Momentous Insurance Brokerage
Diane Brinson, President and CEO

" What kind of insurance do we need to fully cover our custom home with its one-of-a-kind features? "

By Diane Brinson

Simply put, the type of policy needed is a homeowners policy, with some coverage enhancements to address the custom features that increase the replacement cost of the home.

Most policies include an extended replacement cost provision that can extend the amount of coverage from 25 percent to 100 percent of the dwelling limit on the policy. This additional coverage can be used to account for custom, one-of-a-kind features. Some insurance companies offer guaranteed replacement cost, which pays the full amount needed to repair or replace the home, appurtenant structures (gazebos, guesthouses, etc.) and contents, with comparable construction materials, regardless of the declared policy limits. The additional premium for including guaranteed replacement cost will vary depending on the size of the house, but is generally affordable and certainly worthwhile. Not all companies will provide this valuable coverage and those that do will require a current replacement cost appraisal.

When selecting the appropriate homeowners policy, it is important to work with companies that specialize in high-value homes—brokers who understand the exposures and have access to insurance companies that provide broader coverage forms that the homeowner deserves and expects.

High-end insurance companies almost always require an appraisal immediately after binding coverage, which alerts the company of any special features in the home and ensures that policy limits are agreed upon and appropriate. This should be repeated when remodeling or doing major construction. To account for inflation and rising construction costs, most policies include an annual inflation adjustment, from 2 to 10 percent.

With today's declining property values, clients are asking to reduce coverage on their dwellings, not realizing the factors that affect property values are not the same factors that affect replacement cost (see sidebar). An important distinction is that the value of the land the house sits on is the portion of the value that varies the most. Furthermore, the fair market value of land is not insurable. The confusion between real estate values and home replacement values is a longstanding problem. With catastrophic events happening in many parts of the country, insuring the home to value will continue to be a critical issue to address before a major loss occurs.

Another important policy coverage to review is rebuilding to code/building ordinance. Throughout America, municipal building departments have implemented tougher building ordinances and standards to create fewer hazards for the community. A selective group of insurance companies will address this issue and pay up to 100 percent of the dwelling coverage limit.

It is critical that homeowners work with a broker who specializes in the high net worth arena and has the expertise to design policies that adequately cover their homes. ⓦ

UNDERSTANDING HOME REPLACEMENT COST VALUES

The confusion between real estate values and home replacement values is a longstanding problem. The following illustrates the key factors that affect each.

Real estate values have been affected by:
- subprime loan crisis
- foreclosure rates
- new housing starts
- location factors
- land value

Home replacement value factors include:
- material
- fuel and labor costs
- construction code requirements
- changing construction standards and practices
- new technology
- demand for and availability of labor and materials (which rise dramatically in the event of a catastrophe)

"The factors that affect property values are not the same factors that affect replacement cost."

– Diane Brinson

How to reach Diane Brinson

Please call me anytime at 818.933.2700.

**THE LAST BOOK
I READ WAS...**

Improvise, Adapt and Overcome, by Kenneth Keller, *a fast read with a clear message*

IF I WEREN'T AN INSURANCE ADVISOR, I'D BE...

A horticulturist, spending days in the garden and at nurseries

MY HOBBIES ARE...

Art, architecture and design, especially Bauhaus furniture, Danish Modern and clean simple designs of all kinds

About Diane Brinson

Diane Brinson has been in the insurance industry since 1981, serving as an insurance company marketing representative, a direct writer and an independent insurance broker. Before forming Momentous, she was a managing director of a national insurance brokerage, where she was responsible for more than 100 professionals. Her expertise in insurance is rooted in insuring high net worth individuals through accountants, attorneys, family offices and company CFOs, as well as working directly with high-profile clients. Ms. Brinson was recognized by the *Los Angeles Business Journal* as a woman making a difference in 2009. She is well versed in all agency operations, and sits on numerous insurance company advisory boards, including ACE, Chartis, Fireman's Fund, Chubb and Travelers. She has a bachelor of science degree from Florida State University.

Insurance Services Experience
30 years

Website
www.momentousins.com

Email
dbrinson@mmibi.com

Insurance Services Provided
Personal insurance for high net worth clientele; entertainment insurance including film, T.V. and Internet productions, music and touring companies and artists; life, health, disability and employee benefit programs; commercial insurance and professional liability for a wide variety of industries

Certifications
Licensed Fire and Casualty Agent

Momentous Insurance Brokerage | 5990 Sepulveda Boulevard, Suite 550, Van Nuys, CA 91411 | 818.933.2700

New York, NY | **Leading Wealth/Insurance Advisor**

Bruce Gendelman Company
Joseph Gendelman, President and CEO

"Why is group personal excess insurance an option worth considering?"

By Bruce Gendelman, JD, Chairman, and Joseph Gendelman, President and CEO

High net worth individuals have the opportunity to protect themselves with a unique approach to personal excess insurance: the group personal excess policy. This policy can safeguard your assets in the event a lawsuit is filed against you; it covers accidents on your property or on the road, libel or slander charges, not-for-profit board liability and personal employment practices liability, as well as defense costs paid outside of policy limits.

I already have a personal excess policy, why would I need this? Most insurance policies already have property and liability coverage within the homeowners coverage, and some clients have personal excess liability above that limit. However, most insurance companies do not offer limits that meet the exacting needs of affluent individuals and their families. In the event of a lawsuit, if you are not insured with the proper limits, you may be forced to surrender material assets, and even salary may be fair game.

How is a group personal excess policy different from what I have? Group personal excess is a benefit that companies offer either as a mandatory or voluntary program. It replaces the individual excess liability policy that covers persons and their families individually, while maximizing purchasing power as a group. A group may be defined as a company's executives, directors, partners and other senior-level employees. A group may also be defined as a family office or a family pooling together as one unit.

What are some of the advantages of a group personal excess policy?

• **Discounted premiums.** Savings due to the group's buying power are locked in for the entire year even if additional properties, vehicles, etc., are added. Group members pay the same price for the same limit of coverage as fellow participants.

• **Easy customer reporting.** Unlike a traditional personal excess policy, you do not need to notify the insurance carrier when new purchases are made; you can wait until the renewal date without sacrificing automatic coverage.

• **High limits of $5 million to $100 million are available.** Worldwide protection also follows you wherever you go.

• **High limits of UM/UIM available** (uninsured/underinsured motorist). An estimated one in six drivers is uninsured, and those with insurance may not have enough coverage to properly compensate for your loss.

• **Defense costs paid outside of policy limits.** If the defense costs were included within the policy limits, protection could erode quickly and might leave significant out-of-pocket expenses. Participants may also play an active role in selecting legal representation from litigation specialists.

• **Expanded legal defense coverage.** This may be included to reimburse participants for some legal-related expenses, and their personal attorney can participate in the defense strategy.

• **Errors and omissions coverage built in for the sponsoring organization.**

• **Employer-added benefit offering for employees.** The program can be firm subsidized, employee subsidized or a combination of both.

Group personal excess is a specific insurance option for those looking to maximize coverage, flexibility and pricing for employers, employees and family organizations. Personal insurance carriers are continuing to raise the bar regarding product and service offerings. When seeking an insurance firm, make sure the broker has a thorough knowledge and working expertise of the ultra high net worth insurance market. Additionally, a firm that can guide you through this unique product offering and provide valuable advice on group personal excess program design, employer offerings, coverage options and claims mitigation is a must. ⓦ

"A group personal excess policy replaces individual excess liability, maximizing purchasing power as a group."

– Joseph Gendelman

How to reach Joseph Gendelman

Please contact me at 800.845.4145, ext. 13, for an initial consultation.

I NEVER LEAVE HOME WITHOUT...

My BlackBerry. If my clients do not get a response back from me in five minutes, I am in a meeting or on an airplane.

THE LAST BOOK I READ WAS...

The Fishbowl Principle: Building the Ark for the 21st Century, by Bruce Gendelman, Robert Miller and David Taus (I highly recommend it to all the intellectuals out there.)

WHAT MAKES A GOOD CLIENT...

Someone who is smart and challenges you to think outside the box

Bruce Gendelman

Joseph Gendelman

About Joseph Gendelman

Joseph Gendelman has been the presiding president and CEO of the Bruce Gendelman Company since May 2008. Mr. Gendelman's expertise in the high net worth property and casualty market has continued the steady growth and profitability of the family-owned and operated company that his father built 30 years ago. Mr. Gendelman is active in the New York community and is a member of the Young Presidents Organization and various charities. He is a graduate of Emory University.

Minimum Fee for Initial Meeting **None required**	Compensation Method **Fixed fees and commissions**
	Education **BA, Emory University**
Minimum Net Worth Requirement **$5 million**	Professional Services Provided **Ultra high net worth personal property and casualty insurance**
Largest Client Net Worth **High-level Forbes 400**	Association Memberships **Young Presidents Organization**
Insurance Services Experience **9 years**	Website www.gendelman.com Email jgendelman@gendelman.com

Bruce Gendelman Company   30 West 63rd Street, 29th Floor, New York, NY 10023   800.845.4145, ext. 13

"Why should art insurance be considered part of a wealth management program?"

By Katja Zigerlig

For many of us, collecting art is a passion. However, private collections—a term that includes everything from paintings and sculpture to antique furniture, wine and jewelry—are not just culturally and aesthetically valuable. They are also tangible assets that should be addressed in your wealth management plan.

Many collectors bristle at the suggestion that their carefully honed collection is a commodity to be sold. However, acknowledging (and clearly defining) the investment value can help you make smarter decisions when it comes to protecting the collection over time. For example, art collections can be included in trust, estate and wealth planning. Donations of art to charities can ease your tax burden while being a philanthropic gesture to a beloved charitable institution. A collection can also be leveraged to get a loan, offering a discreet form of collateral. Yet these options only work if the art is in excellent condition, and if the value is clearly understood.

Distinct insurance coverage is available for fine art, jewelry, wine, antiques and other collectibles, yet many include these items in a homeowners policy and unknowingly diminish their protection. Regardless of your overall policy limit, homeowners policies generally cap limits on contents coverage. The value of covered items also may be subject to depreciation. Insuring high-value collections appropriately can provide broader, more flexible protection.

My colleagues and I help our clients with a range of factors, including:

- Customized underwriting to ensure precise protection
- Vulnerability assessments and loss-mitigation advice
- Disaster planning for areas prone to wildfires, hurricanes, etc.
- Hands-on claims assistance

We also serve as an ongoing referral resource by maintaining a network of carefully vetted appraisers, conservators, art handlers, shipping specialists, storage facilities and inventory service providers.

Whether you buy for aesthetic or investment purposes, the loss of art—through partial damage or total destruction—requires time, money and planning for conservation or replacement. Proper insurance, updated appraisals and thorough risk management make the foundation of a thorough art/asset protection plan. Independent insurance agents or brokers can point you to the best-in-class providers. **Look for a policy that includes:**

- Coverage for all types of collectibles and art media
- Worldwide protection
- Immediate coverage for new acquisitions
- Coverage for items in transit or on loan for exhibit. ⓦ

THE PRIVATE CLIENT GROUP

The Private Client Group at Chartis employs a team of seven full-time art experts with degrees in art history, anthropology, studio arts, economics and museum sciences. We understand the sophisticated financial and physical risk structures of collections.

Our collections managers assess the vulnerability of collections to risk and make recommendations to reduce the possibility or magnitude of loss.

Our underwriters take loss-prevention measures, collection location and financial risk into consideration to access large insurance capacity for our collections. We also work with an extensive network of art lawyers, conservators, packers and shippers.

Our approach of 360-degree protection helps us deliver the best in service and product for our clients. At the end of the day, no one wants a loss, and our clients want to focus their time and energy on their collections.

"Insuring high-value collections appropriately can provide broader, more flexible protection."
– Katja Zigerlig

How to reach Katja Zigerlig

Please contact me at 212.458.8861 or by email at katja.zigerlig@chartisinsurance.com for an initial consultation regarding the insurance of your private collection.

I'M CURRENTLY READING...

The Keep, *by Jennifer Egan*

I'M MOST INFLUENCED BY...

Creative people who achieve professional success. They are a personal and professional reminder to me that innovative thinking, risk taking and following your vision can be rewarding—specifically designer Martin Margiela, artist Louise Bourgeoise and art historian Griselda Pollock.

WHAT'S ON MY DESK...

A list of the grand cru vineyards of Burgundy—it is a personal and professional passion—so many vineyards to remember!; a large cup of green tea; auction catalogues; and my calendar

About Katja Zigerlig

Katja Zigerlig is an assistant vice president of fine art, wine and jewelry insurance for the Private Client Group division of Chartis. Ms. Zigerlig has almost two decades of professional experience in the art world. Prior to joining Private Client Group, she insured private collections, museums, galleries and exhibitions for AXA Art Insurance Co. She also worked at the Walker Art Center in Minneapolis and interned at the National Gallery of Art in Washington, D.C. Ms. Zigerlig has a BA and MA in art history, with a specialty in 20th-century art. She is a member of several arts-related organizations and speaks internationally. She has been quoted in *The Wall Street Journal, The New York Times, Financial Times, Canadian Underwriter* and *Art & Auction* and has appeared on CNBC's *Power Lunch.*

Number of Private Collections Policies **45,000***	Professional Services Provided **Insurance underwriting and personal risk management consultation**
Aggregate Worth of Art/Collectibles Insured **\$31 billion***	Association Memberships **The Advisory Council of the Appraisers Association of America; the Associates Endowment Committee at the Museum of Modern Art; the Young Collectors Council at the Guggenheim Museum; and a member of the Art Table**
Aggregate Worth of Jewelry Insured **\$6.6 billion***	
Value of Largest Private Client Collection **\$500 million***	Education **MA, art history and 20th-century art, American University; BA, art history, College of St. Catherine**
	Website **www.chartisinsurance.com/pcg** Email **katja.zigerlig@chartisinsurance.com**

*The figures above are based on U.S./Canada policyholder data from the Private Client Group division of Chartis. Information is current as of 4/25/10.

Chartis   Private Client Group   180 Maiden Lane, 27th Floor, New York, NY 10038   212.458.8861

" How do I properly insure my luxury home in a catastrophe-prone area? "

By Ray Celedinas

Recent increases in the number and severity of catastrophic insurance claims from floods, earthquakes, tornados, wildfires and hurricanes are having a negative impact on insurance and reinsurance company losses worldwide. As a result, insurance companies are taking major rate increases, limiting coverage and even reducing exposure by cancelling clients located in catastrophe-prone areas.

And forecasts show no relief in sight from future catastrophes. Germany-based Munich Reinsurance Company states: "The number and intensity of weather-related catastrophes is expected to increase in the coming decades largely on account of climate change. Munich Re therefore anticipates price increases in the loss-affected regions and business segments."

If you own a home located in an area subject to one or more of these events, you are going to need the assistance of an experienced and creative insurance broker/advisor who not only understands your unique needs but also has access to all the insurance markets and tools to properly insure your luxury assets.

Many insurers now shy away from catastrophe-prone areas, but a handful of financially-sound blue-chip companies have special programs for qualifying accounts in high-risk locations.

These luxury market carriers provide a level of service not available from standard market carriers. For example, these are not only the kind of insurance companies that inspect your home for damage after a hurricane, but they also make temporary repairs to mitigate the claim. In California several of these top carriers have even implemented programs to apply fire resistant foam to the exterior of their clients' residences to reduce the probability of damage from wildfire.

Blue-chip luxury carriers have broad coverage terms and endorsements that can be modified to provide what is absolutely necessary without paying for what is not. For example, property insurance in catastrophe-prone areas can be quite expensive; however, in many instances you can reduce personal property and other structures so that your coverage matches up with your actual exposure, thereby reducing your premium. You can further simplify the process by hiring a single broker/advisor to manage your entire insurance program, thereby providing you with one consolidated policy and billing statement as compared to having multiple agents and policies, each with separate billing and expiration dates.

You need to be aware that standard insurance policies in high-risk areas often have exclusions and limitations that can cause serious gaps in your insurance portfolio. The National Flood Insurance Program provides a maximum of $250,000 in building and $100,000 in contents coverage. In most situations, this coverage limitation is insufficient to properly protect a luxury home in a flood- or storm surge-prone area. However, this gap in coverage can be properly addressed with a supplemental excess flood insurance policy. So it is especially important in high-risk areas for the sophisticated insurance consumer to have an advocate who is aware of the myriad of exposures and gaps in insurance coverage.

To properly insure your home in a catastrophe-prone area and to receive the greatest number of solutions tailored to your needs, we recommend you select an insurance broker/advisor that has direct relationships with carriers specializing in the market. ⓦ

Source: BusinessInsurance.com, June 8, 2010

> # "Standard insurance carriers in high-risk areas often have exclusions and limitations that can cause serious gaps in your insurance portfolio."
> – Ray Celedinas

How to reach Ray Celedinas

Ray Celedinas can be reached personally by email at rceledinas@celedinas.com or 800.940.7744 ext. 5605.

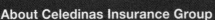

WHAT MAKES A GREAT HNW INSURANCE BROKER...

Expertise in the affluent marketplace and direct relationships with specialized luxury insurance carriers, which allow the broker/advisor to remain completely objective

WHAT SURPRISES YOU MOST ABOUT AFFLUENT PROSPECTIVE CLIENTS...

They have the best in legal, tax and financial advice, but are often poorly counseled about their property and personal liability exposures; they incorrectly assume their assets are adequately protected against physical losses and lawsuits, while their insurance programs often have material deficiencies that expose their assets to catastrophic loss.

WHAT MAKES A GREAT CLIENT...

Great clients are committed to a comprehensive personal risk management program that protects their assets and current lifestyle.

About Celedinas Insurance Group

The Celedinas Insurance Group is one of the oldest and largest privately held insurance brokerage firms in America and is focused on the complex needs of affluent clientele. With an understanding of the challenges unique to high net worth clients who have assets located in catastrophe-prone areas, the company offers an array of options along with objective and unbiased advice. Celedinas Insurance Group is one of the few insurance firms in America with direct access to all five luxury insurance companies, including ACE Private Risk, Chartis, Chubb, Fireman's Fund and PURE High Net Worth. These relationships, coupled with exhaustive analysis of policy terms and conditions, enable Celedinas to consistently exceed its clients' expectations. Areas of specialization include luxury homes and automobiles, personal excess liability, private collections, yachts, aircraft and advanced life insurance planning.

Number of Employees **105**	Largest Client Net Worth **$500 million+**	Website **www.celedinas.com**
Year of Establishment **1959**	Licensing **Licensed to transact business nationally**	Email **rceledinas@celedinas.com**
Insurance Services Experience **50 years**		

Celedinas Insurance Group | 4283 Northlake Boulevard, Palm Beach Gardens, FL 33410 | 800.940.7744
140 Royal Palm Way, Palm Beach, FL 33480

"How do I properly insure my super toys?"

By Robert H. Erdmann, ARM

Many of my highest net worth clients regard their yachts and private jets as the ultimate trappings of their great success. Taking ownership of a 100-foot watercraft or a 10-passenger jet is terrific, but with ownership, specialized and often complicated insurance issues arise and need to be addressed by an expert.

WATERCRAFT

Let us assume you are about to purchase a 150-foot megayacht that carries a $50 million price tag. As a rule of thumb, I recommend my clients purchase special marine liability if their yacht's hull exceeds 50 feet in length and requires a professional crew. Why? The Merchant Marine Act of 1920, or the Jones Act, is a very specialized marine workers' compensation statute that protects both the crew and the owner internationally whether the yacht is at sea or in port.* A well-crafted marine liability policy will cover these exposures when a normal personal excess (umbrella) policy would not. Here is one example:

A crew member from the yacht injures someone while driving a rented vehicle when the yacht is in port. The owner is liable for his crew's actions. So while a carefully crafted yacht policy will guarantee the owner legal and financial protection, I always urge my client to select and vet his crew before hiring. The larger the yacht, the more important it becomes to engage a professional agency to handle the hiring of the crew.

Other factors that affect the scope of yacht coverage include: the waters to be navigated, the countries that will be visited, and whether the yacht will be put out to charter. Even the size and type of tenders accompanying the yacht affect coverage.

Some insurance advisors suggest a level of watercraft liability coverage equal to the purchase price of the craft. So in the case of the $70 million yacht, at least $70 million of liability should be in place in addition to sufficient property coverage to protect the value of the hull, its contents and its various other accessories.

PRIVATE AIRCRAFT

While there are no special statutes, like the Jones Act, that apply to private aircraft and their crews, the owner is still obligated to provide both workers' compensation and health insurance. The owner must also consider numerous other property and liability issues specific to the operation of the jet.

For example, the crash of a private jet almost guarantees a large lawsuit filed by those on the ground who sustain injuries or property damage.

In addition to insuring the replacement value of your aircraft, I always urge my larger aircraft clients to buy high amounts of liability coverage. Limits of $150 million or $200 million are often customary. Additionally, chartering a private aircraft necessitates liability insurance to include all passengers onboard.

And what of the individual who owns both a yacht and a jet? Many clients put both in a limited liability corporation—a prudent way to shield an individual from potentially enormous liability exposure.

To sum up: First, if you purchase any boat over 50 feet in length or own a private aircraft of any size, you need to know what questions to ask about insurance. Second, you need to consult with an expert who understands the complexities and intricacies of insuring your super toy. ⓦ

*Source: www.jonesact.com

"With ownership, specialized and often complicated insurance issues arise and need to be addressed by an expert."

– Robert H. Erdmann, ARM

How to reach Robert H. Erdmann

I can be reached at 978.548.3740.

MY HOBBIES ARE...

Squash, tennis, paddle tennis, golf and coaching youth lacrosse and hockey

THE LAST BOOK I READ...

The Talent Code, *by Daniel Coyle*

WHAT'S ON MY DESK...

Photos of my family

About Robert H. Erdmann, ARM

Robert H. Erdmann, ARM, president, Felton Berlin & Erdmann Insurance Services, has spent almost his entire career in the insurance business and received his associate in risk management designation in 1999. Prior to joining Felton & Berlin, he spent 13 years with Marsh USA Inc., the last six as a senior vice president and office head of the Boston Private Client Services Marsh office. He is an active member of the Boston Estate Planning Council, a member of the Professional Advisors Committee for the Boston Foundation, and sits on the Friends Board of the Northshore Educational Consortium. He is a graduate of Choate Rosemary Hall and Colby College.

For more than 24 years, the mandate of Felton, Berlin & Erdmann Insurance Services has remained unchanged: develop sophisticated personal insurance programs for an affluent clientele. Personal insurance services offered include homeowners insurance, umbrella liability, valuable articles, flood/earthquake, auto insurance, yacht/watercraft and specialty coverage. Partnerships with Chubb, Chartis, Fireman's Fund, ACE and other top-rated insurers afford the agency's clients access to the most effective personal risk management services, delivered by Felton, Berlin & Erdmann Insurance Services' 14 licensed insurance professionals.

Insurance Services Experience 20+ years	**Professional Services Provided** Personal risk management
Website www.feltonberlin.com	**Association Memberships** Boston Estate Planning Council
Email rerdmann@feltonberlin.com	**Credentials** Associate in risk management (ARM)

Felton, Berlin & Erdmann Insurance Services Inc. | 100 Corporate Place, Peabody, MA 01960 | 978.548.3740

"What should I look for when considering insurance for my collector cars?"

By Ronald Fiamma

An estimated 10,000 auto gatherings take place every year in the United States. They range from grand spectacles, such as the Pebble Beach Concours d'Elegance and the Cavallino Classic at the Breakers Hotel, to small gatherings in a McDonald's parking lot, where local collectors show off their favorite rides. No matter the level of participation, the popularity of these events points to an ongoing love affair with the automobile and the continuing growth of car collecting as a hobby. For many enthusiasts it is a life-long passion. Some collect numerous examples of a single marque; others search for a particular elusive automobile with an unmatched provenance and racing history.

Roughly 4 million collector autos are in the United States, and that number is growing. In keeping with the tremendous interest in collecting cars, there exists a specialty niche in the insurance industry to protect them.

The collections insurance sphere is different in that tremendous emphasis is placed on vulnerability assessments, risk management and loss prevention. Whether owning rare old master canvases, a cellar of vintage Bordeaux, or a stable of rare prewar Bugattis, collector clients need to know that everything possible has been done to prevent damage or loss to what in many instances is an irreplaceable item. **Knowledgeable insurance carriers and brokers can draw from experience to consult on topics as diverse as:**

• Have proper appraisals been performed, and is the collection insured to value?

• Is the garage facility properly constructed to withstand tremors or storm surges?

• Has an emergency evacuation plan been put in place?

• Are necessary vehicle repairs or restoration being performed by qualified experts?

• Is the transportation company suited to the needs of the car and the move?

• Has proper international documentation been put in place for a smooth overseas transit?

The intricacies of collector auto coverage are just as important as the pre-loss planning. **Coverage details can vary from carrier to carrier, but some of the more important aspects to look for are:**

• Agreed value coverage
• Worldwide coverage
• Full transit coverage
• Single liability policy for the entire collection
• Market appreciation coverage to account for rising values
• Diminution in value coverage for partial loss
• Automatic coverage for new purchases

Collector auto enthusiasts build collections for a variety of reasons—for aesthetic enjoyment, to diversify an investment portfolio, or sometimes simply to satisfy a lust for a particular car first seen as a teenager. Preferences can range from Auburns, Cords and Duesenbergs to hot rods, concept cars and exotics. Despite what they own, true collectors know that proper protection is always in good taste. ⓦ

A CLAIMS STORY

Our claims experts go to extraordinary lengths to satisfy passionate collectors. One policyholder was involved in a collision that virtually totaled his Ferrari Enzo, one of only 400 ever produced. The extensive damage would require lengthy and complicated repairs.

We offered to reimburse the policyholder for the full value of the vehicle, but he preferred that we attempt to repair it.

The rarity and design intricacies made it nearly impossible to find a qualified technician and replacement parts in the area. We determined that the only craftsmen qualified to complete the repairs were the ones who originally built it—at the Ferrari factory in Italy.

We shipped the damaged remains and flew the policyholder to Italy twice to inspect the progress. When all repairs were completed to the policyholder's satisfaction, the vehicle was shipped back to his residence, and to this day he remains the proud owner of one of these rare beauties.

"Clients need to know that everything possible has been done to prevent damage or loss."

– Ron Fiamma

How to reach Ron Fiamma

Please contact me at 212.458.8843 or by email at ron.fiamma@chartisinsurance.com for an initial consultation regarding insurance for all types of private collections.

MY FAVORITE ESCAPE...
Anywhere on my bicycle

WHAT I'M READING NOW...
The Big Short, by Michael Lewis

WHAT'S ON MY DESK...
A photo I took in Nepal while trekking at 10,500 feet above the clouds, watching the sunrise. It puts things in perspective on a hectic day.

About Ron Fiamma

Ron Fiamma is vice president and director of private collections for the Private Client Group, a division of Chartis. Based in New York, Mr. Fiamma manages the firm's insurance portfolio of client collections of fine art, jewelry, wine and collector automobiles. Prior to joining Private Client Group, he spent six years in the financial institutions division of Chartis underwriting professional liability coverage for investment advisors, hedge funds, family offices and securities broker/dealers. He joined Chartis after many years in the financial services industry as a broker, trader and analyst. Mr. Fiamma received his degree in art history from Vanderbilt University and continued his graduate work in Italy in art history, archaeology and art restoration. He maintains his childhood fascination with vintage automobiles and Formula 1 auto racing.

Number of Private Collections Policies **45,000***	Professional Services Provided **Insurance underwriting and personal risk management consultation**
Aggregate Worth of Art/Collectibles Insured **$41 billion***	Education **BA, art history, Vanderbilt University**
Range of Auto Collections Insured **$10,000 to more than $200 million**	Website **www.chartisinsurance.com/pcg**
	Email **ron.fiamma@chartisinsurance.com**

*The figures above are based on U.S./Canada policyholder data from the Private Client Group division of Chartis. Information is current as of 9/1/10.

Chartis   Private Client Group   180 Maiden Lane, 27th Floor, New York, NY 10038   212.458.8843

South Florida | **Leading Wealth/Insurance Advisor**

Seitlin Insurance & Advisory
Roxana Sora, CIC, AAI, President—Private Client Group
Chad Rustici, Insurance Consultant

" What is the likelihood that I do not have enough personal insurance in place? "

By Roxana Sora and Chad Rustici

In today's busy world, personal insurance seems to just happen. Individuals buy insurance as a series of transactions. The necessary due diligence is rarely performed to assure that all aspects of personal exposure are adequately covered. Do you know if your insurance is up to par with your needs? Are your personal assets exposed? Has anyone ever done an in-depth audit of your personal insurance? We notice that most often the answer to these questions is a resounding no.

Clients and prospects often ask, "What is in it for me?" This question prompted us to look at a group of new clients and to perform a thorough audit on each, comparing the clients' actual personal property and liability exposures to their current in-force insurance. Performed on 26 of our newest clients, the audit revealed that with a large percentage, their coverage did not meet their needs. Our findings were:

- **81 percent** of clients were missing coverage they needed
- **60 percent** were overcharged
- **72 percent** were underinsured
- **75 percent** wanted higher limits for mold coverage on their homeowners policy
- **77 percent** had insufficient liability limits, thereby exposing their net worth to litigation.

An insurance advisor should focus on the specific coverage needs of clients, as well as the limits required to adequately protect their assets.

Exploratory questions should focus on the personal activities of the insured and the person's immediate family. These inquiries help to uncover needs such as workers compensation for domestic staff, excess directors and officers liability insurance for those who participate on charitable or nonprofit boards, and employment practices liability for domestic staff, should a suit arise from an employee charging sexual harassment, wrongful termination, etc.

Once the risk management study is completed, the findings should be compared to the current coverage and credits in place. This allows a broker to prioritize a client's needs and to determine which areas need to be addressed. In addition to any coverage gaps or exposures that are discovered, all applicable credits must be applied.

We also found in our audit process that many of our new clients were missing these valuable services:

Risk Management Services
- Hurricane and wildfire protection units
- Residential risk management assessment
- Residential security analysis
- Complimentary background checks on domestic staff

Collections
- Collection management services for fine arts and antiques

Do you think it is time for you to have someone perform an audit of your personal insurance? ⓦ

WHAT IS INCLUDED IN AN AUDIT?

An insurance audit should include the following:
- Risk evaluation of liability created by either ownership of property or other personal activities by you or your immediate family members
- Risk retention
- Evaluation of current coverage and recommended coverages: homeowners; windstorm; primary and excess flood; automobile; watercraft; collections; personal excess liability; aviation; travel; kidnap and ransom
- Risk mitigation: hurricane preparedness; hurricane damage response; wind mitigation; collection and inventory management; evaluation of protective devices
- Financial-strength rating of carriers

"The necessary due diligence is rarely performed to assure that all aspects of personal exposure are adequately covered."

– Roxana Sora and Chad Rustici

How to reach Roxana Sora and Chad Rustici

We would love to hear from you. You can reach either of us at 305.591.0090 or by email at rsora@seitlin.com or crustici@seitlin.com.

MY MOST INFLUENTIAL BOSS WAS...

Roxy: Steve Jackman, Seitlin's chairman. At the beginning of my career at Seitlin, I was Steve's assistant. He taught me the business and encouraged me to meet challenges head on.

Chad: David Norton, my former manager at State Farm. He convinced me to get into the insurance industry and helped me build the foundation for where I am today in my career.

MY FAVORITE RESTAURANT IN THE WORLD IS...

Roxy: Asia to Cuba in New York and South Beach, and Mr. Chow in South Beach

Chad: New York Prime, Da Campo Osteria and Bentley's in Isla Morada

I NEVER LEAVE HOME WITHOUT...

Roxy: My BlackBerry
Chad: My BlackBerry

Chad Rustici

Roxana Sora

About Seitlin Insurance & Advisory

Since its inception in 1945, Seitlin has redefined the traditional role of insurance agent. Seitlin's success is based on exceeding the expectations of its clients and providing services that allow them to focus on their businesses and their lives. This philosophy has enabled Seitlin to become Florida's largest privately owned agency. Seitlin's Private Client Division was established to provide risk management and insurance solutions to affluent individuals and their families. Given the unique risks faced by Floridians and the ever-changing insurance landscape, we have assembled a team dedicated to meeting these challenges.

Minimum Net Worth Requirement
$5 million

Largest Client Net Worth
$50 million (approximately)

Total Number of Professionals
120

Insurance Services Experience
65 years (Sora and Rustici combined)

Compensation Method
Commissions (insurance products)

Credentials
Accredited advisor in insurance, Insurance Institute of America, and certified insurance counselor, Society of Certified Insurance Counselors

Website
www.seitlin.com

Email
rsora@seitlin.com, crustici@seitlin.com

Seitlin Insurance & Advisory | 9800 Northwest 41st Street, Suite 300, Miami, FL 33178
6700 North Andrews Ave., Suite 300, Ft. Lauderdale, FL 33309 | 305.591.0090

Los Angeles, CA   **Leading Wealth/Insurance Advisor**

Poms & Associates

Seth Ford Gilman, Senior Vice President, Gregg Carpenter, Senior Vice President,
Ryan Dritz, Vice President, Gregory Hughes, Vice President, David Beeton, Account Executive

"Are there advantages to having coordinated insurance policies versus separate coverages and brokers? "

By Seth Ford Gilman

A coordinated insurance portfolio offers numerous advantages. Broker selection, choice of carriers, ongoing management and advice on unique risks play important roles in your insurance program.

One of the key advantages of going through one broker and, ideally, one carrier is the elimination of gaps in insurance due to inconsistent policy language. Utilizing one broker to handle all lines of business allows for reviews of all policies—those reviews catch potential gaps, which allows the broker to advise you how to eliminate them.

In addition to cross credits for having multiple policies with one carrier, the consolidation of insurance companies also leaves little ambiguity when submitting a complex claim. With only one carrier, you typically get one claims contact who will apportion the claim to the various applicable policies, thereby avoiding finger pointing between companies over which one has primary or secondary responsibility.

Another advantage of coordinating multiple insurance policies through one broker is that it allows for effective management of the insurance program as the risk evolves. Just as with your financial portfolio, an insurance portfolio needs reviews and occasional modifications. Through the use of annual (at minimum) insurance reviews, your broker will be able to modify your policies, if needed, ensuring they are best positioned in the insurance marketplace year over year.

One example of this is a client who has grown a considerable art collection. High-value pieces of fine art, jewelry, wine and other collectibles need to be insured separately with a collections policy. Unfortunately, a frequent assumption is that a homeowners policy will adequately cover everything in the home, which is simply not true. A collections policy goes much further than a homeowners policy in protecting high-value items, utilizing broad policy language and a scheduled limit representing present market value. And, in most cases, it is not subject to a deductible at the time of a loss. Any collection of valuable items needs to be managed effectively year to year to ensure that the value of each piece is updated as it appreciates and that the items in the collection are properly maintained, managed and displayed.

Lastly, when reviewing the insurance program on an annual basis, it is important to consider how much liability insurance is enough. In today's litigious culture, it is increasingly important to have high limits of excess liability, often known as an umbrella policy. Excess liability is inexpensive relative to the high limits of insurance that are provided. A good insurance broker will be able to guide you to a liability limit that is appropriate, considering both net worth and lifestyle. Ⓦ

HOW MUCH INSURANCE SHOULD I PURCHASE FOR MY HOME?

We get that question a lot these days given the steep decline in real estate values. You should insure your house for what it would cost to rebuild given current construction costs and similar design and quality of materials. Unfortunately that value may not coincide with what the home could sell for. Each home has unique design features and characteristics that need to be taken into account. Materials that were once commonplace—whether five or 100 years ago—may not be as available today. Also consider changes in building codes, which can increase the cost if you have to rebuild. Our advice is to make sure you have enough insurance in place to rebuild your home to like, kind and quality without overinsuring and spending premium dollars unwisely.

"The consolidation of insurance companies leaves little ambiguity when submitting a complex claim."

– Seth Ford Gilman

How to reach Poms & Associates

You can reach any member of our team at 818.449.9300. We look forward to speaking with you.

Left to right: Gregory Hughes, Gregg Carpenter, Seth Ford Gilman, David Beeton and Ryan Dritz

About Poms & Associates

The growth and care of personal assets for the use and benefit of both today's and tomorrow's generations are no easy tasks. They take hard work, perceptive investment and discerning protection. Preferred Client Insurance Services is a division of Poms & Associates Insurance Brokers Inc., specializing in the analysis and establishment of comprehensive asset-protection programs for affluent individuals and families. The combination of Poms' superior expertise as a leading insurance broker, its unparalleled risk-management expertise, and its staff of uniquely practiced professionals helps to provide affluent clients with insurance programs for assets including homes, automobiles, yachts, aircraft, fine art, jewelry, rare collectibles and more.

Minimum Annual Fee
None required

Minimum Net Worth Requirement
$5 million

Largest Client Net Worth
$1 billion

Insurance Services Experience
79 years (combined)

Website
www.pomsassoc.com

Professional Services Provided
Analysis and establishment of comprehensive insurance programs for affluent individuals and families to protect their assets including homes, automobiles, yachts, planes, fine art, jewelry and collectibles

Education
Gilman: MBA and BS, economics, University of Southern California; Carpenter: BA, University of Southern California, College of Insurance, risk and insurance studies; Dritz: BA, California Polytechnic University, San Luis Obispo; Hughes: BA, political science, University of California, Los Angeles; Beeton: BBA, finance and marketing, Loyola Marymount University

Email **sgilman@pomsassoc.com, gcarpenter@pomsassoc.com, rdritz@pomsassoc.com, ghughes@pomsassoc.com, dbeeton@pomsassoc.com**

Poms & Associates | 5700 Canoga Avenue, Suite 400, Woodland Hills, CA 91367 | 818.449.9300

New York, NY—Fairfield, CT **Leading Wealth/Insurance Advisor**

Ericson Insurance Services
Spencer M. Houldin, President

" What is the most important, but often overlooked, personal insurance coverage? "

By Spencer M. Houldin

Excess liability coverage!

What is excess liability coverage? In its purest form, insurance is a transfer of risk from an individual to an insurance company, either because the insured cannot afford the risk or wishes not to retain it. Most individuals do not have the funds to self-insure against a large lawsuit. Excess liability coverage, also referred to as an umbrella, protects against such an occurrence. While unfortunate, a lost piece of jewelry will not affect one's lifestyle to the same degree as a draining lawsuit. It takes too much effort to amass wealth to leave it vulnerable to the quick strike of a judge's gavel.

Excess liability insurance is typically sold in increments of $1 million and provides protection above the limits provided on your homeowners, automobile, watercraft and other underlying policies. The cost is relatively inexpensive. For example, a $10 million limit costs approximately $1,250 per annum. Our firm has the ability to place limits up to $200 million.

What are the most common losses that trigger excess liability coverage? An automobile accident is the most likely scenario because a permanent disability or fatality could result in a multimillion-dollar judgment. We also see large losses in condominiums and cooperatives when an event in one unit, such as a water leak or fire, causes significant damage to an adjacent unit or to a neighbor's personal property. For examples of actual court cases and judgments, please visit www.iericson.com/worth.

What is the proper limit for one to carry? Although difficult to answer because no one knows what the future may hold, certain lifestyle characteristics can provide valuable guidance. Knowing the client and the client's way of life, net worth and exposure to risk are key elements. The characteristics that expose you to greater risk include such things as membership in a condominium or cooperative association, employing domestic workers, and having young or elderly drivers. Additionally, owning a swimming pool, a sports car, a watercraft or a horse makes a person more vulnerable. After understanding the client's needs and risk factors, we develop various coverage options to aid in the decision-making process.

Caution! Not all excess liability policies are the same! One should make sure the provided coverage is worldwide and will cover the same losses as one's underlying policies on which it sits (referred to as a "follow-form" contract). Some contracts include coverage for domestic-employee suits, such as wrongful termination or sexual harassment. It is important to work with an advisor who understands the contractual differences among insurance companies. Lastly, but certainly not least, it is critical that the insurance company is reputable and financially strong. We place the majority of our clients' policies with Chubb and ACE Private Risk Services. ⓦ

THE NEED FOR EXCESS LIABILITY— AN ACTUAL STORY

The insured was having lunch with a client at a New York restaurant when his cell phone rang. It was the superintendent of his cooperative building. Water was pouring from his co-op into the unit below. The superintendent had entered his premises and found the toilet was clogged. The insured's 5-year-old son was to blame. The concern was not the stain on the neighbor's cloth wall covering or the wet ceiling, but rather the irreparable damage to his multimillion-dollar painting. It was fairly clear that the insured would be responsible for all the damage, including the piece of art. Thank goodness he had a $25 million excess liability policy and would be well covered. Furthermore, his neighbor would be reimbursed for the loss, which keeps peace in the building.

"It takes too much effort to amass wealth to leave it vulnerable to the quick strike of a judge's gavel."

– Spencer M. Houldin

How to reach an Ericson advisor

Please call our office at 646.703.0411 or email Spencer at shouldin@iericson.com.

Left to right: Spencer Houldin, Kurt Thoennessen, Karen Russell and Peter Houldin

About Ericson Insurance Services

Ericson is a 75-year-old insurance firm dedicated to satisfying the personal insurance needs of the high net worth individual. With offices in Connecticut and New York City, Ericson provides insurance in all 50 states through 12 reputable carriers. The firm is comprised of 22 licensed insurance advisors who are specially trained to understand the needs of the affluent consumer. They are extremely engaged in the industry, as evidenced by their principals' activities in 2009, which included testifying in front of both chambers of Congress and making multiple appearances on nationally televised programs.

Minimum Fee for Initial Meeting
None required

Minimum Net Worth Requirement
$1 million

Largest Client Net Worth
$200 million

Insurance Services Experience
20 years

Email
shouldin@iericson.com

Compensation Method
Commissions from sale of property and casualty insurance products

Professional Services Provided
Property and casualty insurance, risk management advice, premium and coverage analysis, claims analysis and advice

Association Memberships
Independent Insurance Agents and Brokers of America; Trusted Choice Agent, Professional Insurance Agents of America

Website
www.iericson.com

South Florida | **Leading Wealth Advisor**

The Bermont/Carlin Group at Morgan Stanley Smith Barney
Adam E. Carlin, MBA
Director of Wealth Management and Portfolio Management Director

"Where do you think the next bubble may be, and what can I do to lessen the impact?"

By Adam E. Carlin

As a result of the historically low interest rate environment that has prevailed for the past two years, the markets have seen a rather substantial increase in the value of many fixed-income assets. This increase in value has not discriminated and thus can be observed in a vast number of types of fixed-income securities, ranging from sovereign and municipal debt to corporate debt.

For those who believe the global economic environment will continue to improve, it is very important to consider that the historically low interest rate environment may change and thus may only be a temporary phenomenon. In fact, if you go back in time, you will be reminded the current rate environment was in large part manufactured by the Federal Reserve as well as other central banks around the world in order to quickly and aggressively deal with the extraordinarily dire economic circumstances that existed at that time.

Thus, investors should not get too comfortable and forget that nothing is ordinary about the current level of interest rates and, consequently, the current valuation of certain fixed-income securities. Quite the contrary, I believe most would argue that the circumstances and events that caused the current interest rate environment were nothing short of truly extraordinary. That said, what would a rational investor expect to happen to interest rates and, as a result, fixed-income prices, when such emergency steps are no longer necessary? I suggest one consider the strong possibility that a commensurate increase in rates may be in order.

With this in mind, some fixed-income investors should again become familiar with the term "caveat emptor" ("let the buyer beware"). **Unfortunately, in this environment some investors, in an attempt to increase their current yield, may have found themselves extending the average maturity or duration of their fixed-income portfolios.** As a result, these same investors may have added longer maturity securities to their holdings. While this strategy may help provide these investors with some incremental increase in yield, I believe one must not forget the likely increased duration risk that may accompany such a decision.

Additionally, it is essential to keep in mind that during such a period of low rates this risk may hide and lay dormant within a portfolio. In my opinion, a word of caution is important for these investors because a portfolio may not show the true signs and consequences of this risk until rates move up and a portfolio's fixed-income prices start to react. In addition, this risk can be particularly pronounced in portfolios with fixed-income holdings that do not have stated maturities, such as many bond funds or, even more so, leveraged bond funds.

For those investors who wish to be proactive and address this potential risk within their portfolio, I suggest the following:

Ask your advisor to review your fixed-income holdings and thoroughly address the potential risks that may be embedded within your portfolio.

Determine whether the amount of risk ultimately found is in fact the amount of risk preferred and/or appropriate given your tolerance for risk as well as your needs. ⓦ

Adam E. Carlin is the director of wealth management and portfolio management director at Morgan Stanley Smith Barney LLC (member SIPC) located in Coral Gables, Fla., and may be reached at 305.476.3302. The views expressed herein are those of the author and do not necessarily reflect the views of Morgan Stanley Smith Barney or its affiliates. All opinions are subject to change without notice. Neither the information provided nor any opinion expressed constitutes a solicitation for the purchase or sale of any security. Past performance is no guarantee of future results. Bonds are affected by a number of risks, including fluctuations in interest rates, credit risk and prepayment risk. In general, as prevailing interest rates rise, fixed-income securities prices will fall. Bonds face credit risk if a decline in an issuer's credit rating, or creditworthiness, causes a bond's price to decline. Finally, bonds can be subject to prepayment risk. When interest rates fall, an issuer may choose to borrow money at a lower interest rate, while paying off its previously issued bonds. As a consequence, underlying bonds will lose the interest payments from the investment and will be forced to reinvest in a market where prevailing interest rates are lower than when the initial investment was made. NOTE: High-yield bonds are subject to additional risks such as increased risk of default and greater volatility because of the lower credit quality of the issues. This material does not provide individually tailored investment advice. It has been prepared without regard to the individual financial circumstances and objectives of persons who receive it. The strategies and/or investments discussed in this material may not be suitable for all investors. Morgan Stanley Smith Barney LLC recommends that investors independently evaluate particular investments and strategies, and encourages investors to seek the advice of a financial advisor. The appropriateness of a particular investment or strategy will depend on an investor's individual circumstances and objectives. © 2010 Morgan Stanley Smith Barney LLC, member SIPC.

"Some fixed-income investors should again become familiar with the term 'caveat emptor.'"

– Adam E. Carlin

How to reach Adam E. Carlin

Please give me a call at 305.476.3302 for a preliminary consultation.

WHAT MAKES A GOOD WEALTH ADVISOR...

Must have the ability to specifically identify what a client's true investment needs are and then have the process as well as the resources (intellectual as well as breadth of staff) to help the client best meet these needs

WHAT MAKES A GOOD CLIENT...

Most importantly, a good client must be rational and have consistent and realistic investment expectations

*Front row- Adam E. Carlin;
Left to right: back row-
Ronald A. Rosenberg,
Richard B. Bermont and
Brian R. Exelbert*

About The Bermont/Carlin Group

The Bermont/Carlin Group at Morgan Stanley Smith Barney, founded in 1974, provides financial services for a limited number of high net worth individuals and families, institutions and businesses. Adam E. Carlin, director of wealth management and portfolio management director, has taught at both the undergraduate and graduate levels at the University of Miami (UM). From 2006 to 2009, he was selected to be in *Research* magazine's Winner's Circle ranking of the top advisors in America. In 2009 and 2010, *Barron's* also named him one of the top advisors. He has been chosen multiple times to attend *Barron's* Top Advisors Summit. Mr. Carlin is involved in a wide range of community, educational, and cultural activities. He serves as co-chair of the UM Sylvester Comprehensive Cancer Center Founders Board, and is a member of the board of trustees for the New World Symphony and Shake-A-Leg Miami. In 2006, he cofounded and helped underwrite the MBA Ethics Fellow Internship program at UM, for which he also cofounded and underwrote the Bermont/Carlin Group Scholars program in support of the university's most outstanding students majoring in finance. Mr. Carlin is also a grand founder and Ibis Society member at UM.

Assets Under Management **$800 million (Carlin); $1.4 billion (group)**	Compensation Method **Asset-based fees and commissions**
Minimum Net Worth Requirement **$5 million (planning services)** **$2 million (investment services)**	Professional Services Provided **Money management, investment advisory** **and planning services**
Largest Client Net Worth **$400 million**	Website **fa.smithbarney.com/carlin/**
Financial Services Experience **16 years (Carlin); 100+ (group)**	Email **adam.e.carlin@mssb.com**

Barron's "Top 100 Financial Advisors," as identified by The Winner's Circle LLC, bases its rankings on qualitative criteria: professionals with a minimum of seven years' financial services experience, acceptable compliance records, client retention reports, customer satisfaction and more. With over 7,000 nominations, advisors are quantitatively ranked based on varying types of revenues and assets advised by the financial professional, with weightings associated for each. Additional measures include: in-depth interviews with senior management, peers and customers, and interviews with the nominees. Because individual client portfolio performance varies and is typically unaudited, this ranking focuses on customer satisfaction and quality of advice.

The Bermont/Carlin Group at Morgan Stanley Smith Barney | 220 Alhambra Circle, 10th Floor, Coral Gables, FL 33134 | 305.476.3302

Los Angeles—Orange County, CA   **Leading Wealth Advisor**

Signature Estate & Investment Advisors LLC
Brian D. Holmes, MS, CFP®, CMFC, President and CEO

" Is California a state to invest in or a state to avoid? "

By Brian D. Holmes

The economic demise of California is greatly exaggerated. It has been portrayed by the media and investment community as economically and politically dysfunctional, taxing to business and facing debts that rival Greece's. While much of this criticism is certainly warranted, it is important to not just focus on what could go wrong, but on what will probably go right.

Although California has been coined as unfriendly to business, it is home to Apple, Google, eBay, Intel, Cisco and Disney. It still has the world's eighth largest economy, accounting for 13.4 percent of the U.S. GDP. It is the country's largest agricultural producer and will continue to be a leader in technology and biotech innovations.

The state that "invented" movies and the Internet has always been an entrepreneurial boom-and-bust place, notably the technology boom in the late 1990s and the subprime mortgage/real estate debacle last decade.

California's unparalleled success with innovation and new economic trends also leads to temporary times of economic hardship, making it the most volatile economy nationwide. Boom-and-bust economies drive temporary revenue gaps as governments spend what they have and fail to build reserves. California has past experience of double-digit gaps as a percentage of annual budgets, but its debt-to-GDP ratio is approximately 6 percent, lower than in Massachusetts, New Jersey, Michigan, New York and Florida.

The state's fiscal mess is real, and tough cuts must take place, but if the past is any indication, the pendulum will swing back. The next California Gold Rush may be just around the corner. Its general obligation bonds are attractively priced and are relatively safe. The stable income is federal and state tax exempt for California residents and is not subject to the alternative minimum tax. These bonds are backed by the taxing power of the state, and attractive yields exist in the short and intermediate California Municipal Class 1 debt (i.e., an intermediate bond at 4.5 percent equals 7.65 percent taxable equivalent at the top bracket). Class 1 municipal debt includes state and local general obligation, school district, power, water, sewer and higher education. The default rate has been less than 1 percent over the past 25 years on this type of debt.

Opportunities will also exist with equities of publicly traded and new companies. Arguably, the world's largest incubation center of technology lies in the Bay Area and Silicon Valley. San Diego's biotech cluster is expanding rapidly, and Los Angeles continues exporting entertainment and is the gateway to Asia with the largest ports in the country.

The University of California system, which continually feeds these three epicenters of innovation, is the envy of the world. Six of the country's top 15 public universities, as reported by *U.S. News & World Report*, are part of the UC system. Cal Berkeley and UCLA occupy the top two spots.

The comparisons between California and Greece should stop at their picturesque coastlines. Although Greece is only 2 percent of the European Union's GDP, the contagion factor recently forced the EU to band together to temporarily protect Greek debt. California is more than one-eighth of the U.S. economy and is critically important to both the U.S. and world economies. **Ben Franklin said it best: "We must, indeed, all hang together or, most assuredly, we shall all hang separately."** I believe investment opportunities will continue to exist in the Golden State, and it will lead our country's economy while producing the next generation of economic innovations. ⓦ

"California's unparalleled success with innovation and new economic trends also leads to temporary times of economic hardship."

– Brian D. Holmes

How to reach Brian D. Holmes

I encourage a short initial conference call and then an in-person complimentary consultation in one of SEIA's four offices. I can be reached at 310.712.2323 or at bholmes@seia.com.

WHAT'S ON MY DESK...
John Wooden's Pyramid of Success

I NEVER LEAVE HOME WITHOUT...
Kissing my wife and children good-bye

IF I WEREN'T A WEALTH ADVISOR, I'D BE...
A university professor

About Brian D. Holmes

Brian D. Holmes, MS, CFP, CMFC, is the president and CEO of Signature Estate & Investment Advisors LLC. For four consecutive years (2007, 2008, 2009 and 2010), Mr. Holmes has ranked in the top 25 in *Barron's* annual list of the top 100 independent financial advisors. He has been in the securities and insurance business since 1984 and is the managing partner of the Century City branch of the John Hancock Financial Network. Mr. Holmes is a past member of the Schwab Institutional Advisory Board and the UCLA Department of Economics Board of Visitors. He received his bachelor of science degree from the University of California, Los Angeles. A longtime resident of Malibu, Calif., he is involved with numerous charities throughout Southern California.

Assets Under Management $1.7 billion (firm)	**Compensation Method** Asset-based fees
Minimum Fee for Initial Meeting None required	**Primary Custodian for Investor Assets** Charles Schwab & Co.; Fidelity Investments
Minimum Net Worth Requirement $4 million (planning services); $500,000 (investment services)	**Professional Services Provided** Planning, investment advisory, money management and private client wealth management services; estate planning
Largest Client Net Worth Confidential	**Association Memberships** Investment Advisor Association, Financial Planning Association, UCLA Department of Economics Board of Visitors, Financial Services Institute, National Association of Insurance and Financial Advisors
Financial Services Experience 27 years	**Website** www.seia.com **Email** bholmes@seia.com

Signature Estate & Investment Advisors LLC | 2121 Avenue of the Stars, Suite 1600, Los Angeles, CA 90067 | 310.712.2323

San Francisco—Bay Area, CA | **Leading Wealth Advisor**

Chrysalis Capital Group LLC
Cheryl A. Lane, President, Chrysalis Capital Group LLC,
FINRA Investment Banker, RIA, CPA, MBA, CTA, Realtor and CBI

"What top three real estate investment vehicles would you recommend?"

By Cheryl A. Lane, President, and Mark Cesare, Registered Representative,
Chrysalis Capital Group LLC

As Realtors as well as investment advisors, we often assist baby boomers with the disposition and replacement of their real estate investments. Baby boomers are generally established real estate investors who have owned their property for a number of years: for example, a couple in their 60s who have been managing their own properties, or the business owner who also owns the real estate associated with the business.

As established real estate investors approach retirement, their investment goals change: They want to liquidate their properties because they want more income; they want to be liberated from the active management of their real estate; and they want to reduce the risk for losing their capital. They also want to accomplish all of this without paying taxes on the transition out of their current property.

The key to their success is Section 1031 of the U.S. Internal Revenue Code. Section 1031 lays out the rules for the tax-deferred exchange of like-kind properties held for productive use in a trade or business or for an investment. In order to get this tax deferral you must replace the property being sold with assets described in various tax rules.

Three investment vehicles that can help real estate investors accomplish all their goals: Delaware statutory trusts, tenant in common properties, and oil and gas royalties. Even though these investments qualify as real estate for tax purposes, they are securities. Realtors cannot sell them; you can only buy them from someone with a securities license. Some states require your advisor to have both licenses.

As investors age, their need for income generally replaces their desire for capital appreciation. Their real estate investments have probably built up significant capital gains that they must access for cash flow to replace employment income. Aging real estate also becomes more work to manage. And as they mature, many owners find that they no longer want to or are able to manage their properties, and their aversion to risk becomes more important. The older you get, the harder it becomes to rebuild your wealth.

Diversification is one of the most important things that an investor can do to protect capital. Ideally an investor spreads the risk of capital loss across several asset classes. This is almost impossible for the person whose wealth is tied up in two or three similar buildings in the same city, making him vulnerable to catastrophic events such as a hurricane, a flood or an earthquake.

Delaware statutory trusts and tenant in common properties provide for fractional ownership of professionally managed properties that can often be higher in quality than those that average investors can purchase by themselves. With fractional ownership, investors can own a slice of several properties in different cities and within several real estate classes, and the properties can be rounded out by diversification with an oil or gas investment: for example, partial interest in a medical office building in Atlanta; an apartment building in Columbus, Ohio; and some oil or gas royalties in Texas. Active management of these investments is not required. These properties must pay investors their share of the cash flow on a monthly basis and the gain when they are sold. Today's programs are projecting 4 to 6 percent cash-on-cash returns, and much of the monthly distributions will be sheltered from income taxes.

These investments are illiquid so they are not appropriate for everyone. But for others, they can be good problem solvers. Ⓦ

"As established real
estate investors approach
retirement, their investment
goals change."

– Cheryl A. Lane and Mark Cesare

How to reach Cheryl A. Lane

I prefer face-to-face meetings with prospective clients. My assistant will happily schedule a convenient time to meet. You can reach her at 415.771.5263.

MY HOBBIES ARE...

Fine dining, karaoke, dancing and spending time with family and friends

I NEVER LEAVE HOME WITHOUT...

My notebook computer and a good book

WHAT'S ON MY DESK...

Desktop computer, dolphin message holder and a Bluetooth headset

About Cheryl A. Lane

Cheryl A. Lane, president and founder of a suite of financial service companies, including Chrysalis Capital Group LLC, has 30-plus years of experience as a private investment banker, financial advisor and professional Realtor. Ms. Lane is a FINRA-registered general securities and municipal bond and financial operations principal, a registered investment advisor, a commodities trading advisor, a certified public accountant with a master's degree in taxation, a certified business intermediary and a life and disability and long-term care insurance agent. Ms. Lane received her master's degree from Golden Gate University School of Taxation and graduated with distinction from Sonoma State University. She was the first woman governor to sit on the board of the National Association of Real Estate Investment Trusts and is a former editor of the "Tax Tips" column for the *San Francisco Examiner*. Believing that mid-market entrepreneurs deserve the same quality of services as those provided by an investment bank, Ms. Lane created the Lane Group of Companies to serve their needs. Chrysalis Capital Group is one of the five companies that she guides under the Lane Group banner.

Minimum Fee for Initial Meeting **None required**	Compensation Method **Success fees for the execution of a liquidity event; commissions on private placements and securitized insurance; asset-based fees (post liquidity transaction)**
Minimum Net Worth Requirement **$5 million**	Primary Custodian for Investor Assets **TD Ameritrade**
Largest Client Net Worth **$11 million**	Professional Services Provided **Business and real estate investment banking, advisory and estate planning, private placement broker-dealer, business transition strategies, mid-market investment banking and tax strategy**
Financial Services Experience **32 years**	Association Memberships **AICPA, CABB, CALCPA, CREW, FINRA, IBBA, MCEPC, NAR, NFA, NCPGC, SFAR, SFEPC, TICA,** *International Who's Who of Entrepreneurs*
Email **cheryl.lane@chrysaliscapital.us**	Website **www.chrysaliscapital.us**

Chrysalis Capital Group LLC   131 Franklin Street, San Francisco, CA 94102   415.771.5263

Houston, TX   **Leading Wealth Advisor**

Stavis & Cohen Financial
Deborah Stavis, CFP®, Chief Executive Officer
Eddie Cohen, CFP®, Chief Investment Officer

" How can I reduce risk and protect my lifestyle while at the same time optimizing investment performance? "

By Deborah Stavis and Eddie Cohen

High volatility and slow growth represent the new normal. A 2 percent one-day gain or loss in the S&P 500 (as a measure of volatility, ignoring even greater swings that often occur intraday) has occurred once every 21 trading days over the past 50 years. In contrast, it has occurred once every four days since September 2008. Volatility over the last two years is occurring at five times the rate of the prior 50 years.

With respect to investment growth, over the past 100 years the stock market has consistently cycled between extended periods (15 to 25 years) of minimal growth and substantial growth. We are in the middle of a slow-growth cycle that began in 2000. For the 10-year period ending December 31, 2009, the S&P 500 was actually down about 9 percent. Over the next three to five years, it is likely that the combination of government spending, high unemployment, rising taxes, higher interest rates, global competition and geopolitical risk will continue the volatility and slow growth.

What, then, should a savvy investor do? For individuals who want both capital preservation to maintain lifestyle and investment performance that beats benchmarks, the answer is far from clear. What is clear is that the old investment playbook no longer applies. The ability to both preserve capital and enhance performance requires a different strategy.

The mathematics of retracement underscores the importance of getting it right and shows the devastating impact of getting it wrong (see sidebar). Gains and losses are not a zero-sum game. Capping losses in declining markets has more impact on overall returns than beating benchmarks in bull markets.

To preserve capital and optimize performance in the new normal, we employ an enhanced dynamic asset allocation strategy. The strategy begins with a global analysis of changing market conditions and fundamental market data. This information is then used to identify high-value global investments and to regularly fine-tune allocations to adjust both risk and reward among various asset classes. At the same time, we allocate a portion of each investor's portfolio to risk-managed alternatives in order to minimize losses, reduce volatility and protect gains.

Risk-managed alternatives, now available in low-fee, highly liquid mutual funds and ETFs, are investments designed to mitigate risk by minimizing volatility and loss of capital during declining markets. By opportunistically adjusting the risk-management component of each investor's portfolio, risk-adjusted returns can be optimized.

No obvious solutions exist for investing in the new normal, but for investors focused on preserving wealth, protecting lifestyle and optimizing performance, enhanced dynamic asset allocation is an approach that merits serious consideration. ⓦ

GAINS AND LOSSES ARE NOT A ZERO-SUM GAME

The more you lose, the harder it is to break even.

- Down 50%
  Must earn 100% to break even

- Down 30%
  Must earn 43% to break even

- Down 10%
  Must earn 11% to break even

Vanguard 500 Index Investor (VFINX) Actual Results:

10/09/07		$1,000,000
03/09/09	Down 57%	$434,000
06/30/10	Up 51%	$658,000
Net Effect	Down 34%	$342,000

In volatile markets, the only way to make more is to lose less.

Registered representative. Securities offered through Cambridge Investment Research Inc., a broker/dealer, member FINRA/SIPC. Investment advisor representative, Stavis & Cohen Financial LLC, a registered investment advisor. Stavis & Cohen Financial LLC and Cambridge are not affiliated.

Indexes mentioned are unmanaged and cannot be invested into directly. Strategies described cannot assure profit or guarantee against loss. Past performance is no guarantee of future returns.

"Capping losses in declining markets has more impact on overall return than beating benchmarks in bull markets."

– Deborah Stavis and Eddie Cohen

How to reach Deborah Stavis and Eddie Cohen

Please contact us at 713.275.7750 to schedule an initial face-to-face meeting.

OUR COMMUNITY INVOLVEMENT...

Committee for the Barbara Bush Foundation for Family Literacy; Advisory Board at the Rice University Susanne M. Glasscock School of Continuing Studies; Board of Visitors for the University of Oklahoma Weitzenhoffer Family College of Arts

WHAT MAKES A GOOD CLIENT...

A leader—someone who cares deeply about family and community, values sustainable personal relationships, and has a strong desire to create and preserve wealth for future generations

OUR FAVORITE CAUSE...

Our deepest commitment is to teaching financial literacy and stewardship of wealth. We have been teaching financial planning courses since 1984 through the Rice University Susanne M. Glasscock School of Continuing Studies.

Deborah Stavis

Eddie Cohen

About Stavis & Cohen Financial

In 2009, Deborah Stavis and Eddie Cohen formed Stavis & Cohen Financial, a Houston-based, privately owned, full-service wealth management firm. Ms. Stavis has served as a financial advisor to Houston families for more than 28 years, most recently as founder and chief executive officer of Stavis Margolis Advisory Services. During her tenure, assets under management at the firm grew to more than $1 billion. She has been recognized multiple times as one of the nation's top 100 wealth advisors by *Worth.* Mr. Cohen is an investment specialist experienced in global investing, dynamic asset allocation, and risk-managed alternatives. Formerly managing director at Brinker Capital, he was instrumental in helping that firm increase assets from $2 billion to $10 billion during his tenure. Stavis & Cohen Financial employs a team of professionals dedicated to helping families with large and complex estates make sound financial choices.

Assets Under Management **$181 million**	Compensation Method **Asset-based investment management fees; annual financial planning retainer**
Minimum Fee for Initial Meeting **None required**	Primary Custodian for Investor Assets **Pershing**
Minimum Asset Requirement **$1 million**	Professional Services Provided **Asset management services and sophisticated estate, financial and retirement planning**
Largest Client Net Worth **Confidential**	Website www.stavisandcohen.com Email dstavis@stavisandcohen.com ecohen@stavisandcohen.com
Financial Services Experience **30 years**	

Stavis & Cohen Financial   1330 Post Oak Boulevard, Suite 2190, Houston, TX 77056   713.275.7750

" With crippling budget deficits and fiscal crises, should I be worried about the safety of my municipal bond portfolio? "

By Donald J. Sorota

The budget troubles facing many state and local governments have clients concerned about the safety and security of municipal bonds, which form the bedrock of their investment portfolios. Declining tax collections during and since the recession have been a major culprit. Investors look at the state of California and its issuance of IOUs and wonder if that is a harbinger of things to come.

Every state except Vermont has some form of constitutional or statutory requirement to maintain a balanced budget. This is forcing tough decisions about raising taxes, reducing expenses, cutting services and deferring capital projects. Although some vendors and others who are owed money may experience difficulty collecting from municipalities, bond holders fare much better because they have a higher claim. For example, California's constitution mandates that general obligation bonds are second only to support of the public school and university systems. Of the $88.1 billion collected for all general fund revenues in California's 2009–2010 budget, $41.8 billion went to education, followed by $5.2 billion to general obligation bond debt service. Roughly $40 billion went for the payment of all other expenses. California's bondholders have that $40 billion cushion standing between them and default.

Historically, the default rates for municipal debt are significantly lower than corporate debt. The 10-year cumulative default rate for all Moody's rated municipal issuers is the same as that of the highest rated (AAA) corporate bond sector—0.19 percent. As one of our municipal bond managers recently highlighted, only 54 out of 18,400 municipal issuers rated by Moody's defaulted on their debt from 1970 to 2009. Of these 54 defaults, 42 were confined to the healthcare and housing sectors.

Still, the current environment does warrant caution. Our recommended managers favor investment-grade municipal bonds of large and liquid issuers, and they avoid issues from smaller communities because they tend to struggle more than large cities during challenging economic times. Generally, essential service revenue bonds, including water, sewer and utility bonds, tend to have steady revenues regardless of the economic environment. Investors in high-tax states such as California and New York, who often own only bonds issued by their home state, should rethink that approach. We believe a portfolio of bonds from issuers across the country provides a very real benefit of diversification to different economic circumstances.

We recommend active management and continuous monitoring of a municipal bond portfolio. Many investors inquire about the rating and analyze the credit risks of a bond only at purchase. That buy-and-hold strategy carries risks. Although defaults on highly rated municipal bonds have been low, credit conditions can change over time. ⑩

"Only 54 out of 18,400 municipal issuers rated by Moody's defaulted on their debt from 1970 to 2009."
– Donald J. Sorota

How to reach to Donald J. Sorota
Please call me at 312.429.3040 to set up an initial appointment.

Left to right: *front row*–Richard K. Black, Steven B. Weinstein, Bryan R. Malis; *back row*–Rebekah L. Kohmescher, Donald J. Sorota, Brett K. Rentmeester, Jason M. Laurie, Michael J. Murray

About Altair Advisers LLC

Altair was formed on June 1, 2002, by members of Arthur Andersen's Chicago Investment Consulting Practice, with an exclusive focus on providing independent investment counsel to high net worth individuals. The firm is employee owned and committed to building long-term successful relationships by providing responsive and highly personal service. Turmoil in the markets and upheaval in the advisor community have clients on the move. According to the Capgemini *2009 World Wealth Report*, "Of all the high net worth individual clients surveyed, 27 percent said they withdrew assets or left their wealth management firm in 2008." Altair has retained more than 95 percent of its clients.

Assets Under Management **$2.5 billion**	Compensation Method **Asset-based and fixed fees**
Minimum Annual Fee **$30,000**	Primary Custodian for Investor Assets **State Street**
Minimum Net Worth Requirement **$5 million (in investable assets)**	Professional Services Provided **Planning and investment advisory services**
Largest Client Net Worth **$1 billion+**	Association Memberships **Chartered Alternative Investment Analyst Association, Chicago Estate Planning Council, CFA Institute, CFA Society of Chicago and FPA**
Financial Services Experience **130 years (combined)**	Website **www.altairadvisers.com** Email **info@altairadvisers.com**

Altair Advisers LLC   303 West Madison Street, Suite 600, Chicago, IL 60606   312.429.3000

Delaware Valley | **Leading Wealth Advisor**

Wescott Financial Advisory Group LLC
Grant Rawdin, JD, CFP®, President and CEO
Lydia Sheckels, CFP®, EVP and CIO
Harold Weinstein, PhD, COO

"Does gold hold allure to you as part of a sound investment plan, or is it a fool's bet?"

By Grant Rawdin

Gold's investment reputation has been burnished recently by its substantial price rise. Is this confirmation of the investment efficacy of gold, or is investment in gold a perpetual-motion machine pedaled by investor fear amid difficult markets? Let us share a brief and unemotional history and perspective about the investment theses for gold.

An oft-cited reason for owning gold is that it is an inflation hedge. Yet from February 1970 through November 2010, gold and inflation had a near-zero correlation—0.001. Think about it, and it rings true: Gold's 286 percent run up during the 2000s came during the decade's historically low 24.6 percent (2.26 percent annualized) inflation rate.

Another investment thesis is that gold is a less volatile investment asset, providing more diversification in a portfolio.

Gold itself has a high standard deviation (higher risk represented by high volatility). Over the past 30 years, gold had annual returns ranging from +136.5 percent to –32.60 percent, yet in the first 25 years of the period, annualized gold returns were relatively flat.

Then what is driving the bull market in gold, and is it sustainable?

All the gold that has ever been mined can fit into two Olympic-size swimming pools. Jewelry accounts for about 70 percent of the demand for gold; industry demand is far behind at 12 percent, with gold used largely for electronics.

The remaining 18 percent of demand is investment related, primarily used by central banks that hold gold as a reserve. Recently, however, individual investors began feverishly mining for returns from gold amid concerns about markets and economies. This has been a primary force behind the recent increase.

Our conclusions and recommendations: Investment prospects for gold are good as long as there are rising demand and limited supply and uncertainty clouds the market. Changes in any of these factors, particularly investor sentiment, will greatly tarnish prospects for gold.

The meteoric rise of gold from 2000 to 2010 is very unlikely to be coined again during the next decade. While many believe there will be inflationary pressures caused by large government deficits, as we stated previously, gold has not been a solution for inflation hedging.

Gold has been part of our model portfolio largely through the earnings of companies that mine and sell gold. There has been some direct exposure to gold, but we believe that opportunity has largely passed.

So, despite history, if you feel a need for a trove of gold, then our recommendation is to buy a modest amount in legitimate coin (to make trade easier) and to store it in your own safety deposit box. And while you do not receive regular capital gain tax treatment upon the sale of gold (assuming you have a gain), like most individual gold investors, you will never sell it. ⓦ

FURTHER RESOURCES ON THIS TOPIC...

There are a multitude of reasons why gold, despite the current mania, is an investment best approached very thoughtfully; only some of these have been explored here. For an excellent story on other startling aspects and issues about gold, please see *National Geographic* magazine, December 2009, "The Real Price of Gold," available online.

For a variety of other information resources and links on wealth management and life issues and advice, please see our e-letter, *Wescott Life* at www.wescott.com.

The Delaware Valley region is defined as the following counties: Pennsylvania—Berks, Bucks, Chester, Delaware, Montgomery, Philadelphia; Delaware—New Castle; Maryland—Cecil; and New Jersey—Atlantic, Burlington, Camden, Cape May, Cumberland, Gloucester, Mercer, Ocean, Salem.

"All the gold that has ever been mined can fit into two Olympic-size swimming pools."

– Grant Rawdin

Harold Weinstein

Grant Rawdin

Lydia Sheckels

About Wescott Financial Advisory Group LLC

Grant Rawdin is founder and CEO of Wescott. An attorney, accountant and CFP, Mr. Rawdin has been named annually among the top 100 wealth advisors in *Worth* and *Barron's*. In addition to client service, he is responsible for the overall management and development of Wescott. Lydia Sheckels is executive vice president and chief investment officer of Wescott. She is responsible for the firm's Investment Research Group, which constructs Wescott's asset allocation model and conducts rigorous manager due diligence. Harold Weinstein, PhD, is the firm's chief operating officer. He is responsible for overall business operations, with innovation for a richer staff and client experience.

Assets Under Management
$1.5 billion (globally)

Compensation Method
Asset-based and fixed fees

Minimum Fee for Initial Meeting
None required

Primary Custodian for Investor Assets
Charles Schwab & Co., Fidelity Investments

Minimum Net Worth Requirement
N/A ($2 million investment portfolio)

Professional Services Provided
Planning, investment advisory and money management services

Largest Client Net Worth
$145 million

Association Memberships **Financial Planning Association (FPA), the National Association of Personal Financial Advisors (NAPFA)**

Financial Services Experience
30 years

Website
www.wescott.com

Email
grawdin@wescott.com

Wescott Financial Advisory Group LLC | 30 South 17th Street, 4th Floor, Philadelphia, PA 19103 | 215.979.1600
200 South Biscayne Boulevard, Suite 3400, Miami, FL 33131 | 305.960.2357

" How should I structure my investments in the wake of the apparent failure of MPT? "

By Gregory S. Horn

We reject the premise that modern portfolio theory (MPT) failed in the market meltdown in 2008. MPT does not suggest that negative returns can be avoided, only that more-broadly diversified portfolios should exhibit less volatility than less-diversified portfolios. Many investors are under-diversified much of the time. We strongly recommend that our clients remain diversified across asset classes and geography, include alternative investments, and do rigorous cash-flow planning when structuring their portfolios. Unfortunately, both individual and institutional investors, on average, exhibit unhealthy under-diversification and returns-chasing behavior.

For example, in the late 1980s, international stocks, particularly Japanese stocks, were posting very high returns. Many investors overweighted these in their portfolios and they were severely punished for it. In the late 1990s, technology and Internet-related stocks were posting unprecedented high returns. Again many investors bulked up on these issues, and they were severely punished for it. In 2008, many investors were overweight in stocks and leveraged, asset-backed investments, and they were severely punished for it. However, while almost all financial assets declined in 2008, portfolios that were less overweight in these asset categories and more broadly diversified

tended to decline less. That is all MPT suggests one can expect.

A 2008 study of the hiring and firing of investment managers by pension plan sponsors found that newly hired managers tended to have outperformed their benchmarks and/or peers in the three years prior to being hired, but tended to underperform during the three years after being hired.[1] Likewise, the fired managers tended to outperform their replacements over the following three years.

Many investors, individuals and institutions alike, seem to view investment management as a great race against market benchmarks, and they are frustrated when their managers fall behind, even for a brief period. Actually, managers who employ strict stock selection criteria may outperform in the long term, but may naturally underperform in periods when the market is forming a bubble or chasing a fad. At these times, investors should review why they selected their managers, and whether they are adhering to their stock selection discipline. If so, sticking with them during periods of relative underperformance may prove wise. In short, if you would like the potential to meaningfully outperform the markets in the long term, you must be willing to accept largely inevitable periods of underperformance when the market is chasing something the manager is not. ⓦ

AN EXAMPLE

We offer the last three years of the 1990s and the first three years of the 2000s as a classic example of growth versus value. Russell Investments publishes numerous equity benchmarks popular with investment consultants. The Russell 1000 series tracks the 1,000 largest U.S. companies by market capitalization and breaks them down into growth and value investing style subsets. As you can see in the table, huge return differences occurred between growth and value. As you might imagine, many investors were overweighting their growth-oriented managers in the first period, only to be punished for it in the second. Investors who maintained their asset and style weightings through this period generally fared better than those who chased growth. In other words, MPT worked, and we believe it still does today.

Russell 1000 Indexes[2]		
YEAR	GROWTH	VALUE
1997-1999 (1st period)	141.0%	67.8%
2000-2002 (2nd period)	-55.5%	-14.7%
1997-2002 (All six years)	7.3%	43.2%

Information contained herein should not be considered investment advice and is subject to change at any time based on market or other conditions.
[1]*Amit Goyal and Sunil Wahal, 2008, "The Selection and Termination of Investment Management Firms by Plan Sponsors," The Journal of Finance, volume 63, (p. 1805–1847)*
[2]*Indexes are unmanaged and cannot be invested in directly. Returns represent past performance, are not a guarantee of future performance, and are not indicative of any specific investment. Source: Russell Investments & Persimmon Capital Management.*

The Delaware Valley region is defined as the following counties: Pennsylvania—Berks, Bucks, Chester, Delaware, Montgomery, Philadelphia; Delaware— New Castle; Maryland—Cecil; and New Jersey—Atlantic, Burlington, Camden, Cape May, Cumberland, Gloucester, Mercer, Ocean, Salem.

> "Managers who employ strict stock selection criteria may outperform in the long term, but may naturally underperform in periods when the market is forming a bubble or chasing a fad."

– Gregory S. Horn

How to reach Gregory S. Horn

Please call 877.502.6840 to reach me or any other member of our team: Todd E. Dawes, senior vice president, partner; Kevin O'Shea, senior vice president, partner; John P. Collins, CIMA, senior vice president, partner; Matt J. Terrien, CFA, chief quantitative analyst; Amy B. Armstrong, vice president, partner; Jodi E. DiFilippo, assistant vice president; and Brad Brubaker, CPA, controller.

I NEVER LEAVE HOME WITHOUT...

My BlackBerry, so my clients can always contact me

THE LAST BOOK I READ WAS...

Lords of Finance: The Bankers Who Broke the World—*it's a historical perspective on the central bankers from post-WWI*

MY HOBBIES ARE...

Golf, travel and wine collecting

About Gregory S. Horn

Gregory S. Horn is the founder and managing partner of Persimmon Capital Management, an SEC-registered, independent investment advisor providing wealth advisory services to family, foundation and pension clients since 1998. Prior to founding Persimmon, Mr. Horn was president and cofounder of Ashbridge Investment Management Inc., growing assets under management from approximately $100 million to nearly $1 billion. Before that, he headed the Personal and Family division of Mellon Private Capital Management. With a team of eight dedicated and experienced professionals, Persimmon is well qualified to support the complex needs of today's most sophisticated investors.

Assets Under Management **$300 million**	Compensation Method **Asset-based fees**
Minimum Fee for Initial Meeting **None required**	Primary Custodian for Investor Assets **Schwab Institutional**
Minimum Net Worth Requirement **$5 million**	Professional Services Provided **Investment advisory and family office services**
Largest Client Net Worth **$200 million+**	Website **www.persimmoncapital.com**
Financial Services Experience **27 years (Greg)** **87 years (investment team, combined)**	Email **ghorn@persimmoncapital.com**

Persimmon Capital Management LP | 1777 Sentry Parkway West, Gwynedd Hall, Suite 102, Blue Bell, PA 19422 | 877.502.6840

Fairfield County, CT   **Leading Wealth Advisor**

The Trischman Group at Morgan Stanley Smith Barney
Harold J. Trischman Jr., Managing Director–Wealth Management
Robert A. Franchini, CFP®, ChFC®, CRPC®, Vice President–Wealth Management
Richard J. Smalley, First Vice President–Wealth Management
Stephanie M. Franchini, CRPC®, Second Vice President–Wealth Management

"Why invest in longer-term bonds?"

By Harold J. Trischman Jr.

At times in the past the difference in yields between short-term bonds and longer-term bonds has been small. These markets are said to have a flat yield curve. During times of a flat curve it is tempting to invest in bonds of shorter maturities because extending to longer maturity dates offers little incremental reward (yield), and the cost of waiting is small.

Today, however, money markets and cash equivalents are generally yielding 1 percent or less, and yet I believe millions of investors are reluctant to buy bonds of any meaningful duration because they are so convinced that yields will be rising soon. I am convinced of this, too, but if one waits with the expectation that rates will rise, the arithmetic suggests that it may not be good enough to be right. You have to be very right. Yields on 5-, 10- and 20-year bonds are not historically high, but their returns are still significant.

My counsel to bond investors is to take out a pen and paper and do some math. If a 4 percent difference (called a spread) exists between cash and a bond yield, then that is another way of saying that cash returns must rise by 400 basis points just to equal what the bond has been paying all along. Certainly rates could rise in the current environment, but what many investors ignore is that the magnitude of the rise and the length of time taken for the rise to occur are essential pieces of the calculation. In this case, time really is money.

Furthermore the yield on tax-free bonds is historically very high when compared to their taxable counterparts, and these conditions may not last forever. In the prior example, if we assume that the bond is tax-exempt (very plausible), then the argument for putting money to work is that much stronger. With income tax rates set to rise for some individuals, the argument for trying to resist playing the interest rate speculation game is quite strong.

What I try to do is prevent investors from being right about interest rates, but wrong about their investments. If you ignore the cost of waiting to invest you can be both right and wrong at the same time. Ⓦ

DOING THE MATH: THE COST OF WAITING

In the five-year scenario of bond holder versus cash holder, even if short-term interest rates increase by 1 percent a year, at the end of five years, the bond holder will come out way ahead—not to mention that the holder can take the earnings during that time and invest in stocks, thereby possibly piling earnings on top of earnings.

Year	FIVE-YEAR BOND		
	Assumed % Annual Rise in Rates	Assumed Cash Yields	Assumed Bond Yields
1	+1.0	0.50%	3.50%
2	+1.0	1.50%	3.50%
3	+1.0	2.50%	3.50%
4	+1.0	3.50%	3.50%
5	+1.0	4.50%	3.50%

Note: These examples are for illustrative purposes only and do not represent the actual performance of any investment. Past performance is no guarantee of future results.

> "What many investors ignore is that the magnitude of the rise and the length of time taken for the rise to occur are essential pieces of the calculation."
>
> – Harold J. Trischman Jr.

How to reach The Trischman Group

We prefer face-to-face meetings with prospective clients. Please feel free to contact any member of The Trischman Group at 203.661.3330.

Seated: Harold J. Trischman.
Standing, left to right:
Robert A. Franchini,
Richard J. Smalley,
Stephanie M. Franchini.

About The Trischman Group at Morgan Stanley Smith Barney

Harold J. Trischman Jr., managing director–wealth management, focuses on the spectrum of complex wealth issues that face high net worth individuals and businesses. His 25 years of experience span estate planning, philanthropy, alternative investments, control and restricted securities, lending, hedging and monetization and investment banking. Robert A. Franchini, CFP, ChFC, CRPC, vice president–wealth management, has spent 14 years in financial services, concentrating on asset management, risk management, trust and estate analysis, estate plan design, liability planning, hedging and monetization and retirement plan design. Richard J. Smalley, first vice president–wealth management, brings 24 years of experience and concentrates on fixed-income investing, particularly tax-free municipal bonds, to help the team's high net worth individuals address their cash-flow needs. Stephanie M. Franchini, CRPC, second vice president–wealth management, has been a member of the Trischman Group since 1999, and her primary role is to facilitate the trading of equities, bonds, futures and commodities within the team.

Assets Under Management $900 million	**Compensation Method** Asset-based fees and commissions (investment and insurance products)
Minimum Fee for Initial Meeting None required	**Primary Custodian for Investor Assets** Morgan Stanley Smith Barney
Minimum Net Worth Requirement $10 million ($2 million investment portfolio)	**Professional Services Provided** Planning, investment advisory and money management services
Largest Client Net Worth $200 million	**Website** fa.smithbarney.com/trischmangroup
Financial Services Experience 70+ years (combined)	**Email** harold.j.trischman@mssb.com robert.franchini@mssb.com richard.smalley@mssb.com stephanie.m.franchini@mssb.com

The Trischman Group at Morgan Stanley Smith Barney | One Fawcett Place, Third Floor, Greenwich, CT 06830 | 203.661.3330

Atlanta, GA **Leading Wealth Advisor**

The Hansberger Group at Morgan Stanley Smith Barney
James C. Hansberger Sr., Managing Director-Wealth Management,
Senior Portfolio Management Director, Financial Advisor

" What is the outlook for equities for the next 10 years? "

By James C. Hansberger Sr.

While we fully recognize the difficulties of the recessions and market declines of 2000–2002 and 2008–2009, we suggest that purchasing growth businesses at reasonable prices always represents an excellent opportunity for capital appreciation. The very fact that these two disappointing periods serve as the bookends of a lost decade for many equity investors makes our argument for outperformance for the next 10 years all the more plausible.

Big ideas come from original thinking and discarding many long-held assumptions. We focus on businesses, not just their stocks, and believe that many companies may be mispriced in the marketplace; hence, we believe markets are often inefficient. Our discipline states that over time a stock can only do as well as the business itself and that the value of that business does not fluctuate as much as the stock. Behind every stock lies a tangible, operating business, and our goal is to identify such opportunities, large and small, and purchase shares at undervalued prices, i.e., growth at a reasonable price.

Our discipline states that the characteristics of great businesses include high returns on equity, above-average corporate profit growth, a balance sheet with limited debt, substantial levels of free cash flow, a management team that owns heavy amounts of the stock, and significant pricing power of goods and services in the marketplace.

The 1970s was an extraordinary time in our financial history. After the post-WWII boom and the record bull market of the 1950s and 1960s, came Vietnam, Watergate and the oil embargo, which caused havoc in the markets. Inflation eventually reached 15 to 16 percent, and interest rates soared above 20 percent by decade's end. Over 1973 and 1974, the DJIA declined 45 percent, and, after a partial recovery in 1975 and 1976, remained flat until the early 1980s. Indeed, in 1982 the U.S. stock market was priced at a level below that of 1965, and we had experienced the worst economic environment since the Great Depression[1]. This time was a watershed period in my career learning curve; surely, adversity is the best teacher of success and achievement. I see similarities today to the world of the 1970s. Investors then, as now, had been disappointed by a decade of flat performance for the market averages as a whole.

We understand that investors today are cautious and risk averse but suggest they focus on probabilities, not possibilities; reality often falls short of anticipation. Investors should properly balance their concerns about risk with the reality that cash and the most conservative investment instruments offer inferior yields and have the inherent risk of a loss of purchasing power if faced with inflation. No risk does indeed offer no return.

With such subpar returns from fixed income, and with concerns of debt and illiquidity in real estate and private equity, we believe equities will become the asset class of choice in the next decade. **We recommend five distinct equity portfolios—core growth, dividend income, emerging markets, aggressive small/mid-capitalization equities, and long/short strategies—together offering diversification and hedging strategies.**

The Hansberger Group has represented the high net worth marketplace for more than three decades, assisting our clients in the creation and maintenance of significant net worth. It all comes down to original thinking—our mantra for more than 30 years—a disruptive growth strategy that decommoditizes a commodity business. We compete on the power of our discipline and original ideas. In a time of advice overload, what is still in short supply are insights and real innovation in investment management. Ⓦ

---

[1]Inflation rates, interest rates, DJIA return information from Bloomberg Markets

This material does not provide individually tailored investment advice. It has been prepared without regard to the individual financial circumstances and objectives of persons who receive it. The views expressed herein are those of the author and do not necessarily reflect the views of Morgan Stanley Smith Barney or its affiliates. All opinions are subject to change without notice. Neither the information provided nor any opinion expressed constitutes a solicitation for the purchase or sale of any security. Past performance is no guarantee of future results.

Chicago, IL **Leading Wealth/Insurance Advisor**

HUB International Personal Insurance
James P. Kane, CIC, President

"Have attitudes changed toward personal risk management in light of recent financial events?"

By James P. Kane

Perhaps the biggest casualty of the financial meltdown has been consumer confidence. The blow that has been struck to the psyche of clients from the massive fraud, misrepresentation and mismanagement will take years to heal. The insurance business has also been adversely impacted. Insurance carriers have recorded unprecedented reductions in premiums due to downsizing and bankruptcies of businesses across the country. In turn, personal insurance programs have seen significant changes in philosophy to managing risk.

A positive outcome from the turmoil in the market has been an increased focus on insurance and risk management by insurance buyers. Today's economy requires clients to take a closer look at their allocation of resources, including what they spend on insurance coverage. For example, we have seen a greater willingness by consumers to move toward higher deductibles as an effective way to manage premium costs. They are also pressing their insurance advisors to identify any and all available discounts. At 8 to 10 percent of the household budget, insurance premiums must be treated as a critical piece of one's financial plan.

Unfortunately, we typically find that affluent consumers are underinsured when it comes to personal liability coverage as well as total replacement coverage for their home. As insurance advisors, these are two of the biggest areas of concern we consistently communicate to clients.

While an insurance review tends to create the same anxiety that one feels in the dentist's chair, gone is the attitude that insurance is a necessary evil to be dealt with only when absolutely required. That attitude has been reset partly out of necessity. The increased attention to personal risk management and insurance has been supported by other financial professionals who seek to enhance the service and support they provide to their clients. Now more than ever, the insurance advisor has become a pivotal member of the financial advisory team.

The challenges in the current economy have reinforced the notion that buying a policy is not always the first, or only solution. **The sophisticated buyer requires an insurance expert who takes a holistic approach to personal risk management, including avoidance, risk transfer or risk assumption.** Many ways to manage risk do not involve insurance. Today, personal risk management must be viewed holistically if we are to meet the expectations of a client base that has weathered the worst economic downturn in more than half a century.

In order to compete in this market, the professional insurance advisor must be proactive in monitoring a client's insurance portfolio or take the chance that a competitor will do it. Conducting a thorough analysis of the client's lifestyle and appetite for risk is the best approach to advising how to manage risk. In the midst of uncertainty, understanding one's risks and making the appropriate investment in insurance will go a long way toward planning for a more secure future. ⓦ

REGULATIONS DO HELP

For me, one of the most understated lessons from the recent downturn has been that the regulation of property and casualty insurers has actually worked. Little attention has been paid to the overall stability of the property and casualty industry amidst one of the worst economies we have seen in a generation.

Conventional wisdom would suggest that current economic conditions would result in a shrinking of capacity or supply of insurance availability. We have witnessed the opposite, with a few notable but expected exceptions (professional liability coverage for financial institutions, to name one). This extraordinary turn of events can be attributed to a number of factors, most significantly an industry that increased surplus during the economic boom. This discipline has allowed the insurance business to absorb the financial blow inflicted by the economic meltdown.

"The insurance advisor has become a pivotal member of the financial advisory team."

– James P. Kane

How to reach James P. Kane

Please call me anytime at 312.279.4856 or connect with me on LinkedIn.

THE LAST BOOK I READ WAS...

Brain Rules, *by John Medina and* Silent Safety, *by Doug Kane and Paul Viollis*

WHAT MAKES A GOOD CLIENT...

There are no bad clients, only bad process on our part if we fail to listen.

MY FAVORITE VACATION...

Our 2009 family visit to Ireland was spectacular and included meeting some cousins for the first time.

About James P. Kane

James P. Kane has dedicated the last two decades to establishing a personal insurance practice built on service that drives growth. In his five-year tenure as president of personal insurance at HUB International, he has established his firm as a premier provider of thought leadership on insurance matters for high net worth clients. HUB has more than 500 personal insurance experts dedicated to their clients' insurance needs and to planning for the unforeseen. Mr. Kane is an active member of his local parish church and the University of Notre Dame Alumni Association.

Largest Client Net Worth
$1 billion+

Insurance Services Experience
25 years

Website
www.hubinternational.com

Professional Services Provided
Risk management service for property casualty exposures

Certifications
Certified Insurance Counselor

Email and Twitter
james.kane@hubinternational.com
Follow James P. Kane on Twitter at twitter.com/kanejp.

" Should I worry that increased access and transparency have actually diminished the productivity of hedge funds? "

By Jeremy Tennenbaum

A long list of factors has impacted the productivity of hedge funds as a group, for better and for worse, but increased access and transparency are far down the list in terms of their importance. That being said, investors should remain confident that they can choose from a broad universe of hedge funds with high levels of productivity.

New strategies are created every year to replace those that are no longer productive. As long as we have capital market innovation, structural inefficiencies and the ability to trade in a variety of markets using multiple instruments, hedge funds will search worldwide to find good opportunities.

Some of the major factors impacting hedge fund productivity include:

01 **Leverage and access to credit.** In the wake of the events of 2008, access to leverage has become more expensive for established players and more difficult to obtain for start-ups. This has reduced the attractiveness of fixed-income strategies that depended on 8:1 or 9:1 leverage (many relative value trades, for instance).

02 **The paring back of investment banking proprietary trading efforts (and, if the Volcker rule is instituted, their elimination).** This is likely to be a positive factor, particularly for multistrategy funds, because investment banking prop desks had easy access to credit and tended to be more highly leveraged than their hedge fund counterparts. This caused spreads to contract in many strategies, negatively impacting returns.

03 **Fund flows.** The flow of monies into and out of different strategies is a critical element of productivity. The first $200 million invested in a strategy might produce returns in excess of 20 percent, the next $2 billion might produce high single-digit returns, and the next $20 billion might produce negative returns. It is hard to estimate flows with a high degree of accuracy, though the impact is clear ex post facto.

Nevertheless, it is essential to follow flows in strategies dependent upon spreads between securities (merger arbitrage, many event-driven strategies and convertible arbitrage, among others) because fund flows can critically impact future performance. For strategies that go long and short, fund flows have not mattered as much. For example, small-cap stocks are richer or cheaper as a result of hedge fund flows.

No evidence shows that improved transparency and access have diminished productivity. Perhaps the reverse is true; if crowded trades had been more transparent we might have avoided upheavals such as the quant fund debacle of August 2007 or the Porsche trap of October 2008. And we suspect investors in Amaranth Advisors and Sowood Capital Management might have preferred more transparency. ⓦ

"No evidence shows that improved transparency and access have diminished productivity."

– Jeremy Tennenbaum

How to reach Jeremy Tennenbaum

I always have my BlackBerry on me, so please contact me via email at jtennenbaum@spoutingrockconsult.com.

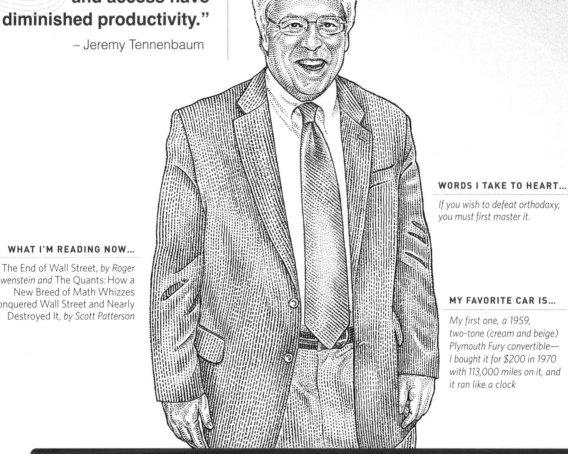

WORDS I TAKE TO HEART...

If you wish to defeat orthodoxy, you must first master it.

WHAT I'M READING NOW...

The End of Wall Street, *by Roger Lowenstein and* The Quants: How a New Breed of Math Whizzes Conquered Wall Street and Nearly Destroyed It, *by Scott Patterson*

MY FAVORITE CAR IS...

My first one, a 1959, two-tone (cream and beige) Plymouth Fury convertible— I bought it for $200 in 1970 with 113,000 miles on it, and it ran like a clock

About Jeremy Tennenbaum

Jeremy Tennenbaum has more than 25 years of investment experience. He has served as the CIO of a billion-dollar family office, has run a venture capital fund, managed equity portfolios, and invested in both public and private companies. He has a broad knowledge of a variety of asset types—embracing marketable and non-marketable securities, equities, bonds and alternatives, both domestic and international. Before joining Spouting Rock Consulting he was affiliated with Continental Grain, Seagate Technology, Wellington Management Co. and Salomon Brothers. He has a master's degree in finance from MIT's Sloan School of Management and a bachelor of arts in politics from Princeton.

Minimum Annual Fee $10,000	Compensation Method Annual retainer, time-based (monthly, weekly, daily) and task-based fees
Minimum Net Worth Requirement $5 million	Professional Services Provided **Investment due diligence (focus on alternatives), investment reporting, asset allocation and investment policy statements**
Largest Client Net Worth $1.5 billion	Association Memberships CFA Institute (and two chapters: CFA Society of Philadelphia and NYSSA), Family Firm Institute, IMCA, Institute for Private Investors
Financial Services Experience 25 years	Website www.spoutingrockconsult.com Email jtennenbaum@spoutingrockconsult.com

Spouting Rock Consulting | 150 Strafford Avenue, Suite 350, Wayne, PA 19087 | 484.253.1216

Chicago, IL—Des Moines, IA   **Leading Wealth Advisor**

The Swanson Group at Morgan Stanley Smith Barney
Keith K. Swanson, CIMA®, Director–Wealth Management
Meredith S. Swanson, CIMA®, Second VP–Wealth Management

" Where in the world should I invest? "

By Keith K. Swanson

In today's environment, it is important to broaden the opportunity set to capture opportunity in the worlds of today and tomorrow. Emerging markets are an asset class that many believe will deliver robust returns in 2011 and beyond. There is a subset of this asset class, however, that is less developed than its emerging market peers and may offer greater growth potential that is yet to be recognized by global equity markets. These frontier markets are countries that due to size, investment restrictions or lower development level are ineligible for inclusion in the emerging market index. The frontier universe includes countries such as Argentina, Vietnam and Latvia. I believe frontier markets offer a compelling case for consideration.

HISTORICALLY LOW CORRELATION
As the credit crisis unfolded in 2008 and as sentiment reversed course in 2009, dramatically high correlations occurred among all asset classes. Frontier markets, however, have maintained low correlation to both developed and emerging markets, and among each other, offering diversification benefits (source: Factset, MSCI and S&P).

COMPELLING DEMOGRAPHICS
Productivity in frontier markets is in part a result of their demographics. Higher projected growth may be attributable to young populations, improvements in technology, large shifts toward manufacturing and away from agriculture, and supportive policy reform. Many frontier markets are not integrated into the world trade structure, deriving a relatively low portion of their GDP from exports. As a result, domestic consumption accounts for the greatest portion of their GDP (source: Morgan Stanley).

CAPITALIZATION DISCONNECT
According to 2009 IMF GDP estimates, frontier markets accounted for a 5 percent share of nominal GDP in the world. Conversely, only 0.8 percent of the world's market cap representation is attributed to the frontier marketplace, according to MSCI. We believe that valuations of companies within these countries may increase to close the gap between GDP and market capitalization.

Frontier markets find themselves in a unique position, with the potential to deliver solid returns in the future. They are small, undervalued and below the radar screen, which may provide for an attractive opportunity. ⓦ

"Frontier markets are small, undervalued and below the radar screen, which may provide for an attractive opportunity."

– Keith K. Swanson

How to reach Keith K. Swanson and Meredith S. Swanson

Please feel free to contact us via phone at 312.917.7512 or email at meredith.s.swanson@mssb.com.

I NEVER LEAVE HOME WITHOUT...

Meredith: Some idea of where I am going

Keith: An 1892 silver dollar that my great-great-uncle gave my father during the Depression so he would always have a dollar

WHAT'S ON MY DESK...

Meredith: Pictures of my nephew, photos from my favorite trips, an orchid and a revolving pile of industry reading material

Keith: Pictures of my wife, children and new grandson, Henry, along with my favorite 1895 historic picture of Telluride's main street

MY HOBBIES ARE...

Meredith: Traveling, training for triathlons, cooking and reading

Keith: Skiing, bicycling and reading

Keith K. Swanson

Meredith S. Swanson

About Keith K. Swanson and Meredith S. Swanson

Keith K. Swanson, director–wealth management, has been designated a family wealth director at Morgan Stanley Smith Barney and an institutional consulting director for Graystone Consulting, a business of Morgan Stanley Smith Barney. He came into the industry more than 35 years ago, remaining with the same firm throughout his career, through a series of mergers and name changes. Mr. Swanson built a team of investment professionals to expand his thriving business. His daughter, Meredith, joined the team to help service the emerging wealth for multigenerational families.

Assets Under Management **$400 million**	Compensation Method **Asset-based and fixed fees, commissions** **(investment and insurance products)**
Minimum Annual Fee **None required**	Primary Custodian for Investor Assets **Morgan Stanley Smith Barney**
Minimum Net Worth Requirement **$5 million**	Professional Services Provided **Planning, investment advisory and money management services**
Largest Client Net Worth **$400 million**	Association Memberships **IMCA**
Financial Services Experience **36 years**	Website **fa.smithbarney.com/swanson** Email **keith.k.swanson@mssb.com** **meredith.s.swanson@mssb.com**

The Swanson Group at Morgan Stanley Smith Barney | 190 South LaSalle Street, Suite 2900, Chicago, IL 60603 | 312.917.7512

Tempe, AZ—Los Angeles, CA   **Leading Wealth Advisor**

**The Meyer, Pickens, Turner Wealth Management Group
at Morgan Stanley Smith Barney**
Kurt Meyer, CIMA®, Financial Advisor, Pamela Pickens, Financial Advisor,
Ryan Turner, CFA®, Financial Advisor

" How can I potentially avoid the next bear market? "

By Kurt Meyer

The obvious answer to the above question is: Do not own investments that are declining but rather buy or own investments that are rising or maintaining their value. Relative-strength investing aims to help you do just that.

As defined by Investor Glossary, relative strength is basically the measurement of the performance of one security relative to another. This analysis may be related to the basic asset classes (cash, domestic stocks, foreign stocks, bonds, foreign currencies, real estate and commodities) or subsets of these classes. By measuring and monitoring the relative performance of various asset classes, investors can focus on outperforming positions relative to their peers. **Additional portfolio management benefits of relative-strength investing may be:**

- A disciplined approach
- Objective, not emotional, decisions
- Reacting and adapting to the investment environment
- Not being afraid to deviate from a benchmark
- Help in removing subjectivity

Ken French, a professor at Dartmouth University, has shown that for more than 80 years relative strength has been an effective return factor, and it has been the strongest of all the various factors he studied. In addition, in the 1996 book, *What Works on Wall Street*, James O'Shaughnessy tested more than 60 different investment strategies and found that by adding relative strength to the common fundamental value strategies, all of the returns were better than when relative strength was not used.

Therefore, when building or reviewing a portfolio, we believe an investor should periodically screen the relative-strength attributes of each major asset class and each individual position to determine whether to overweight, underweight or eliminate an investment. An investor's broad risk/return objectives can then be blended to buy, hold or sell good relative-strength investments while maintaining a mix that meets the investor's risk tolerance.

In its simplest terms, the use of relative-strength analysis may help you overweight investments in any category that is rising at a faster pace than the rest of the investment world. Consequently, this type of analysis may help investors identify the weakest areas of their investments. Ⓦ

LET YOUR WINNERS RUN AND CUT YOUR LOSERS SHORT

The main principles of relative-strength investing are to keep or add money to the assets that are outperforming and to sell or avoid those that are underperforming. If investors can unemotionally exit underperforming assets because of relative-strength analysis, they may go a long way toward mitigating the damage of the next bear market.

In an April 2010 white paper titled, "Relative Strength Strategies for Investing," Mebane Faber of Cambria Investments tested relative-strength models consisting of U.S. equity sectors from 1926 to 2009 and major asset classes from 1973 to 2009 using the French-Fama CRSP data library. The relative-strength measures he used for the studies are common methods based on trailing returns. Some interesting conclusions from the paper were:

- Relative-strength models outperformed buy-and-hold investing in roughly 70 percent of all years
- Approximately 300 to 600 basis points of outperformance per year was achieved
- Relative-strength models outperformed in each of the eight decades tested

"Introducing the issues of wealth and social capital to children is one way to help children live happy, productive lives."

– Kurt Meyer

How to reach The Meyer, Pickens, Turner Wealth Management Group

We would love to hear from you. Please call us at 480.345.4712.

Kurt Meyer

Pamela Pickens

Ryan Turner

About The Meyer, Pickens, Turner Wealth Management Group

The Meyer, Pickens, Turner Wealth Management Group provides family office wealth management and investment services to ultra high net worth investors. Kurt Meyer attended UCLA and Arizona State University, receiving a BS in finance. He began his career as a financial consultant with Merrill Lynch in 1986. He joined Smith Barney, now Morgan Stanley Smith Barney, in 1988. He is a member of the Director's Council, which acknowledges the top 5 percent of financial advisors at Morgan Stanley Smith Barney. Pamela Pickens works from the Newport Beach, Calif., office. She began her career with Morgan Stanley Smith Barney and predecessor firms in 2000. She is a member of the Investment Management Consultants Association and is a liaison for energy advocates, given her close ties to her father, T. Boone Pickens. Ryan Turner attended the University of Notre Dame where he graduated with a BA in finance and captained the soccer team. In 1999, he joined Morgan Stanley Smith Barney.

Assets Under Management
$400 million

Minimum Fee for Initial Meeting
None required

Minimum Net Worth Requirement
$5 million

Largest Client Net Worth
$1.5 billion

Financial Services Experience
45 years (combined)

Compensation Method
Asset-based fees and commissions (investment and insurance products)

Primary Custodian for Investor Assets
Morgan Stanley Smith Barney

Professional Services Provided
Planning, investment advisory and money management services

Association Memberships
CFA Institute, Investment Management Consultants Association

Email
kurt.e.meyer@smithbarney.com

Phone
480.345.4712

The Meyer, Pickens, Turner Wealth Management Group at Morgan Stanley Smith Barney

660 Newport Center Drive, Suite 1100, Newport Beach, CA 92625
80 East Rio Salado Parkway, Suite 810, Tempe, AZ 85281

Los Angeles, CA   **Leading Wealth Advisor**

Morgan Stanley Smith Barney
Larry Palmer, CFP®, CIMA®, Managing Director

" Why do you think ETFs may be a good post-meltdown investment? "

By Larry Palmer

Will Rogers is often credited with saying, "I'm more interested in the return of my investment than the return on my investment." He might have been speaking for many of today's high net worth investors. In this era, exchange traded funds (ETFs) may offer an investment that is long on transparency and liquidity, low in cost and can be highly tax efficient. In my opinion, they are changing the way many people invest.

LONG ON TRANSPARENCY, LIQUIDITY AND EASE

An ETF is structured as a mutual fund but has the ability to trade on an exchange like a stock. Like a mutual fund, an ETF gives investors exposure to a group of securities through the purchase of a single share. Like a stock, shares are traded on exchanges at market-determined prices and bought and sold through brokerage accounts. ETFs closely track indexes, such as the S&P 500, or market sectors, such as gold stocks, oil stocks, etc. Several characteristics may make them attractive to investors.

For one thing, ETFs are easy to buy and own. You buy ETFs just like a stock trade, making them a highly liquid security. ETFs also have a high level of transparency. Unlike with hedge funds and alternative investments, you can go online and look at all the securities in your ETF almost any time.

LOW ON MANAGEMENT AND COST

An ETF may be a low-cost way to passively invest in the publicly traded market. It may be cost-efficient compared to a hedge fund or an actively managed fund because you do not need an active manager. Instead of buying and selling on quarterly reports of a specific company and its stock, with an ETF you are getting representation of a sector in the market.

Also, because ETFs are highly liquid and traded on an exchange, their fees tend to be significantly lower than those charged by hedge fund managers or actively managed equity managers. Depending on the type of account for which they are purchased, commissions or fees may apply.[1]

ETFS: A MATTER OF CHOICE

With ETFs you can thematically invest in almost any sector of the market—commodities, indexes, real estate, etc. In addition, ETFs are easy to understand and have a readily ascertainable market value. For investors who want to take risks and get nothing but alpha*—that is, higher than average performance—ETFs may seem a bit like the plain vanilla of investments. But for a growing number of investors, ETF "vanilla" is not just a flavor of the month, but one for the long term. ⓦ

ETFS: WHY YOU MAY LIKE THEM AT TAX TIME

ETFs can be highly tax efficient because the owner of the ETF is not actively buying and selling securities. Your tax consequence comes if the ETF has dividends or you sell it. So with an ETF you get to control part of the tax liability with the timing of your sale. Another beauty of an ETF is, if you have a tax loss, you can actually sell out the portfolio, harvest the tax losses, and the next day or even the same day, go long on an ETF, which is similar to the position that you just sold for tax purposes.

Exchange traded funds are subject to market risk and may fluctuate in value. Shares may be worth less or more than original cost when they are sold.

Investors should consider the fund's investment objectives, risks, charges and expenses carefully before investing. The prospectus contains this and other information about the fund. To obtain a free prospectus, please call Larry Palmer at 213.486.7105. Please read the prospectus carefully before investing.

> ## "An ETF is structured as a mutual fund but has the ability to trade on an exchange like a stock."
> – Larry Palmer

How to reach Larry Palmer

I prefer face-to-face meetings with prospective clients. Please contact me via phone at 213.486.7105 or via email at larry.palmer@morganstanleypwm.com.

I NEVER LEAVE HOME WITHOUT...

My cell phone, BlackBerry and wallet

MY HOBBIES ARE...

Surfing, swimming, training and travel

WHAT'S ON MY DESK...

Computer, phone, research reports and investment articles

About Larry Palmer

Larry Palmer is a managing director and Corporate Client Group director with Morgan Stanley Smith Barney in Los Angeles. Mr. Palmer and his team assist senior executives and founders of public and private companies with their personal wealth and business needs. Mr. Palmer works extensively with corporate officers and directors on wealth management, including liquidity and diversification strategies for concentrated equity positions, estate planning and asset and liability management. For private companies, he has experience advising founders and upper-level management on exit strategies and accessing growth capital. Within the firm, Mr. Palmer is a member of the Director's Council, which acknowledges the top 5 percent of financial advisors at Morgan Stanley Smith Barney.

Assets Under Management **$1 billion**	Compensation Method **Asset-based fees**
Minimum Fee for Initial Meeting **None required**	Primary Custodian for Investor Assets **Morgan Stanley Smith Barney**
Minimum Net Worth Requirement **$5 million**	Professional Services Provided **Planning, investment advisory and money management services**
Largest Client Net Worth **$6.5 billion**	Association Memberships **IMCA**
Financial Services Experience **27 years**	Website **www.smithbarney.com** Email **larry.palmer@morganstanleypwm.com**

Morgan Stanley Smith Barney | 444 South Flower Street, 26th Floor, Los Angeles, CA 90071 | 213.486.7105

New York, NY | **Leading Wealth Advisor**

Sage Capital Management LLC
Lawrence C. Busch, CFA®, Founder and President,
Ronald Deutsch, CFA®, Managing Director, Howard Gottlieb,
Managing Director, and Geoffrey Kurinsky, Director

" What should I consider when it comes to bonds? "

By Lawrence C. Busch

The performance of capital markets in 2008 and 2009 has served as a wake-up call that bonds are not a mundane asset class to be ignored. Gains and losses in excess of 20 percent were commonplace among bond investments over the past two years. Understanding how to properly manage a bond portfolio begins with a basic understanding of the different types of bond risk and how these risks affect the return on investment:

CREDIT RISK

Bond issuers (corporations, municipalities and governments) are evaluated for their financial strength by rating agencies that assign ratings from AAA (least risk) to C (most risk). Bonds issued by the U.S. government are AAA rated, implying that they have the least amount of risk in their ability to pay interest and principal upon maturity. Bonds rated below BBB are commonly called junk or high-yield bonds and carry higher levels of credit risk with commensurately higher yields. Corporate and municipal bonds are particularly sensitive to economic factors and are often harbingers of both good and bad economic times.

INTEREST RATE RISK

The value of bonds moves inversely to the direction of interest rates. Bonds increase in value when interest rates fall and decline in value when interest rates rise. Longer-maturity bonds have greater interest rate risk or price movement than shorter-maturity bonds. Municipal bonds and corporate bonds generally carry less interest rate risk than U.S. Treasuries because they have exposure to credit and other risks that factor into their valuation. Bonds with higher coupons will tend to have less interest rate risk.

PREPAYMENT RISK

This risk is unique to mortgage-backed securities (MBS) and bonds that are callable. MBS are obligations, issued by public and private institutions, that are backed by a pool of mortgages. Mortgages paid off early can result in a shorter maturity than desired. Bonds that are called at the option of the issuer also shorten the effective maturity.

There are two main considerations when building a portfolio of bonds: diversification of risk and tax efficiency. Diversification of risk requires an understanding of the credit, interest rate and prepayment risk of each bond. Investing in bonds that represent all of these risks is essential to managing a bond portfolio. Tax efficiency requires an understanding of how the income from each bond is taxed. Only after considering the taxes to be paid can you fairly compare the return of one bond to another.

At Sage, our portfolio managers have an average of 20 years of experience in bond portfolio management. This provides our clients with a resource atypical of investment advisory firms. Ⓦ

YEAR-END PLANNING TIPS

Harvest losses: There are sure to be opportunities in your portfolio to sell investments at a loss and reinvest into comparable investments.

Take gains: Carryover losses from last year and loss harvesting in this year can provide you with an opportunity to take gains in positions that substantially appreciated and are not likely to repeat their performance in 2011.

Beware of mutual fund distributions: Many funds (particularly stock funds) make large taxable distributions in December. Check the record date of these distributions before making any new investments.

Roth IRA: Speak to your tax advisor about its potential benefit to your portfolio.

"There are two main considerations when building a portfolio of bonds: diversification of risk and tax efficiency."

– Lawrence C. Busch

How to reach Sage Capital Management LLC

Please refer to our website www.sageny.com for all contact information.

Left to right:
Lawrence C. Busch,
Ronald Deutsch,
Howard Gottlieb,
Geoffrey Kurinsky

About Sage Capital Management LLC

Lawrence C. Busch is the founder and president of Sage Capital Management LLC, an SEC-registered investment advisor that has been providing investment management and financial planning services to high net worth individuals and families since 1999. Mr. Busch has a BS in accounting from Brooklyn College and an MBA from New York University. Ronald Deutsch, managing director, has more than 25 years of portfolio and fixed-income management experience. He received his BS in accounting from Binghamton University and his MBA from Northwestern University. He is a board member of the investment committee of the Binghamton University Foundation. Howard Gottlieb, managing director, has more than 30 years of experience in portfolio analysis, strategic planning and client services. Geoffrey Kurinsky, director, has more than 30 years of fixed-income management experience, including lead portfolio manager of the flagship MFS Bond mutual fund. He received his BBA in accounting from the University of Massachusetts and his MBA from Boston University. He is a board member of the Greater Boston Food Bank.

Assets Under Management **$470 million**	Compensation Method **Asset-based, fixed and hourly fees**
Minimum Fee for Initial Meeting **None required**	Primary Custodian for Investor Assets **Schwab Institutional**
Minimum Net Worth Requirement **$2 million**	Professional Services Provided **Planning, investment advisory and money management services**
Largest Client Net Worth **$100 million**	Association Memberships **CFA Institute, New York Society of Securities Analysts, NFLPA Financial Advisor**
Financial Services Experience **105 years (combined)**	Website **www.sageny.com** — Email **advisor@sageny.com** — Phone **212.584.4110**

Sage Capital Management LLC | 380 Lexington Avenue, Suite 2705, New York, NY 10168 | 1 Bridle Trail, Needham, MA 02492

New York, NY　　**Leading Wealth Advisor**

Further Lane Asset Management
J. Michael Araiz, Chief Executive Officer
Marc Lowlicht, CFP®, MSFP, President–Wealth Management Division

"How do I avoid making the most common investor mistakes? "

By Marc Lowlicht

Common mistakes of any kind are called "common" because a great many individuals make them—sometimes over and over. So if you have made any of the mistakes discussed below, you are not alone. But now is your chance to avoid them in the future.

COMMON INVESTOR MISTAKE
01 Confusing financial planning and investment planning.

An investment plan is just that—a plan that outlines how you will invest your money. It is, as the saying goes, only part of the puzzle. A financial plan, on the other hand, includes every element that touches on your finances: your tax plan, your estate plan, your insurance plans and, yes, your investment plan.

If you and your investment advisor craft a well-thought-out investment plan, that is a good thing. But to have a true and comprehensive financial plan, you also need plans for all aspects of your financial life. And because a financial plan provides a target date by which you can achieve your goal if you stick to it, the plan helps you avoid making rash, emotion-driven decisions during rough patches.

COMMON INVESTOR MISTAKE
02 Not drafting an investment policy statement.

An investment policy statement is a simple yet essential element of sound and smart financial planning. It is quite simply a written document that states your financial goals and objectives and outlines what you plan to do to get there. Think of it as something of a touchstone, something you come back to, that you revisit during good times and bad to remind you that this is why your investments are structured the way they are. This does not mean an investment policy statement is a static document. Lives change, goals change, finances change, strategies may change, and so your description of them should change also. But you should always have a document that outlines them.

COMMON INVESTOR MISTAKE
03 Focusing on return and disregarding risk.

Nearly every day a client tells me about a friend who is getting an incredible return on some investment. And nearly every time, my first question is, "How much risk was involved?" The financial words I live by, and would encourage you to live by also, are these: Focus on risk first and return second. Obviously, the main reason you consider any new investment is that you expect a return. But, as the saying goes, anyone can plan for success. What you need to do is ask yourself: "How risky is this investment, and if it fails, can I (and my finances) handle it?"

COMMON INVESTOR MISTAKE
04 You think you know more than your advisor.

You are smart, extraordinarily good at what you do, and if you are talking to me, you have made lots and lots of money. But with all due respect, you are not a financial advisor. Like professionals in any field, including yours, the best financial advisors not only have exclusive access to vital sources of information, they have advanced degrees in finance, and they have qualified for hard-to-get licenses, such as the CFP. We are trained to understand and notice the subtleties in the world of finance that could make a significant difference in how well your financial plan succeeds.

To put it another way: While I agree you should be an educated investor client, I suggest you focus on managing and growing your own business, and I will focus my full-time efforts on protecting and growing the money you make. ⓦ

"Focus on risk first and return second."
– Marc Lowlicht

How to reach J. Michael Araiz and Marc Lowlicht
Please contact us at 212.808.4800 for an initial consultation.

I NEVER LEAVE HOME WITHOUT...

Michael: My dog, Max

Marc: A picture of my two daughters

MY FAVORITE CAUSE/CHARITY...

Michael: Smile Train, ARF, St. Jude Children's Research Hospital

Marc: The Ronald McDonald House (I have seen this charity at work through personal experience and was very pleased at how it took care of people in need.)

MY HOBBIES ARE...

Michael: Collecting fine art, traveling and horticulture

Marc: Playing ice hockey, playing guitar, reading and anything that involves spending time with my daughters

J. Michael Araiz

Marc Lowlicht

About J. Michael Araiz and Marc Lowlicht

J. Michael Araiz, chief executive officer, has more than 28 years of experience in the trading and valuation of fixed-income instruments, specializing in high-grade and high-yield securities. He is the managing member and CEO of Further Lane Asset Management; the chief executive officer of Further Lane Securities LP; and the sole owner and CEO of Osprey Group Asset Management. Mr. Araiz was a founding partner of MJ Whitman LP and a founding shareholder of EQSF, the advisor to the Third Avenue Family of funds. Marc Lowlicht, president–wealth management division, holds his master of science degree in financial planning from the College for Financial Planning and specializes in implementing sophisticated wealth management strategies through risk management and in understanding client goals and objectives. From 2005 to 2009, he was named one of America's best financial planners by the Consumer's Research Council of America. Mr. Lowlicht has been quoted in numerous business publications including *Forbes* and *Worth*. He is also a regular contributor to *Forbes'* Intelligent Investor Panel.

Assets Under Management
$500 million+

Minimum Fee for Initial Meeting
$1,500

Minimum Net Worth Requirement
$2.5 million

Largest Client Net Worth
$100 million+

Financial Services Experience
28+ years

Compensation Method
Asset-base and hourly fees; commission (brokerage and insurance services)

Primary Custodian for Investor Assets
Pershing and Charles Schwab

Professional Services Provided
Planning, investment advisory and money management services, insurance and corporate benefits

Website **www.furtherlane.com**

Email **maraiz@furtherlane.com**
mlowlicht@furtherlane.com

Further Lane Asset Management | 250 East 54th Street, PH1, New York, NY 10022 | 212.808.4800

New York, NY | **Leading Wealth Advisor**

Rockefeller Financial

Matthew D. Gelfand, PhD, CFA, CFP®, Senior Wealth Advisor
Tamar Manuelian Ioffe, Senior Client Advisor

" Should I choose an active portfolio manager or an indexed portfolio? "

By Matthew D. Gelfand

Investors have debated the merits of active and passive investing for more than 45 years. In 1965, Nobel Prize–winning economist Paul Samuelson published a study on the random behavior of stock prices, and Eugene Fama published what he called the "efficient markets hypothesis." After that, most economists took it on faith that markets accurately reflect all available information and so active portfolio managers cannot beat markets. Thus, the theory goes, investors should opt for low-cost passive or indexed portfolios.

Studies in the 1980s, however, disputed this logic. Hypothetically, if all equity investors bought the S&P 500, say, then no one would play the role of bidding stock prices up and down as company-specific news came out. So, in a sense, passive investors leave opportunities on the table that active managers could pick up.

In addition, the newer line of study called behavioral finance lays out the theoretical groundwork and empirical data that illustrate the many ways that investors can be irrational, creating the potential for more upside for active managers. For example, stock prices tend to fizzle when the weather is poor in New York City or in other cities that have stock exchanges. Also, investors tend to be biased toward stocks of companies in their hometowns or that their neighbors buy. Individual investors tend to trade too much, on average selling stocks that wind up performing better than the stocks they subsequently buy. And, no surprise, company insiders tend to buy and sell at the right time. These anomalies and many others create opportunities—sometimes small or fleeting, sometimes significant or long-lasting—for alert managers to beat the market.

Some markets or asset classes are less efficient than others, and their efficiency can change over time. For example, small-cap stocks, non-U.S. stocks and low-grade bonds tend to receive relatively little coverage from securities analysts, and thus their prices tend to fluctuate more from fair value. Such fluctuations create greater profit opportunities for active stock and bond pickers. That said, there are managers of the most highly covered stocks who outperform consistently. In addition, market volatility itself fluctuates over time. Markets create better trading opportunities when they are more volatile, so active managers are likely to be be more successful at such times.

Investors should also consider active managers from a tax-efficiency point of view. Harvesting losses and deciding when to use those losses as offsets against future gains to minimize capital gains taxes require active management. Changing tax laws also create opportunities for profitable trading—not simply trading when taxes are low, but rather trading when, on net, it is most advantageous. That is a benefit you cannot get with an index portfolio. ⓦ

WHY ELSE SHOULD I GO ACTIVE?
BY TAMAR MANUELIAN IOFFE

Think back to October 2008, when the stock market was lurching downward. Would you have preferred an actively managed portfolio or an index fund? Most investors would answer the former, because, in difficult markets, it is reassuring to know that stocks and bonds have been selectively chosen, and that a portfolio manager can react quickly to news on the markets in general, and on companies in particular. Hence, one feels a greater sense of control over investments.

This is one of the reasons for investing with an active manager versus a passive index. Another is that actively managed portfolios invite more in-depth conversations between clients and portfolio managers on specific holdings. For example, with increasing interest in socially responsive investing and shareholder activism, an actively managed account allows for tailoring investments to be more reflective of a client's values, in addition to meeting financial goals.

"Markets create better trading opportunities when they are more volatile, so active managers can be more successful at such times."

– Matthew D. Gelfand and Tamar Manuelian Ioffe

How to reach Matthew D. Gelfand and Tamar Manuelian Ioffe

You can reach us at 202.719.3020 (Matthew) and 212.549.5275 (Tamar).

Matthew Gelfand

Tamar Manuelian Ioffe

About Matthew D. Gelfand and Tamar Manuelian Ioffe

Matthew D. Gelfand, PhD, CFA, CFP, is a senior wealth advisor with Rockefeller Wealth Advisors. He has 29 years of financial-sector experience. Previously, he was with several advisory firms, including Strategic Investment Group, where he was responsible for more than $1.2 billion in assets, and Calvert Group, a leader in socially responsible investing. He holds a BA from Yale College and a PhD in economics from the University of Pennsylvania. Tamar Manuelian Ioffe is a senior client advisor in the Client Advisory Services Group and a managing director of Rockefeller Financial. Her responsibilities include working with wealthy families, advising on their overall financial planning, and evaluating and supervising their investments. She holds a BBA in international business from Hofstra University and an MBA from Columbia Business School.

Assets Under Management $25 billion (global assets under administration, as of 6/30/10)	Compensation Method Asset-based, fixed and hourly fees; no brokerage or placement fees
Minimum Fee for Initial Meeting None required	Professional Services Provided Planning, investment advisory and money management services; comprehensive wealth management to ultra high net worth individuals, families and institutions; information management
Minimum Net Worth Requirement $30 million (generally)	
Largest Client Net Worth $1 billion+	Website www.rockefellerfinancial.com
Financial Services Experience 125 years	Email inquiries@rockco.com

Rockefeller Financial | 10 Rockefeller Plaza, New York, NY 10020   212.549.5100

Houston, TX | **Leading Wealth Advisor**

Morgan Stanley Smith Barney
Michael Brunner, CFP®, Senior Vice President

" Where do we go from here? "

By Michael Brunner

When you are in the investment advice business, everyone asks: "What is the stock market going to do?" or "Where is the best place to put my money right now?" Most of us have some answer or opinion, but providing the best response requires some overall perspective regarding the larger picture.

To begin, let us get some background on where we have come from regarding our equity markets. Specifically, at the beginning of 1981 the stock market (as measured by the Dow Jones Industrial Average) was trading at 963.99. By the time we got to the end of 1999, that same market was trading at 11,453.98 (Yahoo Finance). Put pen to paper, and you will see the cumulative gain over that period was a stellar 1,092.66 percent. According to Zephyr Style Advisors, that equates to an average annualized return of 13.94 percent. With returns like that, it is easy to adhere to the buy-and-hold strategy. Simply put, it means investing in good companies, letting them grow, and not sweating the ups and downs that occur while you hold them.

I must admit that I adhered to this philosophy to a degree, but now my strategies have changed to some extent. While the 1980s and 1990s were a tremendous time to invest in stocks, so far in this decade the scoreboard tells a different story. The stock market peaked in January 2000 at 11,722.98. At the time of this writing we are sitting at around 10,000. **To put that in perspective, we have gone more than 10 years with a negative annualized rate of return of roughly -0.42 percent** (Zephyr Style Advisors). Some have suggested that this indeed is an anomaly, but again, history suggests otherwise. The Dow Jones Average first crossed 1,000 in 1966, but it did not see 1,000 again until 1976. (For the record, the market went back down and did not pass the 1,000 level again until 1981.) Included in that period were years when the market fell by more than 44 percent (January 1973 to December 1974), and there were other down years as well (Zephyr Style Advisors).

The point is that markets tend to go through stages when the overall bias is either up (as in the period from 1981 to 2000) or flat to down (1966 to 1981). In reviewing the stock market over the course of the last 80 years or so, we see that these trends tend to average about 18 years in duration. So, if you use my starting point of spring 2000 as the time when we had a change in the long-term trend for stocks (MSSB Consulting Services), then that means we have roughly seven to eight more years before we see a new bull market emerge. If that is true, using investment strategies other than buy and hold to achieve positive returns might be in order.

For more information on Michael's alternative portfolios and their performance, email him at michael.l.brunner@smithbarney.com. Ⓦ

"We see that these trends tend to average 18 years in duration."

– Michael Brunner

How to reach Michael Brunner

If you are interested in knowing more about Michael's alternative and tactical investment strategies and performance, email or call his office at michael.l.brunner@smithbarney.com, or 713.658.2786.

MY HOBBIES ARE...

Tennis, bay fishing, grilling (charcoal only—I'm a purist), reading and staying physically fit

I NEVER LEAVE HOME WITHOUT...

Reading glasses, a good book, some running shoes, a bottle of water and a favorite recipe

WHAT'S ON MY DESK...

Texas Monthly magazine, a Marine Corps coaster and more research papers than I care to mention

About Michael Brunner

Michael Brunner has worked for 20 years as an investment and money management professional with Morgan Stanley Smith Barney in Houston. A native of Austin, Mr. Brunner completed his BBA at Texas State University. Upon graduation, he was commissioned as an officer in the United States Marine Corps. After completing his tour of duty, Mr. Brunner began his career in Houston with Morgan Stanley Smith Barney. In 1999, he earned the title senior vice president, and he continues to oversee and manage the investment portfolios of affluent individuals and their families. Mr. Brunner resides in Houston with his wife, Stephanie, and their four daughters.

Assets Under Management $200 million (as of 10/31/09)	**Compensation Method** Asset-based and fixed fees; commissions (investment and certain products)
Minimum Fee for Initial Meeting None required	**Primary Custodian for Investor Assets** Morgan Stanley Smith Barney
Minimum Net Worth Requirement $2.5 million	**Professional Services Provided** Planning, investment advisory and money management services
Largest Client Net Worth $100 million	**Website** http://fa.smithbarney.com/brunner
Financial Services Experience 20 years	**Email** michael.l.brunner@smithbarney.com

Morgan Stanley Smith Barney | 717 Texas Avenue, Suite 3050, Houston, TX 77002 | 713.658.2786

Phoenix—Scottsdale, AZ   **Leading Wealth Advisor**

Harris myCFO™
Michael J. Montgomery, CPA, CFP®, PFS, Managing Director

" How do you properly evaluate and assess 'great' investment opportunities? "

By Michael J. Montgomery

For entrepreneurs, nothing is more exciting than spotting an idea or concept that the general masses have overlooked. A keen eye enables them to take an idea and develop it into a successful enterprise. Along the way, most understand the risks they are taking and perform some degree of homework or due diligence to fully analyze their decisions.

Yet, in stark contrast, when entrepreneurs are asked to buy into another's company or investment, many do not vet these financial activities and opportunities with the same passion, vigilance and diligence as they do when starting their own enterprises. This absence of analysis is typically due to a lack of time, a lack of interest, or perhaps just a genuine absence of understanding.

Unfortunately, the wealth and success of an entrepreneur can be quickly eroded by participating in high-risk, inappropriate and/or ill-conceived ventures.

In the interest of wealth preservation, it is critical for an advisor to approach opportunities presented to clients with a strong and healthy dose of both skepticism and discipline. The end goal is by no means to discredit or challenge a new concept or to always say no, but rather to develop a framework around decision making to ensure that key risks have been considered to the same extent as the purported rewards.

The following are examples of some "great" opportunities presented to some of my clients. These were vetted and analyzed in advance, and while some clients proceeded with the deals, they were better informed of the inherent risks:

• **"No-risk" real estate financing.** A client's short-term bridge loan became long-term when he, acting as the interim creditor, was left holding the bag when the permanent lender backed out of the transaction.

• **Surprisingly cheap jet program.** The memberships were cheap for a reason—the operator's model was not sustainable, resulting in bankruptcy and a loss of participant deposits.

• **Investment fund with impeccable record.** No audited figures, minimal management experience, historical performance generated from a small base of capital, poor infrastructure—all contributed to the fund's failure.

• **Guaranteed principal protected notes.** These instruments offered a 100 percent guaranteed return of principal, plus "some" upside in the equity markets. Guarantees were only as good as the institutions backing them—the issuer of one group of notes went bankrupt. For others, returns were minimal, as the dividend component of the underlying market index was removed, considerably lowering the upside sharing potential for the notes.

Despite the best-laid plans and most rigorous due diligence, things can still go wrong because of: political changes, regulatory reform, natural disasters, unfortunate series of events, etc. However, by ensuring that some basic due diligence tenets are followed and considered, the probability for success, or of minimizing losses, can be greatly enhanced, providing strong support for wealth preservation. ⓦ

BASIC DUE DILIGENCE BEST PRACTICES

Remember these simple adages: "If it sounds too good to be true, it probably is" and "There is no free lunch."

Best practices for a business opportunity:
• Perform social and professional background checks.
• Check management and operations. Are skilled professionals in place?
• Ask why the business is compelling and whether it can indeed make money.
• Avoid deals when there is pressure to close before questions are answered.

For an investment opportunity:
• Review the track record and experience.
• Understand how performance is generated, including the risks taken to achieve that performance.
• What is the form of ownership you will have? Will you own the underlying asset directly? Will you be holding an instrument or derivative that is directly tied to the underlying asset's performance?
• How easily can you redeem out and at what price?
• Understand the fees.
• What can go wrong?

> ## "It is critical for an advisor to approach opportunities with a strong and healthy dose of both skepticism and discipline."
>
> – Michael J. Montgomery

How to reach Michael J. Montgomery

I prefer face-to-face meetings with prospective clients. Please feel free to call me at 480.302.3777.

WHAT'S ON MY DESK...

Two things: pictures of my two daughters as a constant reminder of how fortunate I am, and multiple reference guides for income taxes, investments, insurance, etc. (It is a challenge to stay in tune with all the latest developments.)

I NEVER LEAVE HOME WITHOUT...

My coffee and my BlackBerry. I have few vices, but a large cup of coffee really jump-starts my morning, and my BlackBerry ensures I do not miss a beat on communicating with clients and colleagues.

MY HOBBIES ARE...

Running, hiking and working out. Physical fitness sets the tone for my entire state of mind and attitude and is something I can do and enjoy with my family.

About Michael J. Montgomery

Michael J. Montgomery is managing director of the Scottsdale, Ariz., Harris myCFO Inc. office, serving as a financial strategist and coordinator for wealth management and family office services. He joined Harris myCFO in 2009 and has more than 17 years of experience. He earned a BBA in accounting from Texas A&M and an MBA from Southern Methodist University. He is a Certified Public Accountant, CERTIFIED FINANCIAL PLANNER™ Professional, Personal Financial Specialist, Accredited Asset Management Specialist and a CFA Level III candidate. He is a member of the American Institute of Certified Public Accountants and an associate member of the American Bar Association (real property, trust and estate law section).

Assets Under Management $16.4 billion	**Compensation Method** Asset-based and fixed fees
Minimum Fee for Initial Meeting None required	**Primary Custodian for Investor Assets** Multiple, please inquire
Minimum Net Worth Requirement $100 million	**Professional Services Provided** Planning and investment advisory services
Largest Client Net Worth $1 billion+	**Association Memberships** AICPA, associate member of the American Bar Association (real property, trust and estate law section)
Financial Services Experience 17 years	**Website** www.harrismycfo.com **Email** michael.montgomery@harrismycfo.com

AUM figures are as of 6/30/10 and are applicable to Harris myCFO IAS LLC and certain divisions of Harris N.A. that do business under the brand name Harris myCFO™. All other information is combined for all entities and lines of business under the Harris myCFO™ brand.
Certified Financial Planner Board of Standards Inc. owns the certification marks CFP®, CERTIFIED FINANCIAL PLANNER™ and CFP (with flame design) in the U.S.

Harris myCFO™ | 4900 North Scottsdale Road, Suite 2600, Scottsdale, AZ 85251 | 480.302.3777

Houston, TX **Leading Wealth Advisor**

Morgan Stanley Smith Barney
Murray Snow, Managing Director—Wealth Management

" Is it safe to invest in emerging markets again? "

By Murray Snow

In my opinion, emerging markets are back in style—an impression I get reviewing market performance over recent months and data on fund flows. Investing in developing countries has been long discussed as another way to provide diversification to domestic portfolios, albeit with an unknown level of risk. I believe that much of the volatility experienced by emerging markets in the 1980s and 1990s was the result of politics. From Latin America to Eastern Europe, and in parts of Asia, transfers of political power were often fraught with uncertainty and occasional disorder, usually proving an obstacle to coherent economic policy making. However, on the whole, the major emerging markets have experienced a prolonged period of political calm in the past decade.

The case for investing in emerging markets:

Better economic growth. Rapidly growing economies should lead to faster-growing revenues for firms operating in that economy.

Better demographics. Apart from Eastern Europe, populations are growing faster in the developing rather than the developed world.

Higher productivity growth. Productivity is growing faster in the emerging world than in developed countries and was more resilient in the downturn.

Less debt. Despite the credit crunch, the emerging world is relatively unleveraged.

Bigger slice of the global economic pie. The share of emerging economies in world trade has grown from 19 percent in the early 1990s to 38 percent in 2009. The majority of the world's natural resources are found in the emerging world. These countries control 84 percent of the world's proven oil reserves, 91 percent of natural gas, 84 percent of copper reserves and 73 percent of the world's fresh water.

Finally, the market capitalization of emerging equity markets as a share of world equity markets has risen from less than 1 percent in 1988 to 12.2 percent today, an all-time high.

However, investors must keep some key risks of emerging markets in mind:

• A return to political instability is a key risk for emerging markets.

• Governance has improved but remains weak in many countries.

• Talk of decoupling does not change the fact that most emerging markets are dependent on exports to developed nations.

• Despite improvements, many emerging markets are illiquid and inefficient, which could lead to extra volatility at times of global risk aversion.

• Emerging market countries can vary in risk. ⓦ

WHAT THE MSCI EMERGING MARKETS INDEX MEANS AND HOW IT HAS PERFORMED

The MSCI index was created by Morgan Stanley Capital International (MSCI) and is designed to measure equity market performance in global emerging markets. An investment cannot be made directly into a market index.

22 countries in MSCI:

Brazil	Chile
China	Colombia
Czech Republic	Egypt
Hungary	India
Indonesia	Israel
Korea	Malaysia
Mexico	Morocco
Peru	Philippines
Poland	Russia
South Africa	Taiwan
Thailand	Turkey

Performance:	MSCI[1]	S&P[2]
2009	+74%	+26%
2008	-54%	-37%
2007	+36%	+5.4%
2006	+29%	+15.7%
2005	+30%	+4.9%
2004	+22%	+10.8%
2003	+51%	+28%

There may be additional risk associated with international investing, including foreign, economic, political, monetary and/or legal factors, changing currency exchange rates, foreign taxes and differences in financial and accounting standards. These risks may be magnified in emerging markets. International investing may not be for everyone.

S&P index is an unmanaged, market value-weighted index of 500 stocks generally representative of the broad stock market. An investment cannot be made directly in a market index.

[1]MSCI Barra, 12/31/2009
[2]Standard & Poors, S&P 500, 12/31/2009

References: Andrew Howell, "Special Report: CEEMEA for the Long Run," September 2009, Citigroup Global Markets, pages 7, 15, 17, 22, 1 respectively.

"Emerging markets are indeed likely to grow more rapidly than developed economies for the foreseeable future."

– Murray Snow

How to reach Murray Snow

I prefer face-to-face meetings with prospective clients. My assistant will happily schedule a convenient time to meet. You can reach her at 713.966.2177.

I NEVER LEAVE HOME WITHOUT...

My wedding ring—I feel naked without it—and, of course, my BlackBerry

MY HOBBIES ARE...

Golf, hunting and fly-fishing

WHAT'S ON MY DESK...

Family pictures, economic and market research

About Murray Snow

Murray Snow has more than 20 years of experience in the financial services industry in Houston. He has been recognized in *Barron's* "Top 1000 Financial Advisors", (February 22, 2010, edition*) as well as appearing in the following publications: *Worth, Forbes* and *Texas Monthly*. He was a recent guest on Fox Business News. Mr. Snow perennially ranks in the top 1 percent of all Morgan Stanley Smith Barney financial advisors and serves as co-chairman of the Financial Advisors' Advisory Group, a management task force serving Morgan Stanley Smith Barney's senior directors. He has earned the distinction of managing director—wealth management.

Assets Under Management **$653 million**	Compensation Method **Asset-based and fixed fees, commissions (investment and insurance products)**
Minimum Fee for Initial Meeting **None required**	Primary Custodian for Investor Assets **Morgan Stanley Smith Barney**
Minimum Net Worth Requirement **$2.5 million**	Professional Services Provided **Planning, investment advisory and money management services**
Largest Client Net Worth **$100 million**	Association Memberships **FPA, IMCA**
Financial Services Experience **22 years**	Website **http://fa.smithbarney.com/murraysnow/** Email **murray.snow@mssb.com**

*Barron's "Top 1000 Financial Advisors," February 22, 2010, as identified by *Barron's* magazine, using quantitative and qualitative criteria and selected from a pool of over 3,000 nominations. Advisors in the "Top 1000 Financial Advisors" have a minimum of seven years of financial services experience. Qualitative factors include, but are not limited to, compliance record, interviews with senior management and philanthropic work. Investment performance is not a criterion. The rating may not be representative of any one client's experience and is not indicative of the financial advisor's future performance. Neither Morgan Stanley Smith Barney nor its financial advisors pay a fee to *Barron's* in exchange for the rating. *Barron's* is a registered trademark of Dow Jones & Company L.P. All rights reserved.

Morgan Stanley Smith Barney	5051 Westheimer Road, Suite 2100, Houston, TX 77056	800.666.6069 ext. 2177	713.966.2177
	284 Bellevue Avenue, Newport, RI 02840	401.845.3521	

San Francisco Peninsula—
Silicon Valley, CA

**Leading
Wealth Advisor**

Strategic Global Investment Services
Richard S. Farkas, AAMS, President, Financial Advisor, RJFS

" Why are cash alternatives considered a risk asset? "

By Richard S. Farkas

A subtle shift in thinking can often make a big difference in outcome. If we consider cash alternatives as a risk-asset class, it provides great insights into not only how we approach the risk-oriented markets and asset classes, but also speaks to our world view in general. ("Cash alternatives" referred to here are those measured by one- to three-month U.S. Treasuries.)

Let us consider a couple of observations. Most individuals would consider cash alternatives a risk-free asset, but lately in the United States it has been an income-free asset as well. They do not pay interest, or at least very little; in short, they are at generational-low interest rates. After taxes and inflation, there are times when the real return on cash alternatives can actually be negative, and risk/reward opportunities favor risk rather than risk-free options.

In our view, other riskier assets such as domestic and foreign equities, bonds, commodities and foreign currencies must constantly be compared to cash alternatives to justify putting the money at risk. Unfortunately, there is often a predisposition to believe that investable money must be put at risk at all times. It is rare that investors, professional or otherwise, consider that a final test of risk is comparing the riskier asset in question to cash alternatives on a relative basis.

But they should. In my experience, relative-strength studies performed on an ongoing basis among all asset classes, including cash alternatives, provide an objective view of risk. These studies also foster a built-in sell discipline when a risk-asset class is underperforming relative to cash alternatives.

In the course of relative-strength studies among major asset classes, we have found that cash alternatives become an outperforming asset class in equity bear markets and an underperforming asset class in equity bull markets. That being the case, there is no reason to be all equities all the time, in particular when cash alternatives are the best-performing asset class. That, of course, begs the question, why take the additional risk—with equities or other alternatives—if cash alternatives are outperforming on a relative basis?

To sum up, the fact is that cash alternatives can be considered a risk asset, but not always. Market conditions can affect its risk status, which is literally relative when cash alternatives are included in relative-strength studies with other risky assets. ⓦ

RELATIVE STRENGTH AND LESSONS FROM THE LOST DECADE

Relative strength as a core component of portfolio management discipline and style has a well-documented history of usefulness and long-term success. While the lessons learned from the lost decade will be reviewed by investors and academics alike for decades to come, here are three possible takeaways:

01 Consider cash alternatives as a risk asset.

02 Both offensive and defensive strategies, like all financial endeavors, should be part of an overall game plan for portfolio management.

03 Increasingly we are a global society that operates in multiple currencies, and the disparities among them can influence our decisions about risk depending on the currency we live with.

"After taxes and inflation the real return on cash alternatives can actually be negative."

– Richard S. Farkas

How to reach Richard S. Farkas

I encourage a scheduled 30- to 45-minute conference call to discover the important concerns you have and to get to know each other. Follow up can be determined at that time. You can reach me at 408.371.0500.

MY HOBBIES ARE...

Travel, golf and martial arts

WHAT'S ON MY DESK...

Charts and research of clients' top holdings and a Murano glass bull from my dad's den

I NEVER LEAVE HOME WITHOUT...

Cell phone/PDA, "Honey-do" list and golf clubs

About Richard S. Farkas

Richard S. Farkas is a financial advisor and president of Strategic Global Investment Services, an independent firm (securities offered through Raymond James Financial Services Inc., member FINRA/SIPC). Mr. Farkas was recognized by *Research* magazine in its ETF Advisor Hall of Fame in October 2008. This recognition is based on competence, experience and innovation with ETFs, not on production, AUM or portfolio performance. The firm's services include portfolio management, financial planning and insurance services. Independent research, technical analysis and cost-effective and tax-efficient inventory are hallmarks of Mr. Farkas' strategies. Clientele consists of an eclectic group of successful entrepreneurs, C-level executives, entertainment professionals, martial artists and happy retirees.

Assets Under Management **Confidential**	Compensation Method **Asset-based, fixed and hourly fees, commissions (insurance products)**
Minimum Fee for Initial Meeting **None required**	Primary Custodian for Investor Assets **Raymond James**
Minimum Net Worth Requirement **$500,000 (minimum account size)**	Professional Services Provided **Planning, investment advisory and money management services, insurance and estate planning**
Largest Client Net Worth **$20 million (as of 9/30/09)**	Association Memberships **FPA, Market Technicians Association**
Financial Services Experience **13 years**	Email **richard.farkas@raymondjames.com** · Website **raymondjames.com/richardfarkas**

Strategic Global Investment Services | 1901 South Bascom Avenue, Suite 1550, Campbell, CA 95008 | 408.371.0500

San Francisco, CA—Lake Oswego, OR   **Leading Wealth Advisor**

The Pacific Wealth Group at Morgan Stanley Smith Barney
Sean Gabrio, CIMA®, Senior Vice President, Senior Portfolio Manager
Jim Mead, CFP®, CIMA®, Senior Vice President, Wealth Advisor
Jeff Weiler, Senior Vice President, Managing Partner
Scot Berryman, CFP®, CIMA®, Senior Vice President, Wealth Advisor

" How do I assess my risk tolerance when it comes to investing? "

By Sean Gabrio, The Pacific Wealth Group

It takes many years of hard work and prudent planning to build wealth, but sometimes it may only take one unforeseen "black swan" event to lose a good majority of it. Many have heard the Latin phrase *Primum non nocere*, meaning "First, do no harm," in regard to medical ethics, but few have properly applied this principle to their personal, financial and investment planning.

THE NUMBER ONE RULE

When considering how much risk is appropriate, Warren Buffett reminds us, "Rule No.1: Never lose money. Rule No.2: Never forget Rule No.1." As the chart below outlines, an exponentially larger percent gain is needed to recover capital as the loss increases. In a study by R.A. Prince and David A. Geracioti[1], it was discovered that 92.7 percent of affluent investors were very concerned about losing their wealth. This reality should keep the risk tolerance question at the forefront of planning and investing.

When we meet with prospective clients and referrals, we are often startled to discover the unnecessary risk being taken in an attempt to capture potential upside returns. So how do we assist in determining appropriate risk?

DISCOVERING THE TARGET RETURN

With detailed cash-flow analyses, we strive to help clients walk through a holistic financial plan to uncover the target return needed to maintain current income, as well as to meet inflation-adjusted future income and financial goals. This includes a review of all current investments, real estate, business ownerships, life insurance, trusts, wills and other key holdings and documents.

The newly discovered target return is then utilized to develop an optimized asset allocation designed to produce the least amount of risk. The final step is to filter the myriad of available investment vehicles and to select what we believe will be the best options to build a customized, tax-efficient portfolio. The ultimate objective is to obtain a consistent, total return based upon the least amount of risk that needs to be taken.

We believe that uncovering the target return is a key first step for developing an individual investment policy statement and is critical for the ongoing review process. Though no outcome is ever guaranteed, getting to better "know thyself" through a proper understanding of how much (or how little) risk is needed to meet the desired goals may help to build confidence in the individual's investment planning process. We find that this process helps educate clients and gives them a roadmap to obtain the financial security they have envisioned and spent their lives creating. ⓦ

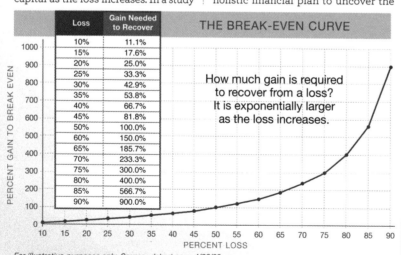

Loss	Gain Needed to Recover
10%	11.1%
15%	17.6%
20%	25.0%
25%	33.3%
30%	42.9%
35%	53.8%
40%	66.7%
45%	81.8%
50%	100.0%
60%	150.0%
65%	185.7%
70%	233.3%
75%	300.0%
80%	400.0%
85%	566.7%
90%	900.0%

THE BREAK-EVEN CURVE

How much gain is required to recover from a loss? It is exponentially larger as the loss increases.

PERCENT GAIN TO BREAK EVEN

PERCENT LOSS

For illustrative purposes only. Source: dshort.com, 4/22/09.

[1] *Russ Alan Prince and David A. Geracioti,* Cultivating the Middle-Class Millionaire, *2005.*

"It takes years of hard work and prudent planning to build wealth, but sometimes it may only take one unforeseen 'black swan' event to lose it."

– Sean Gabrio

How to reach The Pacific Wealth Group

To reach us, call 541.465.1438 for Scot Berryman; 503.552.3393 for Sean Gabrio; 541.617.6018 for Jim Mead; and 503.534.3413 for Jeff Weiler.

Sean Gabrio   Jim Mead   Jeff Weiler   Scot Berryman

About The Pacific Wealth Group

The Pacific Wealth Group consists of four senior partners and portfolio managers, with offices throughout Oregon: Sean Gabrio, CIMA, in Portland; Jim Mead, CFP, CIMA, in Bend; Jeff Weiler, managing partner, in Lake Oswego; and Scot Berryman, CFP, CIMA, in Eugene. The Pacific Wealth Group helps to protect and preserve its clients' wealth by directly managing diversified portfolios with exposure to multiple asset classes, including alternative investments. With their level of achievement at the firm, the partners have access to Morgan Stanley Smith Barney's investment banking offerings, including IPOs, block trades and secondaries, providing qualified investors the opportunity to consistently participate in offerings that are sometimes not available from other firms. As a boutique-like investment advisory practice, the Pacific Wealth Group aims to offer the highest level of service to a select group of ultra high net worth individuals, families, second- and third-generation businesses and nonprofit foundations. Its clients also have direct access to their portfolio decision makers, differentiating the client experience from other advisors.

Assets Under Management $619 million (The Pacific Wealth Group)	**Compensation Method** Asset-based fees and commissions (investment and insurance products)
Minimum Fee for Initial Meeting None required	**Primary Custodian for Investor Assets** Morgan Stanley Smith Barney
Minimum Net Worth Requirement $5 million	**Professional Services Provided** Planning, investment advisory and money management services
Largest Client Net Worth Confidential	**Association Memberships** Investment Management Consultants Association
Financial Services Experience 70 years (combined)	Website www.morganstanley.com/fa/thepacificwealthgroup

Email   scot.berryman@mssb.com   sean.gabrio@mssb.com
jim.mead@mssb.com   jeffrey.weiler@mssb.com

The Pacific Wealth Group at Morgan Stanley Smith Barney | 4800 SW Meadows Road, Suite 400, Lake Oswego, OR 97035 | 866.882.5840

" Besides the obvious, what is a good way to diversify my funds? "

By Todd Rustman

Understandably, people are reassessing their investment strategies in light of the recent market volatility. A simple, but enhanced, approach we take when looking at diversification* is to spend a lot of time with our clients, especially those in the distribution/retirement stage of life, to determine how to match goals with money. We divide time into five-year increments (call them "buckets" if you will) in which each five-year bucket has a goal that we have to be highly confident of fulfilling, even before diversifying the investment portfolio.

For the first five-year bucket, we typically target a 2 to 3 percent return. Why? So that we do not reach for risky returns when we need to make sure that the next five years' worth of income is met. We model a consistent monthly income from this bucket, directing it into the bank accounts of our clients so they risk as little interruption as possible. We use low-risk instruments that most clients have heard of—CDs, fixed annuities, short-term bonds, T-bills, etc. To paraphrase a famous quote, we are more concerned about the return on your money than the return of your money.

The remaining portion of the client's investable portfolio is further segmented into four other five-year buckets, with different targeted rates of return, which guide the diversification process and length of time in the

investments. Furthermore, we work to give our clients a raise every five years by increasing their "take-home" pay by an inflation-adjusted amount—approximately 15 percent every five years, all other things being equal.

We still believe in the benefits of diversification, but the benefits are enhanced when mitigating the effects of longevity risk and/or timing mismatches. By first matching the portfolio buckets with different time frames and income needs, we can reverse engineer a diversified portfolio from a stronger footing. Higher-reaching, more risky (yet higher-return potential) investments are not even considered until the income needs of the next five years are met. In the more time-distant buckets, we place more equities, market alternatives, private equity, private REITs, etc. By covering the closest five years of income we can be comfortable with more risk and volatility, and, of course, higher returns in future years.

As time moves along, each distant-horizon bucket evolves into a lower-return, more stable investment pool from which to draw the next five years of income (and a higher annual/monthly amount).

Diversification is not simply adding an array of investments to a portfolio but rather reverse engineering a portfolio and filling it with diverse investments to help you reach your goals. ⓦ

WINE: AN ILLIQUID LIQUID ALTERNATIVE INVESTMENT

At the end of 2007, Americans officially passed the Italians in wine consumption and became second to the French as the top wine consumers by volume. A diversified portfolio can include the wine industry by:

• Owning a winery or a vineyard.

• Creating a portfolio of physical wine bottles, both investment grade and potential new stars, as well as keeping in-depth documentation on the bottles.

• Wine funds.

• Wine futures. In Bordeaux, futures have been sold since the 1970s, and now there are Burgundy, California, Rhone, Italian and Australian wine futures.

Wine should be looked at as a three- to 10-year investment with no dividend. But bought right (and sold right), it could reap big dividends—if you do not drink the potential profits!

Todd Rustman is a cofounder of Levendi Winery in Napa, Calif.

These investments may have a higher degree of risk to capital. Value of these investments, when redeemed, may be worth more or less than their original cost. Purchasers should carefully assess the risks associated with an investment in these types of assets.

How to reach Todd Rustman

I prefer face-to-face meetings with prospective clients. Please feel free to call me at 800.805.PLAN (7526) or email me at trustman@gr-cam.com.

"Arrange whatever pieces come your way."
– Virginia Woolf

WHAT'S ON MY DESK...

Pictures of my family and four computer screens—never enough information!

I NEVER LEAVE HOME WITHOUT...

Kindle, BlackBerry and a passion for making an impact each day

MY HOBBIES ARE...

Learning, traveling, all sports, wine and picking my battles

About Todd Rustman

Todd Rustman, president of the GRCAM team, has more than 16 years of experience in providing wealth management and MFO services. He has CFP, CFA and CLU certifications, as well as his pilot and real estate licenses. He is a cofounder of several companies, sits on the board of Gen-Next, and is the California representative for the Asset Protection Society. He has been named a top wealth advisor nationally with *Worth* in 2007 and 2008 and was named a five-star wealth manager by Crescendo Business Services for 2009 and 2010.

Assets Under Management
Confidential

Minimum Fee for Initial Meeting
None required

Minimum Net Worth Requirement
$5 million

Largest Client Net Worth
$500 million

Financial Services Experience
16 years

Compensation Method **Asset-based, fixed and hourly fees; commissions (investment and insurance products)**

Primary Custodian for Investor Assets **Pershing and Charles Schwab**

Professional Services Provided **Planning, investment advisory, money management and asset protection services; life settlements**

Association Memberships **Financial Planning Association, CFA Institute, California representative for the Asset Protection Society, and Gen-Next**

Website
www.gr-cam.com

Email
trustman@gr-cam.com

GR Capital Asset Management | 660 Newport Center Drive, Suite 770, Newport Beach, CA 92660 | 800.805.7526

New York, NY   **Leading Wealth Advisor**

Meditron Asset Management LLC
Dr. Walter V. Gerasimowicz, Founder and CEO

" What are the repercussions of a developed country defaulting on its sovereign debt? "

By Dr. Walter V. Gerasimowicz

Recently, the financial world has been turned upside down. Historically, the economies of emerging markets were the ones that required close observation. The International Monetary Fund (IMF) and other authorities advised and constrained the governments of such countries to fight inflation, maintain low debt levels, and control fiscal spending. In the eyes of the IMF, most emerging economies are currently playing by the rules, whereas developed economies—most notably the United States—have in fact (de facto) redefined the concepts of proper economic and fiscal stewardship. A U.S. default is not imminent, but the same cannot be said for the eurozone and a number of its economies.

The European community may have acted too hastily by incorporating certain weak countries into its union. These countries and their economies are referred to as the "PIIGS." The acronym represents Portugal, Italy, Ireland, Greece and Spain. While the United States is comprised of 50 states, the European Union represents 27 sovereign nations that do not have a central government, thus magnifying the flaws in the formation of the union. The current situation appears to mirror past states of affair, such as economic confidence crises and potential run-ups in currency, as reflected in the ever-weakening euro.

The global economy avoided complete catastrophe in 2009 as the result of extraordinary efforts by lawmakers to transfer private sector debt to governments. If a developed country, such as Greece, defaulted on its debt, the scenario would play out with extreme market volatility to the downside, probable currency devaluation, credit market tightening, and higher interest rates. While Greek default would be similar to a major bank failure, the repercussions could trigger a cascade including speculation on which country would be next, and/or which country is "too big to fail." Which of the PIIGS would follow suit: Portugal, Italy, Ireland or Spain? Secondary fallout would also occur as pressure mounted on sovereign credit default swaps and corporate credit spreads, not only in Europe, but around the globe.

An overlay issue with respect to all of these problems is also emerging. To this point, the advocates of free capital markets have been satisfied to permit the financial world to function without many regulatory shackles. This laissez-faire or hands-off approach has been the standard, particularly in the Anglo-Saxon domain. Unfortunately, the current environment is leading politicians to probe deals that investment banks have made in connection with the Greek fiasco, rather than tackling the fundamental, corporate-governance issues that must be solved.

At Meditron, we remain vigilant, in that the interplay of economic and financial actions in today's fast-moving world could lead to severe risks that may not be readily apparent at this particular moment in time. Ⓦ

COMMODITIES AND BIG BANKS FROM: "DR. G'S INVESTMENT KEYS"

Goldman Sachs has predicted that an oil shortage may occur sometime in 2011, while stating that the price of crude oil is expected to reach $110 per barrel.

We find all of this information to be very interesting in that major banks like Goldman are removing millions of barrels of oil from the marketplace. J.P. Morgan, for example, has a supertanker in the Mediterranean and other ships off the coast of Northwest Europe, each storing approximately 1 million barrels, along with storage tanks around the world that hold even more of the commodity than the supertankers.

Together, the three largest banks—Goldman, J.P. Morgan and Morgan Stanley—have control over roughly 120 million barrels of oil.

Therefore, with this much oil off the market, these banks can be very confident in their predictions. At Meditron we are positioning our clients to take advantage of these "expectations."

"If a developed country, such as Greece, defaulted on its debt, the scenario would play out with extreme market volatility to the downside, probable currency devaluation, credit market tightening and higher interest rates."

– Dr. Walter V. Gerasimowicz

How to reach Dr. Walter V. Gerasimowicz

I prefer face-to-face meetings with prospective clients. My assistant will happily schedule a convenient time to meet. You can reach her at 212.634.6330.

WHAT'S ON MY DESK...

An indoor bonsai tree, also known as "The Money Tree," and a brass bull on a marble stand depicting future wealth for our global family of clients

MY HOBBIES ARE...

I enjoy performing with high-level choirs at Carnegie Hall, the Metropolitan Opera and other major venues in and around New York. I serve on various boards such as those for disabled and handicapped individuals.

I NEVER LEAVE HOME WITHOUT...

A feeling of passionate commitment to our clients, their economic advancement and thoughtful consideration of the trust they have placed in us regarding stewardship of their assets and dreams

About Dr. Walter V. Gerasimowicz

Dr. Walter V. Gerasimowicz, founder and CEO of Meditron Asset Management LLC, a global investment advisory firm, deals with all security classes and is on the boards of numerous companies. Previously, he served as the director of Advisory Services and as the chief investment strategist in Lehman's Private Client Services Division, where he was responsible for portfolio allocation, construction and rebalancing, plus risk management and performance attribution. Prior to joining Lehman Brothers, Dr. Gerasimowicz headed the International Portfolio Advisory Group at J.P. Morgan Securities Inc., where he pioneered state-of-the-art techniques. Before joining J.P. Morgan, he was a senior scientist for the USDA and the Naval Research Laboratories in Washington, D.C.

Assets Under Management **$1.1 billion**	Compensation Method **Asset-based, fixed and hourly fees**
Minimum Fee for Initial Meeting **Subject to initial review**	Primary Custodian for Investor Assets **Charles Schwab**
Minimum Net Worth Requirement **$500,000**	Professional Services Provided **Planning, investment advisory and asset management services**
Largest Client Net Worth **$71 million**	Email **wgerasim@meditronassetmanagement.com**
Financial Services Experience **25 years**	Website **www.meditronglobal.com**

Meditron Asset Management LLC | 641 Lexington Avenue, Suite 1400, New York, NY 10022 | 212.634.6330

New York, NY **Leading Wealth Advisor**

Madrigano Group at Morgan Stanley Smith Barney
Jonathan Madrigano, Director—Wealth Management, Family Wealth Director, and
Jared M. Samos, Director—Wealth Management, Financial Advisor, Portfolio Manager

" How do you advise private foundations on spending and investment policies? "

By Jonathan Madrigano and Jared M. Samos

Poets, prophets, financiers and even great medical educators have touted the merits of balance and equilibrium for thousands of years—often tiptoeing the proverbial tightrope, on which balance can bring triumph and instability can bring defeat. Balance, they knew, was vital to success. That same balance can be vital to the success of private foundations. Trustees must find long-term financial stability by balancing spending and investment policies in order to carry forward their donors' charitable endeavors and avoid spending themselves into extinction.

The financial management plan for a private foundation generally has one main purpose: to maximize the resources available to support its donors' mission. The charitable planning process, therefore, requires trustees to balance the expected social impact of their grant-making activity with the desired life expectancy of their endowment. This involves two broad trade-offs: current and future spending versus investment risk and return. The desire to support a high rate of spending may require an aggressive investment policy that will theoretically sustain that high spending level. Regrettably, an aggressive investment policy may result in the endowment suffering larger than expected losses

or even jeopardizing the future of the foundation by violating the trustees' fiduciary duty to manage charitable assets wisely and effectively. Conversely, trustees who prefer a more conservative investment approach may need to reduce spending or spend down the endowment and accept that their foundation may not exist in perpetuity. Either approach affects the social impact of the foundation's grant-making activity, as well as the life expectancy of its endowment.

The rising stock market of the 1990s led some people to call for greater spending levels based on gains realized on endowed portfolios during the bull market. Unfortunately, the days of outsized performance results could not be sustained indefinitely. Those who called for an increase in the annual payout requirements for foundations seemed not to take into account the effect that increased spending levels could pose on the continuance of the foundation on a long-term basis. In retrospect, increased spending targets have posed a formidable challenge for foundations seeking to protect their endowment from serious erosion.

Federal law requires private foundations to spend at least 5 percent of their investment assets each year, subject to certain adjustments. While this target may seem conservative, it

can prove difficult to meet when the capital markets experience a lengthy period of poor performance. Setting spending policy in excess of 5 percent greatly increases the risk that, over time, a foundation will suffer a significant decline in real asset value, which ultimately could lead to sharply lower cumulative spending levels.

While effective portfolio diversification of low-correlated assets may help trustees of private foundations overcome the special challenges they face when balancing spending and investment policy, there is a second option available to advance equilibrium. Rather than basing spending policy on a single year-end endowment balance, the foundation may base its spending on the average of year-end endowment balances over three or even five years. This tends to smooth the overall amount spent on grant making by reducing the impact of a single year's decline in value of the endowment. As asset values fall, the decrease in spending is muted by using average year-end balances. Conversely, as the endowment's value rises, spending does not climb as rapidly. Calculating spending policy based on a trailing average of year-end endowment balances may help advance long-term financial stability by reducing the impact volatile capital markets can have on grant-making activity.ⓦ

"Fortunate indeed, is the man who takes exactly the right measure of himself, and holds a just balance between what he can acquire and what he can use."
– Peter Mere Latham

How to reach Jonathan Madrigano and Jared M. Samos

We are happy to schedule a convenient time to meet. You can reach us at 212.603.6122.

WHAT'S ON MY DESK...

Jonathan: HP calculator, Cases and Materials on Gratuitous Transfers, and a picture of my nephew

Jared: Seven computer screens and a picture of my wife, Roona, and my daughter, Carys

MY HOBBIES ARE...

Jonathan: Reading, writing, cooking and supporting the arts and theater

Jared: Playing tennis, reading and traveling

Jonathan Madrigano

I NEVER LEAVE HOME WITHOUT...

Jonathan: The watch my mother gave me when I graduated from law school

Jared: My BlackBerry

Jared M. Samos

About Jonathan Madrigano and Jared M. Samos

As a Family Wealth Director at Morgan Stanley Smith Barney, Jonathan Madrigano educates principals of private companies that are pre-IPO, as well as individual clients whose wealth has the potential to change the essential nature of their descendants' lives. The core of his group's strategy is his single-minded commitment to client advocacy and to the elimination of potential, or perceived, conflicts of interest. As Madrigano Group's portfolio manager, Jared M. Samos is involved in every stage of the investment consulting process. He oversees an integrated team that includes investment professionals, technical analysts and administrative personnel. Prior to joining Madrigano Group, Mr. Samos worked as a Portfolio Analyst at the Union Bank of Switzerland. He was also an aide to President Clinton in the White House's Office of Counsel to the President.

Assets Under Management
$1 billion (as of 9/30/09)

Minimum Fee for Initial Meeting
None required

Minimum Net Worth Requirement
$5 million

Email jonathan.madrigano@
morganstanleypwm.com
jared.m.samos@morganstanleypwm.com

Compensation Method
Based upon asset value or cents-per-share commission

Professional Services Provided
Money management and comprehensive family office services

Association Memberships
Madrigano: New York State Bar Association; Samos: George Washington University Alumni Association, Pi Kappa Alpha Alumni Association

Madrigano Group at Morgan Stanley Smith Barney | 31 West 52nd Street, 23rd Floor, New York, NY 10019 | 212.603.6122

Chicago, IL—La Crosse, WI | **Leading Wealth Advisor**

Trust Point
Mark Chamberlain, JD, CPA, Senior Vice President
Darwin Isaacson, CPA, PFS, Executive Vice President
Brian Koopman, CFP®, CPA, CTFA, Vice President

"We want to make a substantial donation to a charity. Should we worry about reduced income once we retire?"

By Mark Chamberlain, Darwin Isaacson and Brian Koopman

Creating a charitable remainder trust may allow you to accomplish your goals—and more. In fact, you may be able to:

- Increase your lifetime income stream
- Obtain a current charitable income tax deduction
- Reduce the amount of your estate that is subject to estate taxes

Several types of charitable remainder trusts are available. We will focus on the charitable remainder unitrust (CRUT). A CRUT is a trust that pays an income stream to the donors (you and your spouse) for life. After the death of the second spouse, the balance (remainder interest) is paid to the designated charity or charities. The CRUT also allows you to make additional contributions.

Low-basis, highly appreciated, publicly traded stocks are ideal assets to contribute to a CRUT. Why? Because in order to diversify out of a large stock concentration, the donors normally would incur a significant capital gains tax hit. Capital gains tax rates are expected to increase in both 2011 and 2013. Contributing the stock to a CRUT meets the donors' charitable intent, allows for diversification, and normally will increase the income stream to the donors.

Normal dividend yields on stocks are 0 to 3 percent. The minimum required payout for a CRUT is 5 percent, which is why your income stream is likely to increase. The distributions the CRUT makes to the donors (income beneficiaries) are usually taxable in the year they are received.

The starting point for the income tax deduction is the fair-market value of the stock on the date of the contribution. The amount of the current charitable deduction is based on the calculated value of the remainder interest. This calculation considers the ages of the couple, the payout percentage and an IRS interest rate factor called the Section 7520 rate.

EXAMPLE:
Donors' age: 63
Value of contributed stock: $1 million
Payout rate: 6 percent
Estimated charitable contribution deduction: $250,000

The CRUT is excluded from the couple's estate, which reduces estate taxes. The amount of the federal estate tax exemption varies with political winds, so this may be an important estate planning tool in 2011 and beyond. ⓦ

DOES A CHARITABLE REMAINDER TRUST MAKE SENSE NOW?

Would you like to increase your current cash flow and avoid paying capital gains tax? Or take a substantial charitable income tax deduction this year while also reducing future estate taxes? Care to leave a greater portion of your estate to loved ones and benefit your favorite charity for generations to come?

Creating a charitable remainder trust can make it possible to receive all of these benefits at once. A charitable remainder trust provides what is truly a win-win situation: You benefit through increased cash flow, a substantial charitable income tax deduction and no capital gains tax. Your family benefits through decreased estate taxes and you may include heirs as income beneficiaries.

Ironically, if lawmakers do not act before the end of 2010, both income and estate taxes will rise significantly. This would make a charitable remainder trust even more attractive.

"Low-basis, publicly traded stocks are ideal assets to consider contributing to a CRUT."

– Mark Chamberlain, Darwin Isaacson and Brian Koopman

How to reach Trust Point

You can reach any member of our team at 608.782.1148 or 800.658.9474.

Front row, left to right: Janet Bahr, Kent Handel and Brian Koopman; *back row*–Randy Van Rooyen, Mark Chamberlain and Darwin Isaacson

About Trust Point

Trust Point's Wealth Management Group provides wealth management and advisory services to high net worth individuals and families. Members of the WMG group include Randy Van Rooyen, CFA®, the head of Trust Point's investment department; veteran administrator Janet Bahr, CTFA; Mark Chamberlain, JD and CPA; Brian Koopman, CPA, CTFA and CFP®; Darwin Isaacson, CPA and PFS; and Kent Handel, president and CEO of Trust Point Inc. With nearly $2 billion in assets and 97 years in business, Trust Point is one of the oldest and largest independent trust companies in the nation. Trust Point is a leading provider of services ranging from investment and personal-trust management to retirement plan administration.

Assets Under Management
$1 billion (team)
$2 billion (globally)

Minimum Annual Fee
$25,000 (investment services)

Minimum Net Worth Requirement
$5 million (in investable assets)

Largest Client Net Worth
$200 million

Financial Services Experience
144 years (combined)

Compensation Method
Fixed fees (planning services), asset-based fees (investment services)

Primary Custodian for Investor Assets
Bank of New York

Professional Services Provided
Investment advisory services, tax and financial planning

Association Memberships **American Institute of Certified Public Accountants, CFA Institute, and State Bar of Wisconsin**

Website
www.trustpointinc.com

Email
mchamberlain@trustpointinc.com
disaacson@trustpointinc.com
bkoopman@trustpointinc.com

Trust Point | 230 Front Street North, La Crosse, WI 54601 | 608.782.1148 | 800.658.9474

Phoenix–Scottsdale, AZ—Denver, CO   **Leading Wealth Advisor**

Morgan Stanley Smith Barney
Martin J. Erzinger, CIMA®, Director–Wealth Management, Senior Investment
Management Consultant, Corporate Client Group Director

"What are the advantages and disadvantages of DAFs and private foundations? "

By Martin J. Erzinger

Two very powerful philanthropic choices are available to you and your family for your planned giving: donor advised funds, or DAFs, and private foundations. Both options offer many advantages distinct to the way they are set up, so the objective is to choose which best fits your philanthropic goals.

DAFs have become a significant player in charitable giving in the last 10 years. Now the fastest-growing charitable vehicles of family philanthropy in America*, they offer an ease of administration that many families find appealing. At the same time, private foundations serve a myriad of purposes for high net worth families, particularly those that want a high degree of control and flexibility.

To help you decide which form of planned giving best serves your needs, below are brief overviews of DAFs and private foundations, including breakouts of their advantages and disadvantages.

WHAT IS A DONOR ADVISED FUND?

A DAF is a charitable giving vehicle administered by a third party and created for the purpose of managing charitable donations on behalf of an organization, family or individual. A donor advised fund offers the opportunity to create a low-cost vehicle for charitable giving as an alternative to direct giving or creating a private foundation.

DAF Advantages
- Immediate tax deduction
- Avoidance of capital gains tax—individuals can donate appreciated securities directly to a DAF and realize the full value as a deduction without incurring any capital gains tax
- Separation of tax planning and charitable decisions—immediate tax advantages can be achieved now, contributions can be made to charities later

DAF Disadvantages
- All recommendations advisory—the board of trustees for the host charity is free to accept or reject, in whole or in part, all recommendations
- Donated securities normally sold immediately

WHAT IS A PRIVATE FOUNDATION?

Private foundations are legal entities set up by an individual, a family or a group of individuals to support charitable endeavors, primarily through the distribution of grants. For example, the Bill & Melinda Gates Foundation is one of the largest private foundations in the United States, with billions of dollars in assets. However, most private foundations are much smaller, and the majority have less than $1 million in assets. As their name implies, private foundations do not normally solicit funds from the public. Family-created private foundations often include the participation of children who have an opportunity to test drive the experience of being on a board of directors, helping to make investment and donation decisions.

Private Foundation Advantages
- Foundation organizers nominate their own board of trustees
- Establish their own organizational guidelines and bylaws
- Act as the final authority in making their own investment and grant-making decisions
- Hire family members as staff to assist in pursuing their philanthropic mission—provided family members are qualified and their compensation is reasonable and necessary
- Donors have more flexibility in the types of assets they can donate (real estate, for instance)

Private Foundation Disadvantages
- Necessity to adhere to private foundation rules
- The higher expense of setting up and running a private foundation
- Having to pay the mandatory 2 percent tax on income of trustees

"Two very powerful philanthropic choices are available to you and your family for your planned giving: donor advised funds and private foundations."

– Martin J. Erzinger

How to reach Martin J. Erzinger

Potential clients may always call my office at 800.503.2813, ext. 4846. If I am not available, my staff will coordinate a time that is convenient for you.

WHAT'S ON MY DESK...

Wall Street Journal, *the* Financial Times, Barron's *and family photos*

I NEVER LEAVE HOME WITHOUT...

BlackBerry and wallet

MY HOBBIES ARE...

Golfing, swimming and skiing

About Martin J. Erzinger

Martin J. Erzinger is a director in private wealth management at Morgan Stanley Smith Barney in Denver. He is dedicated to ultra high net worth individuals, their families and foundations. By providing advice founded on a culture of excellence and driven by global insight, Mr. Erzinger is devoted to helping clients preserve and grow their financial, family and social capital. He brings 30 years of capital markets experience and expertise to the planning, design and implementation of clients' wealth strategies. He is backed by a deep team of professionals with multiple disciplines. He has served on numerous boards and investment committees and is a current director and trustee on the University of Colorado Foundation Board.

Assets Under Management **$1 billion**	Compensation Method **Asset-based fees and commissions (investment and insurance products)**
Minimum Fee for Initial Meeting **None required**	Primary Custodian for Investor Assets **Morgan Stanley Smith Barney**
Minimum Net Worth Requirement **$5 million**	Professional Services Provided **Planning, investment advisory and money management services**
Largest Client Net Worth **$800 million**	Association Memberships **IMCA**
Financial Services Experience **30 years**	Email **martin.j.erzinger@morganstanleypwm.com**

Morgan Stanley Smith Barney | 370 17th Street, Suite 2800, Denver, CO 80202 | 303.572.4000 | 800.503.2813

Los Angeles, CA   **Leading Wealth Advisor**

The Glowacki Group LLC
Michael Glowacki, CFP®, CPA, MBT, Founder

"What should I do when Bill Gates and Warren Buffett call for my pledge?"

By Michael Glowacki

Bill and Melinda Gates and Warren Buffett are calling on other billionaires to pledge at least half of their net worth to philanthropy. If you are a bit cynical, you might say they are doing it out of guilt or for the tax benefits. However, if you go deeper, there is another explanation.

For individuals who have reached their financial goals, what better way is there to move to the next level of success—a level at which they can express their values by directing change or enhancing the support of their charitable causes? These changes could live well beyond their lives and the lives of their children and grandchildren. And, if you do not agree with the way Congress spends your money, here is a way to be more proactive with what would otherwise be tax dollars.

With tax rates likely to increase in 2011, the government may be making it worthwhile to redirect your taxes to philanthropy. In fact, depending on how you give your assets, it could cost you as little as 25 cents to give a dollar away.

The next question is how much and how to give. To the right is a table of a few charitable planning strategies that you can use to maximize tax advantages while maintaining your need for control, timing and personal lifestyle

needs. A little warning, though—some of the best philanthropic planning strategies are irrevocable. You will want to make sure that you can afford to give without downgrading your lifestyle or taking from the dreams you have for your children and grandchildren. What is the cost of those dreams? If you are like most individuals, you have no idea. **Consequently, you should follow these steps before you commit your funds:**

1. Write out what you want to change or maintain in your community, the country, or the world.

2. Determine if you want to give your time, a portion of your wealth, or both, and in what proportion. Even your own foundation can require a

substantial time commitment.

3. Calculate how much money you need for your lifestyle for the rest of your life.

4. Calculate how much you want to give to charity, your family and other heirs during and after your life.

5. Determine if and how you want recognition for your gift. Be honest!

6. Work with a philanthropic coach, your charity's planned giving officer, and your planning team to determine the best strategy to implement your gifts.

With some careful thought and planning, your philanthropy can have the same lasting impact as Gates' and Buffett's, while meeting your financial and personal goals. ⓦ

CHARITABLE PLANNING STRATEGIES			
Charitable Remainder Trusts	Donor Advised Funds	Appreciated Securities	Appreciated Real Estate
Charitable Lead Trusts	Charitable Bargain Sales	Life Insurance	Flip Unitrusts
Pooled Income Funds	Retained Life Estates	Charitable Gift Annuities	Qualified Personal Residence Trusts
Foundations	Bequests	Appreciated Art & Collectibles	Retirement Plan Bequests

"If you do not agree with the way Congress spends your money, here is a way to be more proactive with what would otherwise be tax dollars."

– Michael Glowacki

How to reach Michael Glowacki

I prefer face-to-face meetings with prospective clients. My assistant will happily schedule a convenient time to meet. You can reach Beth at 310.473.0100.

WHAT I'M READING NOW...

Philanthrocapitalism, *by Matthew Bishop and Michael Green;* Time to Think, *by Nancy Kline;* More Money Than God, *by Sebastian Mallaby*

WHAT MAKES A GOOD CLIENT...

A family or individual who knows, or is interested in discovering, the purpose for wealth and how money can be used to support that purpose

WHAT MAKES A GOOD WEALTH ADVISOR...

A professional who can combine coaching with advising to help clients focus on the "why" along with the "how"

About Michael Glowacki

Michael Glowacki, founder of The Glowacki Group LLC, which provides comprehensive wealth management and family office services, has more than 30 years of financial, investment, tax and planning experience. He began his career as a certified public accountant with Grant Thornton, the fifth-largest national accounting firm in the United States. Subsequently, he was a CFO for a real estate company, a start-up venture and a family office. While holding these positions, Mr. Glowacki earned his master of business in taxation and became a Certified Financial Planner. He is also a certified professional coach and integrates coaching into his work with affluent clients. As a financial coach, Mr. Glowacki asks his clients relevant questions, which enables him to better understand their intent and to provide tailored planning for their wealth management.

Assets Under Management **$260 million**	Compensation Method **Asset-based and retainer fees**
Minimum Fee for Initial Meeting **None required**	Primary Custodian for Investor Assets **Charles Schwab**
Minimum Net Worth Requirement **$5 million**	Professional Services Provided **Planning, investment advisory services and philanthropic consulting**
Largest Client Net Worth **$120 million**	Association Memberships **FPA, NAPFA, IMCA, AIP**
Financial Services Experience **30+ years**	Website **www.glowackigroup.com** Email **mg@glowackigroup.com**

The Glowacki Group LLC | 11400 West Olympic Boulevard, Suite 1500, Los Angeles, CA 90064 | 310.473.0100

Los Angeles, CA   **Leading Wealth Advisor**

Morgan Stanley Smith Barney
Rebecca Rothstein, Managing Director—Wealth
Management, Family Wealth Director

" What are the reasons for choosing a perpetual vs. a limited-life foundation? "

By Rebecca Rothstein

While existing in perpetuity is the norm for the majority of family foundations, a small segment of families plan to limit their foundations' life spans or are in the process of spending down their assets. A larger segment is currently undecided, either because they have not yet discussed the issue or because of uncertainty about their family's future involvement.

If you are in the latter and larger segment, a report issued by The Foundation Center offers some insight into why families choose one course over another. For example, the Center reports that foundations planning to exist in perpetuity are most likely to do so for family-related reasons. These include engagement across generations, shared responsibility and family unity, and a concern for the long-term needs of people and causes assisted by the foundation.

For families that plan to limit a foundation's life span, the two leading reasons cited were the founders' desire not only to have a greater impact during their lifetimes, but also to be directly involved in how the money is spent. The Center also reports that when a founder is still living it increases the chance that a foundation will consider alternatives to perpetuity, or leave the door open for future consideration.

When a recession depletes foundation assets while the need for charitable funding increases, you might consider the limited-life foundation option. Increasingly, many perpetual foundations are considering this powerful option. In Morgan Stanley Smith Barney's opinion, your foundation should consider adding language to its governing documents providing direction to your trustees in the event of unforeseeable situations that may put the foundation's goal of perpetuity in opposition to its charitable mission.

When considering perpetuity versus limited-life, ask yourself the following:

1. Why do we exist?

2. Have our children and grandchildren expressed and demonstrated an interest in continuing this work and running the foundation?

3. Is perpetuity our sole objective?

4. If we increase our funding within our mission areas, even if it depletes our foundation's assets, will we better meet the needs of our constituency and ultimately our purpose for existing?

5. Do we not exist precisely for times like these, and should we not step up to the challenge?

Your answers to these questions will not only provide direction, they will reaffirm for all why the foundation exists in the first place. Ⓦ

WILL THE ECONOMIC CRISIS IMPACT A LIFE SPAN OF FAMILY FOUNDATIONS?

The decline in foundation assets, coupled with the increased need for funding by a vast majority of non-profit institutions, may result in a greater proportion of private foundations—including yours—deciding to spend down their assets or even folding themselves into donor advised funds.

Of course, if yours is one of the larger endowed family foundations, it will likely forge on. But if it is one of the smaller and newer family foundations that have not had much time to grow, it may not be as lucky. At a minimum, these challenging times should give your family a reason to consider why your foundation was formed in the first place, and to think deliberately about its life-span options.

"You might consider the limited-life foundation option."

– Rebecca Rothstein

How to reach Rebecca Rothstein

I prefer face-to-face meetings with prospective clients. My assistant will happily schedule a convenient time to meet. You can reach her at 310.285.2623.

MY HOBBIES ARE...

Cooking, baking, skiing, sailing, exercising

I NEVER LEAVE HOME WITHOUT...

My pedometer and BlackBerry

WHAT'S ON MY DESK...

Three keyboards and five screens, one cordless headset

About Rebecca Rothstein

With 22 years of industry experience, Rebecca Rothstein and her skilled team focus on advising high net worth investors on their current and long-term needs. A managing director in the Morgan Stanley Smith Barney Beverly Hills branch, Ms. Rothstein focuses on estate, tax and financial planning. She also works extensively with corporate officers/directors regarding liquidity and diversification strategies for concentrated positions. Frequently named to *Barron's* list of America's top 100 wealth advisors* (number 29 in 2009 and number 44 in 2008), Ms. Rothstein was also named the number 1 woman advisor in America by *Barron's* in 2005, 2007 and 2009. *Barron's* "Top 100 Financial Advisors," as identified by The Winner's Circle LLC, bases its rankings on qualitative criteria: professionals with a minimum of seven years of financial services experience, acceptable compliance records, client retention reports, customer satisfaction and more. With over 7,000 nominations, advisors are quantitatively ranked based on varying types of revenues and assets advised by the financial professional, with weightings associated for each. Additional measures include in-depth interviews with senior management, peers and customers, and interviews with the nominees. Because individual client portfolio performance varies and is typically unaudited, this ranking focuses on customer satisfaction and quality of advice. Ms. Rothstein resides in Hidden Hills, Calif., with her husband and four sons.

Assets Under Management $2 billion (as of 3/31/09)	**Compensation Method** Asset-based fees and commissions (investment and insurance products)
Minimum Fee for Initial Meeting None required	**Primary Custodian for Investor Assets** Morgan Stanley Smith Barney
Minimum Net Worth Requirement $2 million	**Professional Services Provided** Planning, investment advisory and money management services
Largest Client Net Worth $750 million	**Email** rebecca.s.rothstein@smithbarney.com
Financial Services Experience 22 years	**Website** http://fa.smithbarney.com/rebecca_rothstein/

Barron's rating may not be representative of any one client's experience because it reflects a sample of all the experiences of Ms. Rothstein's clients. The ratings are not indicative of Ms. Rothstein's future performance. Morgan Stanley Smith Barney does not pay a fee to *Barron's* in exchange for the rating.

Morgan Stanley Smith Barney | 9665 Wilshire Boulevard, Suite 600, Beverly Hills, CA 90212 | 310.285.2623

The Parthemer King Group at Morgan Stanley Smith Barney
Aaron R. Parthemer, CFP®, NFLPA, Registered Player Financial Advisor
Senior Vice President–Wealth Management

" How much money will I need for a safe retirement? "

By Aaron R. Parthemer

The best answer I could give is that there is no such thing as a typical answer. You need to throw out all rules of thumb and simple answers and know that only by reviewing your personal situation will you discover your answer. In my 16 years of advising clients, I have seen nearly every situation imaginable and have learned that no magical number or rule can be applied.

To illustrate, in our work with professional athletes it is not infrequent to see individuals who will spend as little as 10 percent of their life expectancy earning their money while they will spend more than 60 percent of their life expectancy trying to live off that money. The probability analysis that we use will give us an incredibly wide variance in results and make it nearly impossible to create a high degree of certainty of never running out of money, regardless of how much money they have.

On the flip side, among entrepreneurs and corporate executives it is not uncommon that clients may never truly retire and will continue to earn income well beyond the normal retirement age from consulting work or by sitting on the boards of other companies. These individuals will typically spend 60 percent of their life expectancy earning money while spending their nest egg over 10 percent or less of their life. In running the probability analysis for these individuals, it becomes statistically nearly impossible for them to run out of money, and they will often have large surpluses remaining at the end of their lives.

In addition to understanding the number of years spent accumulating wealth compared to the number of years of spending from the assets, another factor that will dictate the amount of money needed to retire will be the spending habits of the individual. It is often assumed that an individual's spending will decrease dramatically upon reaching retirement. This seldom is what actually happens. The lifestyle in retirement is often a by-product of the spending habits during the working years. Those who are focused on aggressively saving while they are accumulating assets will typically lower their expenses that much more in retirement, while those who are often wasteful or not big savers will tend to continue to live a more lavish lifestyle while in retirement. Therefore, in response to the question of how much it takes to retire, I would submit that it is an impossible question to answer absent of detailed financial planning along with a thorough understanding of the client's career goals, spending habits and general attitude toward spending and saving money. ⓦ

THE REAL ESTATE FALLACY

Residential real estate values can be deceptive in a declining market; reduced prices from the market height may not be the great deal that they seem. When determining if real estate is priced properly, include the reversion to the mean theory.

In the late '90s through 2006, many people believed it was normal for a home to appreciate by double digits each year. However, a study released by Fidelity Investments in 2007 showed that the performance of the residential real estate market in the United States from 1963 to 2006 was a mere 1.35 percent per year. During this period, there were three sharp downturns, including the recent one that cut as much as 50 percent of value in less than five years.

Therefore, if you take the historical rate of return for the particular area and compare it to more recent rates of return, you can extract the amount of decline the property should have experienced in order to get its annual return back to that historical average, or reversion to the mean.

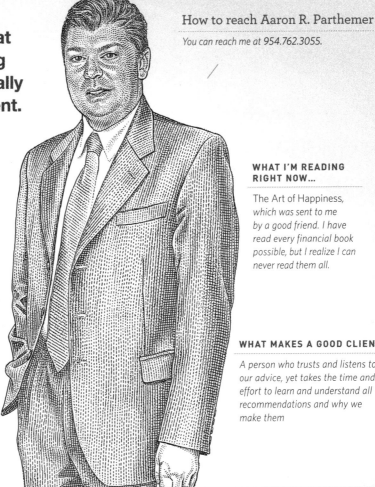

"It is often assumed that an individual's spending will decrease dramatically upon reaching retirement. This seldom is what actually happens."

– Aaron R. Parthemer

How to reach Aaron R. Parthemer

You can reach me at 954.762.3055.

WHAT I'M READING RIGHT NOW...

The Art of Happiness, which was sent to me by a good friend. I have read every financial book possible, but I realize I can never read them all.

I NEVER LEAVE HOME WITHOUT...

An optimistic view of what that day is going to bring. In a world full of pessimism, I attempt to make the most out of each and every minute.

WHAT MAKES A GOOD CLIENT...

A person who trusts and listens to our advice, yet takes the time and effort to learn and understand all recommendations and why we make them

About The Parthemer King Group

In 2000 Aaron R. Parthemer began working with his first professional athlete, taking the time to understand the unique financial issues and other aspects that impacted him and those to come. He partnered with Sylvester King, who brought nearly 20 years of high net worth banking experience to the practice. They completed the team with the addition of Tiffany Taylor, who took over all administrative and other day-to-day duties, and Scott Brady, who had been the assistant and right-hand man to one of the world's top professional golfers. Today, the team manages a substantial number of professional athletes and other high net worth individuals. They retain a financial practice that is tailored to each and every client, regardless of profession.

Assets Under Management **$260 million (as of 9/3/10)**	Compensation Method **Asset-based fees and commissions (investment and insurance products)**
Minimum Fee for Initial Meeting **None required**	Professional Services Provided **Planning, investment advisory and money management services**
Largest Client Net Worth **$300 million**	Primary Custodian for Investor Assets **Morgan Stanley Smith Barney**
Financial Services Experience **16 years**	Association Memberships **Financial Planning Association**
Email **aaron.r.parthemer@mssb.com**	Website **http://fa.smithbarney.com/theparthemerkinggroup/financialplanning.htm**

The Parthemer King Group at Morgan Stanley Smith Barney | 350 East Las Olas Boulevard, Suite 1200, Fort Lauderdale, FL 33301 | 954.762.3055

WORTH FINANCIAL INTELLIGENCE | VOLUME ONE | ①①⑨

"How can I offer a cost-effective and compliant retirement plan to the employees of my closely held business?"

By Carina Diamond

A retirement plan can be a strong employee retention and recruiting tool, but it is often neglected or misunderstood. Here are a few tips to help you properly manage your costs and compliance requirements, while maximizing the benefits of your company's plan.

Fee transparency. Be aware of what your plan is really costing your business and employees. Two costs that are often hidden are the internal management fees of the investments and the asset-based, or "wrap" fee. These should be added together to calculate the true cost of your plan, a figure very helpful in comparing your plan with alternatives. Be sure your advisor has fully disclosed these. If you have not shopped your plan within the past few years, you may be paying too much. Survey the market every few years to make sure current fees are competitive. As plan assets grow, investment fees should decrease.

Employee education. You spend money and time to maintain your retirement plan, but do your employees appreciate it? An effective education campaign can make a huge difference in employee retention and satisfaction. Does your advisor help employees with investment decisions, both in groups and individually? If your advisor is not providing regular employee meetings, you are not getting your money's worth, and you may be setting yourself up for legal issues.

Plan design. If you and your highly paid executives are not able to contribute as much as you would like to, a review of your plan design may be in order. There are plan designs approved by the IRS that allow contributions to be skewed toward older, higher-paid employees, which generally are the owners and executives. Employee education can sometimes help by increasing participation by the rank and file, which may assist in meeting non-discrimination requirements. As laws change, your advisor should recommend enhancements such as the Roth 401(k) option, which can increase employee excitement and appreciation.

Investment—policy and review. We recommend maintenance of a formal Investment Policy Statement, and we help our clients draft and maintain them regularly. Investment choices should be monitored at least quarterly, and a formal review should be conducted at least annually. Changes to the choice of funds available should be made when warranted. If your advisor does not recommend at least a few changes to your investment lineup annually, that could be a red flag that the appropriate due diligence is not being conducted. ⓦ

WHY SHOULD I CONSIDER A ROTH 401(K)?

You may have heard about the tax benefits of a Roth IRA but been advised you earn too much to participate, or found the contribution limits too low. A Roth 401(k) is open to all plan participants regardless of earnings, with a contribution limit of $16,500 to $22,000 per year, depending on age. Monies are contributed to the Roth 401(k) after tax. Distributions (your contributions plus earnings) are tax-free as long as you are at least 59 ½ years old and have had the account for at least five years. If you roll your balance to a Roth IRA, you may be relieved of taking required minimum distributions as well, providing valuable estate planning benefits.

The decision of whether to utilize the Roth or traditional pre-tax option is complex. For many people, much of their savings is already in pre-tax accounts (retirement plans and IRAs). All of these funds are fully taxable upon withdrawal, at the highest ordinary income tax rates then in effect. Regardless of which direction tax rates take in the future, having some funds in a Roth provides additional flexibility and opportunities for tax planning. Who would not like to have a pot of money at retirement that has no taxes associated with it?

"If you have not shopped your retirement plan within the past few years, you may be paying too much."

– Carina Diamond

How to reach Carina Diamond

Please call me at 330.598.2208.

WHAT MAKES A GOOD CLIENT...

Open and full disclosure of goals and concerns; questioning when a concept isn't explained clearly; and availability for regular meetings and communication

IF I WEREN'T A WEALTH ADVISOR, I'D BE...

A child psychologist. I find that most adult behavior toward money is rooted in one's own childhood experiences with their weekly allowance, competition in gym class, and sibling rivalry.

WHAT MAKES A GOOD WEALTH ADVISOR...

Listening more than speaking, ability to motivate and coach, and humility

About Carina Diamond

Carina Diamond, managing director of SS&G Wealth Management LLC, has 25 years of experience advising individuals and businesses on personal financial planning and investment management. She ran a trust company for a community bank and the retirement plan division for a large Midwestern bank. Ms. Diamond speaks nationally on topics including best practices for businesses, communication and retirement plans. Her honors include the Sapphire Award for Women of Excellence in Financial Planning. Ms. Diamond was the top-ranked female advisor for Multi-Financial in 2008 and 2009. She is an active board member for the Diabetes Association of Greater Cleveland, co-chairing the endowment committee. She is also a member of the John Carroll University Entrepreneurs Association and the Financial Planning Association.

Assets Under Management $200 million	**Compensation Method** Fixed and hourly fees, commissions (insurance and investment products)
Minimum Annual Fee None required	**Primary Custodian for Investor Assets** Pershing LLC
Minimum Net Worth Requirement $500,000	**Professional Services Provided** Financial planning, personal investment management and corporate retirement plans
Largest Client Net Worth $20 million+	**Association Memberships** Financial Planning Association
Financial Services Experience 25 years	**Website** www.SSandGwealth.com **Email** cdiamond@ssandg.com

SS&G Wealth Management LLC | 32125 Solon Road, Cleveland, OH 44139 | 330.598.2208

"How much can I withdraw from my portfolio each year during retirement?"

By Kim Foss-Erickson

Four percent is often offered as the standard answer to the question of annual portfolio withdrawals during retirement. However, just as one-size-fits-all does not work when you are shopping for a suit or a new home, your retirement withdrawal rate must be tailored to reflect the size of your portfolio, risk tolerance, lifestyle and even your life expectancy.

A common misconception is that the 4 percent solution advocates withdrawing 4 percent annually. In fact, research supports withdrawing 4 percent in year one of retirement and adjusting that amount in future years to reflect inflation. **If you retire with a $2 million portfolio, you can safely withdraw $80,000 this year, followed by $80,000 indexed for inflation in subsequent years.**

William Bernstein's research first established the ability to support a 30-year retirement based on an initial 4 percent withdrawal, assuming a broadly diversified portfolio—60 percent equities/40 percent bonds—generating an average annual return of 7.5 percent (with annual inflation running at 3 percent). William Bengen later found that a portfolio comprised of three asset classes—20 percent small-company stocks, 45 percent large-company stocks, and 35 percent five-year Treasuries—could increase the first withdrawal to 4.4 percent.

While broad-based diversification to exploit low correlations between asset classes can enhance returns, a down market occurring early in retirement poses a threat to sustainable withdrawals. What is more, with longevity continuing to increase, your retirement may span more than three decades. Accordingly, especially in today's uncertain market, we may need to adjust the 4 percent solution.

For example, Jonathan Guyton recently looked at several diversified portfolios from 1973 through 2003, a timeframe consisting of two bear markets and a period of abnormally high inflation. He found that forgoing an inflationary adjustment to the withdrawal rate following a down year, with no future make-up adjustment, supported a 5.4 percent initial withdrawal rate, sustainable for 40 years, in a 65 percent stock portfolio.

Of course, "safe" and "sustainable" are subjective terms. Some investors are comfortable with a 90 percent chance they will not outlive their money. Others want an absolute guarantee. Given that we do not know how long our portfolio will need to support us, or what the market holds, I view 4 percent as a starting point for constructing a sustainable retirement income stream. The key to ensuring you do not run through your assets too quickly is committing to ongoing portfolio reviews to assess market conditions and to integrate emerging research. Ⓦ

ESTABLISHING A RELIABLE RETIREMENT INCOME STREAM

In "Spending Rates, Asset Allocation, and Probability of Failure," James Davis, of Dimensional Fund Advisors, explores how choices about spending and asset allocation impact retirement income streams. Davis finds that in seeking to balance the desire for stable consumption against the fear of running out of money, there is no optimal spending/investing formula. However, his study illustrates many key principles, including:

• Investors are more likely to maintain their living standards in retirement utilizing low spending rates and reasonably large stock allocations. A long retirement coupled with a low stock allocation translates into a high probability of declining consumption.

• High spending rates, even over short periods, can negatively impact future income streams.

I would note that by considering only two asset classes, Davis' analysis understates the potential benefits of diversification.

> "Research supports withdrawing 4 percent in year one of retirement and adjusting that amount in future years to reflect inflation."
>
> – Kim Foss-Erickson

How to reach Kim Foss-Erickson

Face-to-face is my meeting preference, but when that is not convenient, I always have my BlackBerry in hand. Or you may contact my director of client services, Joanne Nuguit, RP, at 916.786.7626 or at joanne@empyrionwealth.com to arrange a complimentary consultation.

WHAT'S ON MY DESK...

An in-and-out box, my Franklin day timer, and fresh roses from my late mother's backyard to remind me what this journey is all about—family

I NEVER LEAVE HOME WITHOUT...

Two things: 1) Plan B because life is all about how you handle Plan B; and 2) a plate of homemade chocolate chip cookies for the client(s) I will meet during the day

MY HOBBIES ARE...

Running (especially after my 5-year-old son), core training, water and snow skiing, and creating "look books" for my close friends and family

About Kim Foss-Erickson

Kim Foss-Erickson, president and founder of Empyrion Wealth Management, has worked for more than 25 years in the financial services industry, 20 at the helm of Empyrion. She consistently is named one of the nation's top wealth managers by *Bloomberg Wealth Manager*, has appeared on *Good Morning America* and *Today*, and has contributed to the Associated Press, *Washington Post*, *San Francisco Chronicle* and to *Secrets of the Wealth Makers: Top Money Managers Reveal Their Investing Wisdom*. She is a certified financial planner and certified private wealth advisor. She is a member of the Investment Management Consultants Association.

Assets Under Management **$200 million**	Compensation Method **Asset-based and hourly fees**
Minimum Fee for Initial Meeting **None required**	Primary Custodian for Investor Assets **Charles Schwab**
Minimum Net Worth Requirement **$1 million**	Professional Services Provided **Retirement, estate planning and investment advisory services**
Largest Client Net Worth **$60 million**	Association Memberships **Financial Planning Association, Investment Management Consultants Association, and National Association of Professional Women**
Financial Services Experience **26 years**	Email **kim@empyrionwealth.com** Website **www.empyrionwealth.com**

Empyrion Wealth Management Inc.   3741 Douglas Boulevard, Suite 130, Roseville, CA 95661   916.786.7626

San Francisco—Bay Area, CA   **Leading Wealth Advisor**

Cypress Wealth Advisors
Sean J. Figueroa, CFA®, CFP®, Principal and Cofounder
Barbara H. Young, CFP®, Principal and Cofounder
Steven W. Enos, CFA®, Principal and Cofounder
David A. McInnis, Principal

" Which often overlooked securities can help minimize my tax exposure? "

By Barbara H. Young

Dynamic relationships exist among risk, return, tax consequences and liquidity when analyzing any investment. It is imperative to fully understand a client's needs and sensitivities regarding all these aspects before determining the appropriate investment portfolio. Clearly, high after-tax returns are the ideal target, but incorporating the client's appropriate level of risk and liquidity needs are also critical components. Some assets that have favorable tax consequences, such as private real estate partnerships, venture capital and private equity, provide little liquidity, and depending on the specific investment, they can increase the risk of any particular portfolio.

One investment we have found to be attractive from a tax standpoint, as well as providing liquidity and mitigating risk, is a master limited partnership (MLP). MLPs own hard assets, produce or transport vitally needed energy commodities, have major financial and operating advantages over potential competitors, and generate relatively stable and predictable cash flow. MLPs are traded on the securities exchanges as publicly traded instruments and are actually considered to be units in a partnership that is publicly traded. The tax advantage to MLPs is that they are legally structured as a partnership; the income is taxed to the limited partners (unit holders); and there is no double taxation as there is in a corporate structure. The partnerships are required to distribute their excess cash flow to their unit holders. Because the industries that are legally allowed to form as MLPs are restricted primarily to real estate, oil and gas, natural resources, etc., most of them have tremendous depreciation or depletion as an operating expense, thereby drastically reducing the taxable operating income. Commonly, the cash flow distributed to the limited partners (unit holders) is far in excess of the share of net operating income that is taxable to each limited partner. The cash is distributed as a return of capital and reduces the tax basis, deferring tax payment until the units are sold.

We are finding the midstream oil and gas MLPs attractive. These are primarily involved in the ownership and operation of pipelines and the transportation and storage of oil and gas. The outlook for energy demand indicates continued growth, and these MLPs transport the commodity to meet the demand. And because they are involved in transport and storage, they are fairly immune to the price fluctuations of oil and gas.

We find MLPs to be a great income-producing investment; a liquid investment; an investment that when well researched and appropriately purchased can provide upside appreciation; and an investment that provides current tax advantages with the deferral of most taxes until sale of the securities. Ⓦ

> ## "One investment we have found to be attractive from a tax standpoint, as well as providing liquidity and mitigating risk, is a master limited partnership."
> – Barbara H. Young

How to reach Cypress Wealth Advisors

We prefer face-to-face meetings with prospective clients. Please contact David A. McInnis at 415.489.2100 to schedule an appointment.

Steven W. Enos

Sean J. Figueroa

Barbara H. Young

MY HOBBIES ARE...

Steven: *Coaching my kids, golf and wine*

Sean: *Trail running and golf*

Barbara: *Gardening, hiking and reading*

WHAT'S ON MY DESK...

Steven: *Lots of paper!*

Sean: *Family pictures and a clock from my first job as an intern research analyst*

Barbara: *Mementos of my children*

I NEVER LEAVE HOME WITHOUT...

Steven: *My sense of humor*

Sean: *My cell phone*

Barbara: *My PDA*

About Cypress Wealth Advisors

Barbara H. Young, Sean J. Figueroa and Steven W. Enos, principals and founders of Cypress Wealth Advisors, hold various responsibilities including oversight of investment and estate strategies for families and charitable entities. Before Cypress, Ms. Young was the founding president and CEO of Springcreek Corp. and a vice president at Chase Manhattan Bank. Mr. Figueroa served for 10 years as portfolio manager, director of business development and principal at Stein Roe Investment Counsel. Mr. Enos' 20-plus years of experience in managing portfolios for high net worth clients include senior positions at Stein Roe Investment Counsel and Wells Capital Management. David McInnis, principal, has over 23 years of experience advising high net worth clients, family offices, private equity/LBO and venture capital firms.

Assets Under Management **$456 million**	Compensation Method **Asset-based and fixed fees**
Minimum Fee for Initial Meeting **None required**	Primary Custodian for Investor Assets **Charles Schwab**
Minimum Net Worth Requirement **$10 million**	Professional Services Provided **Planning, investment advisory and money management services**
Largest Client Net Worth **$200 million**	Association Memberships **CFA Institute, Security Analysts Society of San Francisco**
Financial Services Experience **139 years (combined)**	Website **www.cypresswealth.com** Email **dmcinnis@cypresswealth.com**

Cypress Wealth Advisors   101 California Street, Suite 1025, San Francisco, CA 94111   415.489.2100

Dallas, TX—Milwaukee, WI | **Leading Wealth Advisor**

Baird Family Wealth Group
Robert W. Baird & Company Inc.
David Klenke, CFP®, CFA, CPA

" How should I adjust my investment strategy in a rising tax environment? "

By David Klenke

While you should always consider how taxes lower returns on your portfolio, you especially need to contemplate and prepare for the rising tax environment we face. As legislated, by 2013 interest income will be taxed at 43.4 percent, capital gains at 23.8 percent, and dividend income at 43.4 percent. These are increases of 24 percent, 59 percent and 189 percent respectively. In addition, we expect the estate tax to be reinstated at a rate above 50 percent in 2011. These increases will significantly impact returns and the wealth you transfer to the next generation.

How do you adjust to this new environment? The most successful families will form a family strategy by integrating their investment plans. This typically begins with a sound foundation in asset allocation— a mix of cash, bonds, stocks and other investments.

With today's technology, a person can easily build optimized allocations by using assumptions about the future. But these assumptions are rarely adjusted to take into consideration real-world taxes. Often times this is because most of these allocation models are built with a focus on institutions and pension funds that pay no tax. But individual investors do. So we have found that adjusting assumptions to include the reality of taxes enables construction of a portfolio with greater wealth potential.

When constructing a tax-sensitive portfolio, we think of asset classes as either tax efficient or tax inefficient. Some examples of tax-efficient classes under current law would be stocks and private equity because their returns come in the form of capital appreciation or dividend income that is taxed at 15 percent. In contrast, an inefficient investment now would include anything, such as hedge funds, in which the primary return component is taxed as ordinary income.

Before January 1, 2011, when income and estate tax rates will begin to move up (see callout below), thereby changing the inefficient/efficient equation, you should consider:

· Decreasing your allocation to once-efficient asset classes
· Changing your portfolio's balance of value and growth stocks
· Reviewing the after-tax returns of your bond portfolio

Furthermore, large families need to think in macro terms, considering a holistic family allocation. What may result is an allocation in which the first generation holds the less-efficient and less-risky assets, and the following generations, with longer time horizons, hold the high-growth assets. Taking this approach may lead to the heirs (or a trust) reaping most of the financial growth while lowering both the income and estate tax burden for the family as a whole. This ultimately results in more wealth. Ⓦ

ASSET-CLASS TAX EFFICIENCY VERSUS NEW TAX RATES

From an after-tax standpoint, we believe new tax rates expected to begin in 2011 (see chart) will make currently tax-inefficient asset classes (fixed income, hedge funds, etc.) more attractive on a relative basis compared to traditionally efficient assets (stocks, private equity, etc.).

Expected Future Income Tax Rates (top tax bracket)				
	Capital Gains	Dividends	Interest	Earned Income
2010	15%	15%	35%	35%
2011	20%	39.6%	39.6%	39.6%
2012	20%	39.6%	39.6%	39.6%
2013	23.8%	43.4%	43.4%	40.5%
% increase	59%	189%	24%	16%

"Rising tax rates should be moved near the top of the list of the many risks faced by successful families."

– Baird Family Wealth Group

How to reach Baird Family Wealth Group

Please call 214.373.2974 in Dallas or 414.765.7092 in Milwaukee or see our website at www.bairdfamilywealthgroup.com to contact any member of our team.

Left to right: Denise Davis, John Mockovciak, Chris Didier, Dave Klenke, Bryn Feyen, Ed DeFrance

About Baird Family Wealth Group

The Family Wealth Group is a multi-family office committed to providing customized and comprehensive wealth management services to successful families. The Group's depth of investment and planning expertise, combined with the highly personalized attention they offer, allows them to simplify their clients' financial life while providing clients with world-class portfolio management. The Family Wealth Group is part of Robert W. Baird & Co. Since 1919, Baird's commitment to keeping clients first has made the company a trusted partner to individual investors, families, corporations, institutions and municipalities. Baird has grown to meet the needs of its clients while maintaining the core values that have kept the company strong. Baird is employee-owned, and its employees are passionate about what they do, knowing from experience that the best way to do it is with their clients' best interests in mind.

Minimum Fee for Initial Meeting **None required**	Compensation Method **Asset-based, fixed and hourly fees**
Minimum Net Worth Requirement **$25 million**	Primary Custodian for Investor Assets **Robert W. Baird & Co., Northern Trust and BNY Mellon**
Largest Client Net Worth **Confidential**	Professional Services Provided **Financial strategy, analysis consulting, planning and investment advisory services**
Financial Services Experience **21 years (on average)**	Association Memberships **CFA Institute and American Institute of Certified Public Accountants**
Email **dklenke@rwbaird.com**	Website **www.bairdfamilywealthgroup.com**

Baird Family Wealth Group	5950 Berkshire Lane, Suite 1300, Dallas, TX 75225	214.373.2974
	777 East Wisconsin Avenue, 29th Floor, Milwaukee, WI 53202	414.765.7092

McLean, VA — Washington, DC   **Leading Legal Advisor**

Holland & Knight LLP
Leigh-Alexandra Basha, JD, LLM Tax
Partner and Chair—International Private Wealth Services

" What are some of the tax and estate planning traps that arise when advising a multinational client? "

By Leigh-Alexandra Basha

Planning for a multinational client is rich in complexity and creativity. While clients everywhere wrestle with similar issues—ensuring that the family business succeeds with the next generation; balancing equities among children with differing needs and capabilities; providing for a spouse who may not be the parent of all the children; giving to charity; and addressing family governance—the multinational client presents additional challenges. Some of these include planning to minimize the double taxation that often arises with the client connected to multiple jurisdictions; circumventing the constraints on inheritance imposed in most civil law jurisdictions; and coordinating an estate plan using multiple wills or trusts without causing them to have conflicting results.

In advising the international client, the advisor always needs to partner with counsel in the other jurisdictions to ensure the plan is appropriate globally. In some instances, one may be able to use the tax arbitrage of different countries to avoid tax altogether. Occasionally, an income tax or estate tax treaty will minimize the double taxation, but not always. Each treaty was negotiated individually, so no

two treaties are alike. Most of the non-English-speaking world is based on civil law. When a client has assets in a civil law jurisdiction, one must be mindful that the use of the common law trust can create a multitude of problems. That means the typical U.S. plan of a pour-over will into a trust with bypass and marital trusts may not work and could tie up the estate for years. Also, the forced heirship rules that exist in most civil law countries may require clients to leave up to 75 percent of their estate to their children (even recalcitrant ones), to the exclusion of the surviving spouse.

Navigating these conflicts-of-law issues also presents planning opportunities. Depending on the countries involved, the use of offshore trusts, life insurance policies, and pre-immigration planning can save the client income tax, as well as estate, gift and inheritance taxes. Knowing where to be taxed and where not to be taxed, how to take advantage of treaty benefits, and, when necessary, determining the best source of funds to pay more than one Uncle Sam, are some of the benefits an advisor experienced in representing the multinational client can bring to the attorney-client relationship. ⓦ

FOREIGN CLIENTS: BEWARE OF TRAPS FOR U.S. BENEFICIARIES

It is crucial for advisors in other countries to take into consideration U.S. tax laws that apply to U.S. beneficiaries. Without proper planning, those beneficiaries may be subject to expensive problems including:

01 The new IRC Section 2801 successions tax, which imposes the highest transfer tax rate on gifts or bequests from a covered U.S. expatriate

02 The onerous throwback rules that are essentially an interest charge on accumulated income within a foreign non-grantor trust

03 The anti-deferral regime of controlled foreign corporations and passive foreign investment companies that may expose the U.S. beneficiary to a penalty

04 Exposure to foreign compliance issues, which could leave a U.S. beneficiary cleaning up a tax mess if an asset was not properly reported to the foreign owner's home country

05 Inadvertent gift tax due to improper structuring

06 The multitude of U.S. tax-filing requirements that may be triggered by a gift or inheritance from a foreign individual

While one does not want to look a gift horse in the mouth, the U.S. beneficiary often must do so.

"Forced heirship rules may require clients to leave up to 75 percent of their estate to their children (even recalcitrant ones), to the exclusion of the surviving spouse."

– Leigh-Alexandra Basha

How to reach Leigh-Alexandra Basha

Please contact me by phone at 703.720.8081 or email leigh.basha@hklaw.com.

I NEVER LEAVE HOME WITHOUT...

My passport, BlackBerry and American Express

WHAT'S ON MY DESK...

Photos of my four beautiful children; Dictaphone; and fortune cookie slip that reads: "Opportunity knocks only once. Be alert."

MY HOBBIES ARE...

Thanks to frequent-flyer miles, traveling to far-off places on the spur of the moment with my husband and children; playing tennis

About Leigh-Alexandra Basha

Leigh-Alexandra Basha is a partner in Holland & Knight's Private Wealth Services Group and chairs its International Private Wealth Services Practice. She focuses on complex domestic and international estate planning and related tax planning and tax controversy work. She chairs the IBA's Individual Tax and Private Client Committee and is the immediate past chair of the ABA's International Tax Planning Committee. She is a fellow of the American College of Trusts and Estates Counsel, an academician of the International Academy of Estate and Trust Lawyers, and the secretary of STEP Mid-Atlantic. Ms. Basha speaks nationally and internationally, including as a visiting professor in France. She has been recognized as a Washington super lawyer and a Virginia super lawyer by *Super Lawyers* magazine, leading 100 counsel in *Citywealth* (London), and as one of Washington's best by *The Washingtonian* magazine.

Association Memberships
American College of Trusts and Estates Counsel, International Academy of Estates and Trusts Lawyers, International Bar Association

Bar Admissions
Virginia, 1985; Maryland, 1986; Washington, D.C., 1986

Legal Experience
25 years

Professional Services Provided
International tax planning (both inbound and outbound); domestic and international estate planning; tax compliance including voluntary disclosure of undisclosed offshore accounts and income, IRS disputes, audits, etc.; estate administration including multinational estates, conflict of law issues, forced heirship, estate and inheritance tax issues, treaty benefits, QDOTs and estate tax reporting; business succession planning

Website
www.hklaw.com

Email
leigh.basha@hklaw.com

Holland & Knight LLP | 1600 Tysons Boulevard, Suite 700, McLean, VA 22102 | 703.720.8081

New York, NY   **Leading Wealth Advisor**

PwC's Private Company Services
Richard Kohan, JD, Personal Financial Services (PFS) Principal

" How will the new federal healthcare act impact my personal income tax planning? "

By Richard Kohan

The healthcare act will, in part, fund its initiatives through tax increases that directly affect high net worth individuals—notably a 0.9 percent hike in the Medicare hospital insurance tax on wages above a certain threshold, and a 3.8 percent tax on certain net investment income. Both tax provisions, which take effect in 2013, have nuances that high net worth individuals will need to note carefully.

INCREASED MEDICARE/HI TAX
The Medicare tax increase of 0.9 percent (which raises the tax rate from 1.45 percent to 2.35 percent) applies to household taxable wages or self-employment income above $250,000 for married couples filing joint returns; $125,000 for married persons filing separate returns; and $200,000 for all other taxpayers.

UNDER-WITHHOLDING
Note that your employer is not required to withhold the additional 0.9 percent if your earnings are not over $200,000. Therefore, if both you and your spouse are employed and your combined wages exceed $250,000, you could end up under-withholding and owe additional tax. Bear in mind also that if you and/or your spouse have self-employment income, the impact of the tax should be assessed on a household basis.

NEW TAX ON NET INVESTMENT INCOME
The net investment income to which the new 3.8 percent tax applies includes income from interest, dividends, annuities, rents, royalties not associated with

a trade or business, net capital gain and working-capital interests. The tax also extends to income from pass-through entities in which the taxpayer does not materially participate.

MINIMIZING YOUR TAX LIABILITY
Because the tax is levied on passive activities but not on active trade or business income, you should analyze your participation in a business with your tax advisor to assess whether you are active or passive with respect to the activity, or to determine what steps you could take to become active in the business. Also, you might consider accelerating some of your investment income into periods predating the tax's effective date, January 1, 2013. For example, if selling a stock and realizing a capital gain makes sense from an investment standpoint, making the sale before January 1, 2013, would ensure that the gain is not subject to the new tax.

Conversely, when you can defer deductions, such as investment management fees and investment interest expense, it would be beneficial to pay those expenses after January 1, 2013, so that they reduce your net investment income. You should consult your personal tax advisor before pursuing any of the options discussed here.

THE BIG PICTURE
The impact of these tax increases will be compounded in 2011 if the Bush tax cuts expire as scheduled, returning the two top ordinary income tax rates to 36 percent and 39.6 percent, with long-term capital gains taxed at 20 percent. Ⓥ

KEEP AN EYE ON YOUR HEALTH SAVINGS ACCOUNT, TOO

The healthcare act imposes new restrictions on the use of health savings accounts (HSAs), flexible spending accounts (FSAs) and Archer medical savings accounts (MSAs). Starting in 2011, the legislation effectively eliminates the deduction for over-the-counter drugs not prescribed by a doctor. That year will also see an increase in the penalty for distributions from HSAs and Archer MSAs that are not used for qualified medical expenses—up from 10 percent to 20 percent for HSAs, and from 15 percent to 20 percent for MSAs. As for the maximum contribution to an FSA, that will be $2,500, starting in 2013. This amount, however, will be indexed annually for inflation.

Effective tax planning rests upon a solid understanding of core tax concepts and wealth management strategies. PricewaterhouseCoopers' *2010 Guide to Tax and Wealth Management* provides a broad overview of these concepts and strategies, as well as helpful tools. Download it for free at pwc.com/pfs.

> **"The tax provisions of the healthcare act have nuances that high net worth individuals will need to note carefully."**
>
> – Richard Kohan

How to reach Richard Kohan

I prefer face-to-face meetings with prospective clients. Please feel free to call me at 646.471.1421.

I NEVER LEAVE HOME WITHOUT...

My BlackBerry, running shoes and Kindle

WHAT'S ON MY DESK...

Pictures of family, computer, clock, phone, calculator and a cup of coffee

MY HOBBIES ARE...

Spending time with my family, reading, running, motorcycle riding, traveling, and supporting the arts

About Richard Kohan

Richard Kohan is a personal financial services (PFS) principal in PwC's Private Company Services practice in New York. He is the national strategic leader of the PFS focus on high net worth individual (HNWI) clients and a trusted advisor to HNWI clients. Mr. Kohan speaks on leading-edge tax, investment, wealth transfer, business succession, charitable giving, family office and other planning topics. He earned a BS in political science from Syracuse University, a JD from Western New England School of Law, and an LLM in tax from Boston University School of Law. Mr. Kohan is a member of the American and Connecticut bar associations.

Minimum Fee for Initial Meeting
None required

Minimum Net Worth Requirement
$5 million

Largest Client Net Worth
$5 billion+

Financial Services Experience
26 years

Email
richard.kohan@us.pwc.com

Compensation Method
Fixed and hourly fees

Professional Services Provided
Personal wealth management advisory services, including: investments; estate, gift, generation skipping planning; charitable giving; family office structuring; and financial planning for high net worth individuals and families

Association Memberships
American and Connecticut bar associations

Website
www.pwc.com/pfs

PwC's Private Company Services | 300 Madison Avenue, New York, NY 10017 | 646.471.1421

" How can I minimize my estate taxes? "

By Morgan Stanley Smith Barney LLC,
Courtesy of Brian Strachan, Managing Director and Senior Investment Management Specialist

You may want to consider some creative lifetime gifts. Charitable trusts can offer you several financial benefits, including the potential deferral of capital gains taxes, as well as possible gift and estate tax savings. They may also serve as effective vehicles for transferring wealth.

A charitable remainder trust is a tax-exempt way to distribute income from the trust to beneficiaries for a period of time, after which remaining assets are distributed to charities of your choice. You determine the time frame of the trust—it can last a lifetime or for a fixed term of up to 20 years—as well as the amount of annual payouts. The annual payout for the length of the trust or the life expectancies of the beneficiaries (which would be you or your spouse) cannot exceed 50 percent or be less than 5 percent of the value of the trust. A private foundation or donor-advised fund may be named as the charitable remainder beneficiary.

Highly appreciated assets owned by the trust can also be sold without an immediate capital gain, which may allow for an increase in current income as well as an income tax deduction. However, the type of assets gifted and the type of charity receiving the gifts, as well as your adjusted gross income, are all taken into consideration when determining your charitable income tax deduction. What is more, there may be income tax due on your annual payouts from the trust.

Charitable lead trusts (CLTs) are funded with assets that are expected to appreciate. The charity of your choice receives a fixed annual payout from the trust, and the remainder goes to your family members at the end of the charity's payout term.

Charitable lead trusts are not tax exempt. The value of the donor's initial gift to the trust is determined by three factors: a government-set interest rate, the length of the trust, and the payout to charity. When the government-set interest rate is low, the value of the donor's gift is reduced for gift tax purposes. So CLTs are particularly attractive in periods of low interest rates.

A grantor retained annuity trust may allow you to transfer assets to remainder beneficiaries of the trust, usually your children, at a reduced transfer tax cost. By transferring assets to the trust, you would receive in return an annuity, reducing or zeroing the gift amount. If the asset appreciation exceeds the rate upon which the annuity is based, the assets remaining in the trust after the final annuity payment may be transferred to your children at a reduced tax cost.

A limited liability company (LLC) or a family limited partnership (FLP) may help reduce the size of your estate for transfer-tax purposes. The LLC or FLP is made up of managing or voting interests and nonvoting interests, and you could gift the nonvoting interests to your children and grandchildren[1]. Because the nonvoting interests gifted to your children and grandchildren lack voting rights and are not readily marketable, they might be discounted for gift tax valuation purposes[2]. **Ⓦ**

[1] You should consult with your legal or tax advisor about LLC or FLP planning and the potential tax consequences. The IRS may challenge this planning and take the position that gifted LLC or FLP interests and/or underlying LLC/FLP assets are includable in the donor's estate.

[2] You should consult with a qualified appraiser to determine the appropriate amount of the valuation discounts. Tax laws are complex and subject to change. Morgan Stanley Smith Barney LLC, its affiliates and Morgan Stanley Smith Barney financial advisors do not provide tax or legal advice. This material was not intended or written to be used for the purpose of avoiding tax penalties that may be imposed on the taxpayer. Individuals are urged to consult their personal tax or legal advisors to understand the tax and legal consequences of any actions, including implementation of any estate planning strategies or investments described herein.

[3] Total team assets include assets not held at Morgan Stanley Smith Barney.

[4] Source: Barron's "Top 100 Financial Advisors," February 2009 and April 2008, as identified by magazine, using quantitative and qualitative criteria and selected from a pool of more than 800 nominations. Advisors in the "Top 100 Financial Advisors" have a minimum of seven years of financial services experience and $600 million in assets under management. Qualitative factors include, but are not limited to, compliance record, interviews with senior management and philanthropic work. Investment performance is not a criterion. The rating may not be representative of any one client's experience and is not indicative of the advisor's future performance. Neither Morgan Stanley Smith Barney nor its financial advisors pay a fee to Barron's in exchange for the rating. Barron's is a registered trademark of Dow Jones & Company L.P. All rights reserved.

[5] Advisor is ranked on individual assets or percentage of contribution team. Some individuals on list are not part of teams and assets reflect only their state ranking. Algorithm includes revenues produced, but is not published. The Winner's Circle is an organization independent of the firms' involvement and does not receive compensation from the more than 100 participating firms or affiliates, financial advisors or the media in exchange for ranking purposes. Each advisor on this year's Research Winner's Circle teams lists was filtered down from a national list of securities firms, banks, independent firms and more. The Winner's Circle team vetted each series 7 registered advisor through a host of quantitative and qualitative criteria, including assets managed, revenues, experience levels, acceptable compliance records and u4 forms, discussions with management and more.

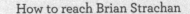

"Charitable trusts can offer you several financial benefits, including the potential deferral of capital gains taxes, as well as possible gift and estate tax savings."

– Brian Strachan

How to reach Brian Strachan

I am happy to speak directly with prospective clients. The best way to contact me is by phone at 617.570.9240 or email at brian.s.strachan@morganstanleypwm.com.

I NEVER LEAVE HOME WITHOUT...

My briefcase and calendar

WHAT'S ON MY DESK...

Calendar, computer and to-do list

MY HOBBIES ARE...

Watching my children play sports, boating and exercising

About Brian Strachan

Brian Strachan is a managing director of wealth management and a senior investment management specialist with Morgan Stanley Smith Barney, where he also serves on the Director's Council and is responsible for overseeing approximately $1.25 billion in assets as of November 30, 2009.[3] By utilizing the resources of Morgan Stanley Smith Barney, Mr. Strachan and his team advise clients on all aspects of wealth planning, including asset allocation, estate and trust planning, risk management, cash management and philanthropic services. He has been featured in numerous publications including *Worth*, *Research* magazine and *Barron's*. He was recognized by R.J. Shook's Winner's Circle Top 100 Financial Advisors in both the April 2008 and February 2009 issues of *Barron's*.[4] The Strachan Group at Morgan Stanley Smith Barney was recognized for its commitment to service by *Research* magazine as one of the top 25 advisor teams in the country in 2007.[5] Mr. Strachan is an active member of the Boston Estate Planning Council and serves on the board of The Carroll School in Lincoln, Mass. He received a BS from the Whittemore School of Business at the University of New Hampshire. Mr. Strachan, his wife, Aleece, and their four children reside in Wellesley, Mass.

Assets Under Management **$700 million (as of 11/30/09)**	Compensation Method **Asset-based, fixed and hourly fees, commissions (investment and insurance products)**
Minimum Fee for Initial Meeting **None required**	Primary Custodian for Investor Assets **Morgan Stanley Smith Barney**
Minimum Net Worth Requirement **$2 million**	Professional Services Provided **Planning, investment advisory and money management services**
Largest Client Net Worth **$500 million+**	Association Memberships **IMCA**
Financial Services Experience **22 years**	Website **fa.smithbarney.com/thestrachangroupsb/story.htm**
	Email **brian.s.strachan@morganstanleypwm.com**

Morgan Stanley Smith Barney | 28 State Street, Boston, MA 02109 | 617.570.9240

San Francisco Peninsula—
Silicon Valley, CA

**Leading
Wealth Advisor**

Navigation Group Inc.
Carlo A. Panaccione, CFP®
Cofounder and Registered Principal

" What are the pitfalls to avoid when I receive a windfall? "

By Carlo A. Panaccione

Without question, those ads for state lotteries are enticing. One of my favorites is, "All you need is a dollar and a dream." Unfortunately, without proper management, a dream windfall—whether it comes from a winning lottery ticket, your company stock or a family member—can become a nightmare.

Because most windfalls result not from lotteries but from the passing of a close relative or a single stock issuance, emotion can play a big part in how you react to your sudden good fortune. Reactions range from individuals who spend their newfound wealth on literally anything their heart desires to those who change nothing—not the structure of their lives nor the structure of whatever delivered the windfall in the first place.

The best course of action, in my view, is a middle ground between these extremes. First, after learning of your windfall, stop and take a deep breath. Then look at your situation objectively. Begin by evaluating the actual value to you. You need to determine if your lifestyle can survive the windfall.

For example, you suddenly own a spectacular oceanfront home...with a lot of maintenance and support issues. Your net worth just went way up, but the property may cause a serious drain on your existing assets. Or perhaps you have inherited a thriving business... in an industry you know nothing about.

Or, let us say you were an early hire at a start-up company and your stock grants went from $60,000 to $60 million. While you now have substantial wealth, holding on to a highly concentrated and highly appreciated stock position leaves your wealth extremely vulnerable to company-specific risk factors, and change may cause unintended tax consequences.

Clearly, understanding the complexity of your situation is essential to formulating a plan that ensures it impacts your life positively. Before you sell that house or that business or cash out that $60 million block of stock, take another breath, and with a professional as a sounding board, consider your options (see sidebar).

Of course, not all windfalls benefit a single individual, and in fact, most do not. So while you evaluate the financial boon itself, be aware of other beneficiaries, in particular, those who may have the proverbial ax to grind. Be inclusive and transparent in your planning to lessen any potential protests or problems.

Once you have a clear sense of the potential pitfalls and opportunities, take yet another breath and reexamine your own financial goals. Based on my experience, the core essentials needed for life to be good do not change after a windfall. But if you plan well, you can make your life even better. Ⓦ

AFTER THE WINDFALL

Sudden ownership of a thriving business or a successful IPO stock can be a dream come true, but it can also complicate your life overnight.

While your gut may tell you to immediately sell your new business, take the time to consult a firm specializing in business strategies. You may determine the business is your life's passion, or you may find its greatest value is in a well-structured sale.

If IPO stock is your windfall, consider a protection strategy, such as a prepaid forward contract, that may greatly limit your risk and allow you to diversify without causing immediate tax consequences. Other strategies to consider are generation skipping trusts, irrevocable life insurance trusts or, for charitable intentions, donor-advised funds.

Finally, remember this: If a windfall does not produce income or capital gains, it is a toy—one that could become very costly to own.

Carlo A. Panaccione of Navigation Group is a registered principal with securities offered through LPL Financial, member FINRA/SIPC. California insurance license 0714349. Financial Planning offered through Navigation Group.

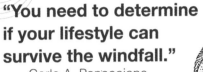

"You need to determine if your lifestyle can survive the windfall."
– Carlo A. Panaccione

How to reach Carlo A. Panaccione
I encourage you to call my office and set up a phone consultation. We can discover a lot about each other in an initial phone call and determine what our next step should be. You can reach me at 650.595.1700.

WHAT'S ON MY DESK...
Pictures of my family, a 103-year-old coin bank given to me by one of my first clients and Swanson's Unwritten Rules of Management

I NEVER LEAVE HOME WITHOUT...
Telling my family I love them, checking the charge on my iPhone and cleaning up after the dogs

MY HOBBIES ARE...
Entertaining family and friends, cooking, skiing, wine and every sport my children play

About Carlo A. Panaccione

Since 1986, Mr. Panaccione has provided the financial advice, education and services that have qualified him for inclusion on top advisors lists such as *Barron's, Worth* and *Medical Economics*. He has also been called upon for his insight and expertise by CNBC, ABC News, Fox Business, the *Wall Street Journal*, Forbes.com, Reuters, the Associated Press and Bankrate.com, among others. Mr. Panaccione cofounded Navigation Group in 1998 in response to client requests for independent and unbiased professional wealth planning and management services tailored to specific individual needs. He believes that treating clients like family means more than enjoying their company and caring about their interests. It also means assuring that clients receive professional advice, a sincere advocate and a level of service so high that Navigation Group is considered family.

Assets Under Management Confidential	**Compensation Method** Asset-based, fixed and hourly fees, commissions (insurance products)
Minimum Fee for Initial Meeting None required	**Primary Custodian for Investor Assets** LPL Financial
Minimum Net Worth Requirement $2.5 million	**Professional Services Provided** Planning, investment advisory and money management services
Largest Client Net Worth $50 million	**Association Memberships** Financial Planning Association
Financial Services Experience 23 years	**Website** www.navigationgroup.com **Email** carlo@navigationgroup.com

Navigation Group Inc. | Three Lagoon Drive, Suite 110, Redwood Shores, CA 94065 | 650.595.1700

WEALTH TRANSFERENCE & SUCCESSION PLANNING

NAVIGATION GROUP INC.

San Francisco, CA   **Leading Wealth Advisor**

The Private Bank, Union Bank, N.A.
Dexter F. Lowry, CFP®, CTFA, Vice President, Regional Manager
Personal Trust, Wealth Management Group

" What steps should I take in choosing a trustee? "

By Dexter F. Lowry

One of the most important decisions a family can make is who to nominate as their trustee or successor trustee. Too often the selection is almost automatic and done for emotional reasons—my spouse, my eldest child, my children as co-trustees. A hasty nomination can lead to unintended consequences with potential for strife between the trustee and the beneficiaries. Families and their advisors should discuss this important role and thoroughly review the duties and liabilities of a trustee, the potential assets the trustee will be responsible for managing, and the family dynamics that may come into play during the administration of the trust.

An individual trustee is adequate in many situations, and the trustor should always inform the individual of the consideration. That will allow both parties an opportunity to discuss the role and expectations. Family members serving in this capacity often waive or charge only a nominal fee, which will result in a cost savings for trusts of a more modest size. Family members may also be more familiar with a family-owned business that becomes a trust asset, as well as with the intentions of the trustor toward its continuance. Furthermore, the beneficiaries may feel more comfortable dealing with a family member.

The use of a corporate trustee should also be considered during the drafting stage of a trust agreement. Corporate trustees can provide objective advice to help the grantor create the intended legacy. A discussion with a corporate trustee also provides the family and their advisors an opportunity to identify any issues and to review trust objectives with an independent party. Corporate trustees can provide the objectivity and experience in the very areas that can lead to trouble with a less-experienced individual trustee. A well-staffed corporate trust department has specialized sections and/or employees who are experienced in areas such as managing investment securities, real estate, closely held businesses, family partnerships and limited liability companies, and mineral, oil and gas interests.

When a family is considering the nomination of a corporate trustee, we suggest that the appropriate family members arrange to meet with more than one trust department. This will allow the family to get a sense of how a corporate trustee actually operates and manages its decision-making process. Issues that are important to the family can be addressed, which will give both parties a better sense of the long-term viability of the trust being considered. ⓦ

TRUST SITUS

Families that are tax sensitive should not overlook the possibility of establishing the administration of an irrevocable trust in a state with no tax on accumulated income or capital gains. Avoiding state income tax may not be possible in their home state, and families should not assume they are limited to using that state's tax and trust law.

Before selecting a trustee, a review of the appropriate state tax laws regarding fiduciary income should be undertaken by the family's tax and legal advisors to determine if a tax situs in another state should be considered. A number of trust companies maintain offices in states without an income tax for the very purpose of providing that advantage to their clients.

"A hasty nomination can lead to unintended consequences with potential for strife between the trustee and the beneficiaries."

– Dexter F. Lowry

How to reach Dexter F. Lowry

Please give me a call at 415.705.7173 for a preliminary consultation.

THE LAST BOOK I READ...

*Physics for Future Presidents
by Richard A. Muller*

WHAT'S ON MY DESK...

A Bose radio tuned to classical music

MY HOBBIES ARE...

Foreign travel, horseback riding, hiking and cross country skiing

About Dexter F. Lowry

Dexter F. Lowry is a vice president and a trust office manager of the Northern California Division of The Private Bank. He has more than 35 years of trust account experience. He joined Union Bank of California in 1988 as a vice president in the Trust and Investment Management Group. He had prior experience with Citicorp Trust and First Interstate Bank. A native of Tallahassee, Fla., Mr. Lowry is a graduate of Valley Forge Military Academy and the University of Colorado. He is a Certified Financial Planner and a Certified Trust and Financial Advisor. Mr. Lowry is a past president of the San Francisco Estate Planning Council. He resides in San Francisco with his wife, Kathie.

Minimum Fee for Initial Meeting **None required**	Primary Custodian for Investor Assets **Union Bank, N.A.**
Minimum Net Worth Requirement **$10 million (planning services)** **$1 million (investment services)**	Professional Services Provided **Trust and estate planning, investment advisory and money management services**
Largest Client Net Worth **Confidential**	Website **www.unionbank.com**
Financial Services Experience **39 years**	Email **dexter.lowry@unionbank.com**

The Private Bank, Union Bank, N.A.   350 California Street, 18th Floor, San Francisco, CA 94104   415.705.7173

Phoenix—Scottsdale, AZ | **Leading Wealth Advisor**

GenSpring
Mark Feldman, CPA, CFP®, PFS
Senior Partner, Phoenix Local Family Office

" Why is it so difficult to sustain wealth through the generations? "

By Mark Feldman

Research suggests the odds of sustaining wealth across generations are as low as 30 percent. This is expressed in the common saying, "From shirtsleeves to shirtsleeves in three generations." Since our founding in 1989, we at GenSpring have worked to sustain family wealth, and a primary focus is helping families break the shirtsleeves-to-shirtsleeves cycle.

Why do so many families fail at sustaining wealth? The reasons vary. Surprisingly, research shows that less than 3 percent of these failures stem from poor estate planning and poor investment returns. Obviously, other factors—nonfinancial factors—play an important role. While understanding these failures might provide some useful insights, allow me to turn the question around: What do successful families do? Through collaboration with experts, internal research and our work with more than 700 of the country's wealthiest families, we have identified 25 nonfinancial best practices that enhance the ability to sustain wealth.

These best practices are summarized in a white paper we published. (If you would like a copy, send an email, and we will send it to you by return email with no cost or obligation.) The 25 best practices can be divided into six categories: family cohesiveness, governance, strategic planning, philanthropy, mentoring and trusts and estates. Allow me to highlight some of these categories and best practices.

FAMILY COHESIVENESS

Family cohesiveness refers to a family's common bonds and desire to work and play together. Families should continually build and strengthen bonds so that their money and legal structures are not the only things keeping them close. A best practice that promotes family cohesiveness is a family mission statement. Families that create a values-based mission statement and then judiciously employ it realize benefits both in their interactions and in the process of making family decisions.

GOVERNANCE

Family governance, or the practice of making informed decisions as a family, becomes increasingly important as time passes because the complexity of decisions grow. The development of a family governance system begins when family leaders start involving younger members in family meetings. For first-generation families, these meetings often start with planning the next vacation. As a family grows in size and complexity, so should the meetings.

MENTORING

Mentoring heirs is an important component of preparing them to be responsible stewards of the family's wealth. Financial education is the mentoring best practice that instills family members with the competence to make good financial decisions.

By adopting these 25 best practices, you will enhance your ability to sustain wealth through the generations. ⓦ

THE 25 BEST PRACTICES OF MULTIGENERATIONAL FAMILIES

Family Cohesiveness
Family history and culture; family mission statement; shared values; teamwork and communication; family member well-being

Strategic Planning
Understanding of economics; wealth objectives; planning for major life events

Mentoring
Financial education; parenting skills; support for entrepreneurship; family support network; money smarts

Governance
Family governance; family meetings; family policies; conflict resolution; succession planning

Philanthropy
Support for philanthropy; shared philanthropy; strategic philanthropy

Trusts and Estates
Communicating intentions; grantor and beneficiary mentoring; selection of trustees and advisors; trustee and beneficiary relationships

> "**Surprisingly, research shows that less than 3 percent of these failures stem from poor estate planning and poor investment returns.**"
>
> – Mark Feldman

How to reach Mark Feldman

I prefer face-to-face meetings with prospective clients. Please feel free to call me at 602.385.7567.

WHAT'S ON MY DESK...

"The Pig of Happiness"...the story of a little pig that decided to become so happy (and succeeded) that everyone coming in contact with him became happy, too!

I NEVER LEAVE HOME WITHOUT...

Thanking my lucky stars that I have a home that is comfortable and safe for my family and me

MY HOBBIES ARE...

Spending time with my children, community service, golf and travel

About Mark Feldman

As a senior partner at GenSpring's Phoenix Local Family Office, Mark Feldman provides wealth management and family office services for ultra high net worth individuals and families in the United States and internationally. He oversees client relationships of all types, including single- and multi-generational family groups, corporate executives and institutions. Mr. Feldman holds CPA, CFP and PFS designations. He is active in the community and serves on the boards of directors of the Arizona Science Center and Free Arts of Arizona, and he is a member of Greater Phoenix Leadership.

Assets Under Management **$1.99 billion**	Compensation Method **Asset-based, fixed and hourly fees**
Minimum Annual Fee **$35,000**	Primary Custodian for Investor Assets **Charles Schwab**
Minimum Net Worth Requirement **$10 million**	Professional Services Provided **Planning and investment advisory services**
Largest Client Net Worth **Confidential**	Association Memberships **Arizona Society of CPAs**
Financial Services Experience **26 years**	Website **www.genspring.com** · Email **mark.feldman@genspring.com**

GenSpring | 2355 East Camelback Road, Suite 750, Phoenix, AZ 85016 | 602.385.7567

New York, NY | **Leading Wealth Advisor**

Beacon Wealth Management
Mark S. Germain, MBA, CFP®, Founder and CEO

" Is it wise for wealthy families to create their own business to pave way for significant savings when transferring assets? "

By Mark S. Germain

True story. When I advised a client, who is a doctor, that the gentleman's farm he owned was actually a tree farm and hence a significant tax planning and estate planning business, his jaw dropped. When we started to create an actual business plan and added up the numbers, he could not put the papers down. Business ideas are limited only by the imagination of the thinker. An open mind can lead to many cost-saving opportunities. Here are two such illustrations.

THE FARM
In the case of the doctor, he had a farm that was being planted and harvested by a nearby farmer. In addition, he had some very tall trees and additional land not utilized. Our recommendation was to create a business plan. It was a classic win-win that provided our client with significant income tax savings, discounted gifting of the farm, and, subsequently, a bond portfolio to justify the cash flow for maintaining the farm.

THE CAPTAIN
Another client was retired and enjoying his new adventures as a captain on a chartered tall sailing ship. In concert with his tax professional, we created his own charter business through which he takes passengers for fun-filled,

worry-free excursions in the Caribbean aboard his schooner. Today he spends most of his time on the water; his travel is free, his vacation is free, and he does what he loves.

A final incentive for starting a business is that the transfer of business assets during your lifetime may be subject to a discount in value. Consider the following: If I transfer $1 million of interest in the stock of my business to my son in the form of restricted nonvoting stock, I may need to use only $700,000 of my gift exclusion, effectively saving tax on $300,000 of value. Moreover, if I make it a joint gift, I may be able to double the savings. The estate tax law also offers considerable tax-saving opportunities that include discount and tax deferral if the asset is swapped.

Creating a business is a useful planning strategy for asset transfer, current tax savings, and creating wealth. The financial umbilical cord that exists between business and life can help build and sustain wealth and preserve the accustomed and preferred way of living. Structuring asset pools, real estate, trusts, succession and estate planning strategies offers significant savings and benefits. The value derived in creating a family business is considerable; it is a valuable strategy for many of our clients. ⓦ

A CONVERSATION WORTH HAVING

On January 1, 2011, the largest tax hikes in history may hit. The top income tax rate may rise from 35 to 39.6 percent. The death tax will return with a 55 percent top rate on estates worth more than $1 million. The capital gains tax will rise from 15 to 20 percent. The dividends tax may rise from 15 to 39.6 percent.

Imagine protecting more of your hard-earned wealth by simply talking to your professional advisor and creating a plan that requires you to do nothing more than live your life as you did before. Many families are sitting on a potential cash-flow generator without knowing it. All you need is an open mind and to put your plan into action now rather than later. Then you can begin reaping the benefits of considerable tax savings.

"The value derived in creating a family business is considerable; it is a valuable strategy for many of our clients."

– Mark S. Germain

How to reach Mark S. Germain

Call my office to set up a phone consultation. In an initial call, we can make sure our values align and that you're open to the high level of customer service we deliver. Then we can determine next steps. You can reach me at 201.447.9500.

MY MOST INFLUENTIAL PROFESSOR/TEACHER...

My eighth-grade art teacher, Ms. Hillerhouse. She saved me from quitting.

WHAT MAKES A GOOD WEALTH ADVISOR...

A blunt, honest and client-focused listener

WHAT MAKES A GOOD CLIENT...

A blunt, honest and inquisitive mind

About Mark S. Germain

Mark S. Germain is the founder of Beacon Wealth Management. A relentless tactician, Mr. Germain has managed his clients' financial lives with passion and precision for more than 25 years. In addition to his work building wealth management strategies for professionals, Mr. Germain educates professionals on all facets of asset protection, investment growth, tax reduction and financial planning. After completing his BS in economics and accounting, Mr. Germain earned his MBA in finance and taught accounting at Northeastern University. He is currently an adjunct professor at Fairleigh Dickinson University where he teaches CFP candidates the financial planning process.

Assets Under Management **$200 million**	Compensation Method **Asset-based, fixed and hourly fees**
Minimum Fee for Initial Meeting **None required**	Primary Custodian for Investor Assets **TD Ameritrade**
Minimum Net Worth Requirement **$1 million**	Professional Services Provided **Planning, investment advisory and money management services**
Largest Client Net Worth **$50 million**	Association Memberships **FPA, IMCA, CFP®**
Financial Services Experience **26 years**	Website **www.beaconwealthmanagement.com** Email **mark@bwmllc.com**

Beacon Wealth Management   65 Harristown Road, Glen Rock, NJ 07452   201.447.9500

Chicago, IL – Milwaukee, WI   **Leading Wealth Advisor**

Cedar Street Advisors
Mitch Prosk, MBA, JD
Vice President and Senior Client Advisor

" What are the main hurdles for the successful transition of a privately held family business? "

By Mitch Prosk

The ultimate goal of a succession plan for a privately held family business is to preserve and nurture harmony among family members. Well-drafted plans often address several critical issues, including: ownership and management succession; compensation of active and nonactive family members; employment policies; estate planning; and other areas. While these issues are important, one critical factor, if not addressed, could impede the successful transfer of the business, thus making planning for all other issues moot. The factor: estate taxes.

Planning for the successful transition of a family business starts with the owner making every effort to reduce the estate tax burden. This is especially important in today's environment in which the government's need for revenue is generating increased speculation that Congress will focus on reducing wealth transfer opportunities. If Congress acts, it could threaten the viability of privately held businesses passing to the next generation.

Complex estate planning techniques that allow the transfer of income to the next generation can ease the estate tax burden when the owner passes away. These allow the next generation to pay taxes at the highest marginal tax rate, rather than the historically higher estate tax rate, so less is paid in taxes to the government, resulting in more wealth transferring to family members. Additionally, transferred income provides the next generation more flexibility when determining how to pay estate taxes—either with cash or through selling the business. This is significantly better than having no choice other than to sell the family business to pay the estate tax burden.

Planning for the successful transition of a family business is an ongoing process that must take into account not only family dynamics, but also ever-changing tax and estate planning laws. A skilled team of professional advisors can help owners navigate even the most complex business planning needs. Ⓦ

THE FAMILY BOARD APPROACH

Establishing a board that consists of the business owner's professional advisors, which may include a financial advisor, an attorney, an accountant and a company director, can help increase the probability of a successful transfer to the next generation.

In the case of succession planning, the role of the family board is to provide expertise, insight and good judgment by establishing a transition plan, conveying how the patriarch/matriarch would run the business, assisting with execution of the plan, and providing continuity between the generations.

While each member of the board is a specialist in a particular field, a coordinated effort among these professionals is essential in order to avoid conflicting advice that does not represent the owner's overall interests.

"**Planning for the successful transition of a family business starts with the owner making every effort to reduce the estate tax burden.**"

– Mitch Prosk

How to reach Mitch Prosk

I prefer face-to-face meetings with prospective clients. Please feel free to call me at 414.287.8853.

I NEVER LEAVE HOME WITHOUT...

My BlackBerry and saying good-bye to my family

WHAT'S ON MY DESK...

My computer, an assortment of investment articles, and pictures of my family

MY HOBBIES ARE...

Jogging, basketball, and any activity with my son

About Mitch Prosk

Mitch Prosk is a vice president and a senior client advisor with Cedar Street Advisors, a specialized wealth advisory firm serving owners of privately held businesses and senior level corporate executives of public companies, as well as affluent families residing across the country. Prior to joining the firm, Mr. Prosk served as account manager for an affiliate of Goldman Sachs. He earned a BS in construction engineering from Bradley University, a JD from DePaul College of Law, and an MBA with a concentration in finance from DePaul Kellstadt School of Business. Mr. Prosk resides in Shorewood, Wis., with his wife and 3-year-old son.

Assets Under Management Confidential	**Compensation Method** Fixed fees (planning services) and asset-based fees (investment services)
Minimum Annual Fee None required	**Primary Custodian for Investor Assets** Marshall & Ilsley Trust Company N.A.
Minimum Net Worth Requirement $25 million	**Professional Services Provided** Planning, investment advisory, money management, and tax preparation services
Largest Client Net Worth Confidential	**Association Memberships** State Bar of Illinois, Family Office Exchange
Financial Services Experience 11 years	**Website** www.cedarstreetadvisors.com **Email** mitch.prosk@cedarstreetadvisors.com

Cedar Street Advisors | 111 East Kilbourn Avenue, Suite 200, Milwaukee, WI 53202 | 414.287.8853

San Francisco—Bay Area, CA   **Leading Wealth Advisor**

Mosaic Financial Partners Inc.
Norman Boone, CFP®, Founder and President

" How do I successfully prepare my children to succeed me in our family business? "

By Norman Boone

The short answer would be: Start early. While many families do a good job of creating a succession plan, too few formally prepare their children, from a young age, to inherit the business. Also, most plans assume a long life for the founder. Tragically, this is sometimes not the case.

In our view, it is never too early to begin teaching children the skills they will need within the family business. As family-member employees, expectations of them will differ greatly from what will be expected of others; as a result there will be additional capabilities they must learn and master.

We are not saying this is easy. We know from advising innumerable families of all configurations just how difficult and emotional preparing children for launch can be. But we also know if a successor takes an elevator ride straight to the top, you will have an entitled and poorly trained individual managing your legacy, which ultimately will become a drain on the business and on the family.

While we become deeply involved with our clients and their children, as a third-party facilitator, we bring a discipline and neutrality to the process that parents understandably cannot. Because emotions can overwhelm objectivity, having a forum to openly discuss the difficult issues that occur when mixing family and business is critical to family harmony. So we help families create their own Family Council, which provides an opportunity for families and family members who may or may not be in the business to:

· Address difficult family issues, not business issues
· Learn the basics about the business because the family's well-being rests on its success
· Become familiar with their parents' estate plans
· Be aware of business succession plans, including policies for employment, compensation, qualifications for ownership and successor development, and how they affect each family member

· Enhance family harmony through greater understanding of one another
· Have a forum to make family decisions, and make all opinions welcome

Successful Family Councils carry both a privilege and responsibility. Each family should develop its own guidelines, codes of conduct and responsibilities and expectations that guide this forum.

For each family member desiring a career in the family business, drawing up a unique comprehensive development and training plan is essential. This plan should include everything from education requirements for various company positions, to extracurricular activities, to on-the-job training.

If you have a business with children in it, you inevitably have challenges, but you also have wonderful opportunities to strengthen your family and build your enterprise. Clarifying and communicating roles and expectations, preferably with the assistance of an effective facilitator, is key to a successful succession. ⓦ

"You cannot achieve success-ful succession without first securing family harmony, busi-ness success and your per-sonal financial security."

– Norman Boone

How to reach Norman Boone

Call me at 415.788.1952 or email me at norm@ mosaicfp.com. We like to meet with prospective clients, without charge, so they have a chance to evaluate us and so we can be sure we can add value for them. We have offices in San Francisco and Lafayette.

MY HOBBIES ARE...

Traveling, movies, current events and sports

WHAT'S ON MY DESK...

Pictures of family, travel mementos, my personal and business goals, a "To Do" list for the day, a crystal ball

I NEVER LEAVE HOME WITHOUT...

My BlackBerry

YOUR MANAGERS: ESSENTIAL TO THE SUCCESSION PLAN

Your top-level managers are in a pivotal position to mentor successors and foster a successful transition. We suggest you negotiate an agreement with them that outlines: **1.** How they would run the business should you pass on before your children are ready to take over; **2.** How they will mentor your children and incorporate them into the business.

Of course, you must abide by the plan for it to work. For example, just three weeks after he started at the family company, a son of a client went on a one-week ski vacation. When his manager objected, he explained that "My dad planned the trip and insisted I go." We met with the father and helped him see how he had undermined the authority of his son's supervisor. He committed to avoid doing so in the future because he wanted his son to be as successful and respected a leader as he has been.

About Norman Boone

Norman Boone is the founder and president of Mosaic Financial Partners Inc., a fee-only, independent wealth management firm located in San Francisco and in nearby Lafayette, Calif. Since 1994, *Worth*, *Barron's* and *Medical Economics* magazines have consistently cited Mr. Boone as one of the best financial advisors in America. He has served on the national board of the Financial Planning Association and is the co-author of the acclaimed *Creating an Investment Policy Statement: Guidelines and Templates*. He is a regular contributor to industry journals and is often quoted in the press.

Assets Under Management **$350 million**	Compensation Method **Asset-based, fixed and hourly fees**
Minimum Fee for Initial Meeting **None required**	Primary Custodian for Investor Assets **Charles Schwab**
Minimum Net Worth Requirement **$1.5 million**	Professional Services Provided **Personal planning, financial coaching, money management services and family business consulting**
Largest Client Net Worth **$30 million**	Association Memberships **FPA, Planned Giving Council (Northern California), Estate Planning Council (San Francisco, East Bay)**
Financial Services Experience **31 years**	Website **www.mosaicfp.com** | Email **norm@mosaicfp.com**

Mosaic Financial Partners Inc. \| 140 Geary Street, 6th Floor, San Francisco, CA 94108 \| 415.788.1952

Mesirow Financial, The Mesirow/Korengold Team
Richard S. Mesirow, Senior Managing Director, Investment Advisory
Steven N. Mesirow, CFP®, CFS®, Managing Director, Investment Advisory
Richard H. Korengold, Managing Director, Investment Advisory

"How can we balance the desire to leave most of our estate to charity and also benefit our children and grandchildren?"

By The Mesirow/Korengold Team

Recently, a long-standing client of ours passed away, leaving a significant estate to her family.

The primary beneficiaries' personal needs were already being met, but they were challenged with the choice of retaining the additional assets or allocating them to family and/or charitable institutions.

Below is an outline of the steps we took to help the family achieve their financial and charitable goals.

SETTLE ESTATE MATTERS
First, we worked closely with the estate attorneys and accountants to understand the trust structure, amount and timing of the bequests, and tax payments. We made suggestions regarding disposition of certain assets for liquidity and other needs.

REVISIT FAMILY NEEDS
We then initiated meetings to understand what was now most important to our clients. We helped confirm that their financial needs were being met, and asked to what extent they wished to further benefit their own children and grandchildren. We confirmed the importance of charitable contributions and posed questions of how to handle donation amounts, timing and potential recipients.

FORMULATE A PLAN
Working together with the clients, we quantified their grandchildren's college education needs while also providing the grandchildren with a modest nest egg. Next we focused on providing some assets for the clients' children, which left them with a significant portion to give to charity. It was decided to gift the charitable portion over the clients' lifetimes, so they could see the benefits of their giving and make changes and offer direction when necessary.

EXECUTE THE PLAN
The clients chose to utilize an existing community foundation versus establishing their own charitable foundation. Our plan proposed gifting in three stages: one-third immediately after the IRS had cleared the estate tax return; one-third over the next five years; and one-third to be given at an undetermined time in the future or upon the passing of the clients. This allowed for flexibility should the circumstances of the clients or the foundation change.

CLIENT BENEFIT
We took the lead role in this two-year process, and we were able to help our clients achieve a balance between their family needs and their charitable desires. A trusted family wealth advisor is a necessity for those who wish to have their financial planning needs accurately understood and their investment management goals properly met. Our clients have peace of mind for now, and will leave a wonderful family legacy for the future. ⓦ

UNDERSTANDING YOUR NEEDS IS THE KEY TO SUCCESS

We believe that all families are complex and the issues that face them are unique.

Because we worked with this family for 50 years, we were able to draw upon our prior knowledge to address this situation, and help them develop a plan that could meet their multigenerational needs. We understood their values, beliefs and goals as they related to their situation. We used this information to develop a written plan and lay out a road map that helped the clients have comfort and confidence in their decisions. By design, the plan is flexible to accommodate changes in family circumstances, market conditions or unforeseen events.

It is important to develop a close relationship with your wealth management team. Performance is not about beating a market average; it is about meeting your needs, preserving principal, growing principal and finding innovative solutions to meet your family goals.

"A trusted family wealth advisor is a necessity for those who wish to have their financial planning needs accurately understood and their investment management goals properly met."

– Richard S. Mesirow

How to reach The Mesirow/Korengold Team

The Mesirow/Korengold Team can be reached at 847.681.2341.

Left to right: Steven N. Mesirow, Richard S. Mesirow, Richard H. Korengold

About The Mesirow/Korengold Team

The Mesirow/Korengold Team is a wealth management group at Mesirow Financial. Founded in 1937, the firm is an independent, employee-owned private company with more than $40 billion in assets under management. As trusted family wealth advisors, The Mesirow/Korengold Team has more than 90 years of collective experience in the industry. The team members leverage their distinct talents and are able to utilize the resources of their uniquely diversified firm to provide their clients with comprehensive wealth management services. The foundation of the team's practice is based upon personal relationships. The team is proud that many of their client associations span decades, serving the needs of multiple generations within the same family. They look forward to working with clients who value close personal relationships based on the highest levels of service and integrity.

Assets Under Management $325 million (Mesirow/Korengold Team)	**Compensation Method** Asset-based and fixed fees
Minimum Fee for Initial Meeting None required	**Primary Custodian for Investor Assets** Mesirow Financial, Inc. (plus multiple secondary)
Minimum Net Worth Requirement $2 million	**Professional Services Provided** Planning and investment advisory services
Largest Client Net Worth Confidential	**Website** www.mesirowfinancial.com
Financial Services Experience 90 years (combined)	**Email** rkorengold@mesirowfinancial.com

Mesirow Financial, The Mesirow/Korengold Team | 610 Central Avenue, Suite 200, Highland Park, IL 60035 | 847.681.2341

" How can I avoid the shirtsleeves-to-shirtsleeves scenario for my heirs? "

By Timothy E. Flatley

Our country is on the verge of an unprecedented transfer of trillions of dollars in family wealth. What family would not want to create a better world for their children and grandchildren?

Unfortunately, many families share a similar wealth life cycle. The first generation, in shirtsleeves, creates wealth. The second generation enjoys it, while members of the third generation find themselves back in shirtsleeves. It can be more challenging to preserve wealth than to create it.

Numerous books tell how to raise children with wealth and how to build values that maximize the use of affluence. We are writing to share Sterling's experiences over the past 29 years in working with high net worth families and the transfer of wealth to their children.

In many families, the discussion of wealth transfer is considered taboo until the time the heir stands to inherit the wealth. This creates a situation in which that person, who may be emotionally unstable due to the loss of a loved one, is forced to make significant financial decisions without proper direction. Education concerning the family's wealth and how to manage it should occur over an extended period of time.

Experience has demonstrated that receiving unrestricted access to wealth at a young age can produce many undesirable results. In response, the definition of a "young age" for our clients has increased over time. A recent trend in wealth transfer is to require minimum ages as old as 40 or 50 before unrestricted access is granted.

Another potential problem is appointing trustees from among friends and loved ones who may not have the expertise required to properly oversee a trust. Blending the responsibilities between corporate trustees and individuals can address this.

Probably the hardest issue to manage is the consumption rate of the family assets. Due to recent economic conditions, many portfolios are smaller and are not producing the returns that existed when lifestyles were being set. This requires honest conversations to reach agreements regarding the level of portfolio consumption that will preserve the family assets for future generations.

A substantial number of estate planning strategies—family limited partnerships, GRITs, GRATs, charitable remainder trusts, ILITS, etc.—can reduce estate taxes and help protect the assets. To determine which of these make sense for your family, we suggest the development of a family vision statement on wealth and a careful analysis of the financial needs of each generation. Discussing wealth within the family can be difficult, but facilitators can assist the process. The balance of the advising team would include an estate attorney, a wealth manager and a tax advisor.

We frequently encounter families who created estate plans more than 10 years ago and who have not updated them since. Make sure an estate plan is updated on a regular basis, especially considering we are in the midst of substantial tax-law changes. ⓦ

"If there's a will, prosperity can't be far behind."
– W.C. Fields

How to reach Timothy E. Flatley

We have offices in both Berwyn and Wilkes-Barre, Pa. Please contact me at 610.560.0400.

Left to right: Robert Orbin, Michelle Smaltz, Timothy E. Flatley, Lisa Curcio and Sean Flatley

Check out the rest of the Sterling team at our website.

About Sterling Investment Advisors Ltd.

Sterling Investment Advisors recognizes that each situation—educating children, building retirement wealth, insuring against loss, reducing taxes, planning estates, setting up trusts, etc.—brings its own complexities. Our team concept results in our clients developing a support group of professionals to delegate the management of these issues. Sterling Investment Advisors, an independent wealth management firm, is recognized as one of the top 10 independent investment advisors in Philadelphia by *Barron's* WCO. The firm was named in the 2009 Philly 100 for the third time in five years; has 29 years of investment experience with an independent orientation; and utilizes proprietary trading strategies, with assets held at Charles Schwab.

Assets Under Management $280 million	**Compensation Method** Asset-based, fixed and hourly fees
Minimum Fee for Initial Meeting None required	**Primary Custodian for Investor Assets** Charles Schwab
Minimum Net Worth Requirement $1 million	**Professional Services Provided** Planning, investment advisory and money management services
Largest Client Net Worth $30 million	**Association Memberships** Association for Corporate Growth
Financial Services Experience 29 years	Website www.sterling-advisors.com	Email flatleyt@sterling-advisors.com

Sterling Investment Advisors Ltd. | 1055 Westlakes Drive, Suite 150, Berwyn, PA 19312 | 610.560.0400 | 877.430.7382

Chicago, IL—Carmel, IN | **Leading Wealth Advisor**

Oxford Financial Group, Ltd.™
Jeffrey H. Thomasson, CFP®
Robert W. Hauswirth, MBA, CFA®, CFP®, CPA, PFS
Charles L. Heekin

" What does it really mean to be an independent financial advisor? "

By Jeffrey H. Thomasson, Robert W. Hauswirth and Charles L. Heekin

The term "independent financial advisor" can mean different things. For some firms, it seems to mean that they do whatever they want—independent, ironically, of their clients' best interests.

Independence, as it relates to financial advisory firms, has three distinct but interconnected facets: independence of advice, independence of ownership, and independence of client experience.

Independence of advice is fairly straightforward: Eliminate conflicts of interest that might affect recommendations made to clients. Truly independent advisors will have no proprietary products and no revenue-sharing agreements with other money managers, will accept no soft dollars or 12b-1 fees, and will have no financial affiliations with other institutions. Their only source of revenue is fee for service. They will have a fiduciary relationship with their clients, and their advice will be determined by their clients' best interests. Period.

Independence of ownership is, at first glance, less straightforward, but equally important. Why? Because the owners of a company ultimately determine how the firm—and all of its divisions—will operate and compete in the industry. Financial advisory firms that are small parts of large institutions compete for corporate resources. They often have financial performance targets and may have to cross-sell other lines of business. Minor shifts in direction at corporate headquarters can affect them.

Independent advisory firms are employee-owned and go to great lengths to ensure they control their own destiny. Independent ownership allows them to focus exclusively on their clients' needs.

Independence of client experience means customized advice that is handcrafted for unique circumstances. Each client has a different set of objectives and constraints, and the right solutions have to be tailored for each one. The best independent advisors will not force clients into model allocations, will not try to mass customize portfolios, and will never recommend a strategy unless it is precisely the right thing for a particular situation.

The next time an advisor touts independence, ask this: What does it really mean to be an independent financial advisor? You will know the answer. But will they? ⓦ

THREE HIDDEN FEES TO WATCH FOR

In a time when asset values are under pressure, many banks, trust companies and wirehouses depend on a variety of fees to support revenue growth from advisory clients. Some of these fees are hidden in places you might not expect, and trying to find them can be like playing a financial version of Where's Waldo.

01 **Custody and trade settlement:** Often, there is an individual "ticket" charge for each trade that is settled in a separately managed account, in addition to a percentage-based custody fee. In high-turnover accounts, these charges can add up quickly.

02 **Internally managed products:** Who in their right mind would pay (or charge) 50 basis points for an internal money market fund? But it happens, and clients often do not notice.

03 **Soft dollars:** These are above-market commissions for trades directed to specific brokers, which are then effectively kicked back to managers to pay for equipment and research services.

"Independence of client experience means customized advice that is handcrafted for unique circumstances."

– Oxford Financial Group, Ltd.

How to reach Oxford Financial Group, Ltd.

To reach Oxford Financial Group, call 317.843.5678 for Jeffrey H. Thomasson or 312.846.6000 for Robert W. Hauswirth and Charles L. Heekin.

MY AREAS OF CHARITY AND COMMUNITY INVOLVEMENT INCLUDE...

Jeffrey: Youth services, humanitarian activities, museums, education, arts and culture

Robert: Education, health and human services, arts and culture

Charles: Arts and education, children's charities and environmental causes

A GOOD WEALTH ADVISOR...

Jeffrey: Sincerely appreciates that clients expect and demand value for their money

Robert: Understands that client relationships are truly the foundation of the business

Charles: Is committed to delivering consistent and unbiased advice

MY HOBBIES ARE...

Jeffrey: Antiques, art collecting, film, painting, opera, music and theater

Robert: Golfing, racquetball, running, biking, theater and film

Charles: Sports, scuba diving, hiking, travel, historical literature and live music

Left to right: Charles L. Heekin, Jeffrey H. Thomasson and Robert W. Hauswirth

About Oxford Financial Group, Ltd.

Founder Jeffrey H. Thomasson is CEO and managing director of Oxford Financial Group, Ltd. He is committed to serving clients' financial and investment planning needs and has been doing so for more than 25 years. He obtained the Certified Financial Planner designation through study in the fields of investment, insurance and retirement and estate planning. He received the Indiana University Kelley School of Business Distinguished Entrepreneur Award. Robert W. Hauswirth is a director in Oxford's Chicago office, where his focus is providing clients with comprehensive investment and financial advice, which he has been doing for more than 15 years. He earned his MBA from Northwestern University's Kellogg School of Management. Charles L. Heekin is a director in Oxford's Chicago office, focusing on business development and advising clients. His experience includes 10 years on Wall Street working in capital markets, advising professional money managers, financial institutions, charities and endowments.

Assets Under Management $8.4 billion (globally)	**Compensation Method** Fixed fees (planning services) and asset-based fees (investment services)
Minimum Fee for Initial Meeting None required	**Primary Custodian for Investor Assets** The Trust Company of Oxford, Fidelity and Schwab
Minimum Net Worth Requirement $5 million (planning services) $2 million (investment services)	**Professional Services Provided** Planning and investment advisory services
Largest Client Net Worth Confidential	Website www.ofgltd.com
Financial Services Experience 64 years (combined)	Email jthomasson@ofgltd.com rhauswirth@ofgltd.com cheekin@ofgltd.com

Oxford Financial Group, Ltd.	980 North Michigan Avenue, Suite 1080, Chicago, IL 60611	312.846.6000
	11711 North Meridian Street, Suite 600, Carmel, IN 46032	317.843.5678

Chicago, IL   **Leading Wealth Advisor**

Harris myCFO™
Kristine M. Givens, CPA, MST, Managing Director

" Is a single family office right for my family? "

By Kristine M. Givens

A family's financial situation generally becomes more complicated when they realize significant wealth from a liquidating event (e.g., selling a business). In addition to making investment decisions at that time, most families review their estate plan and philanthropic goals as well as a myriad of other issues. Some families establish their own single family office to deal with their increased needs; others engage a multifamily office or similar team of advisors.

Families choose to establish their own family office for many reasons. They enjoy running a business. They want to retain control over their wealth. They want the convenience of having an office dedicated to their needs and believe a single family office provides the highest level of confidentiality, independence and advocacy. While these are all compelling reasons favoring a single family office, establishing and maintaining one is expensive.

Forming a single family office requires start-up costs for technology, staffing and facilities. Depending on the services that will be provided to the family, the office may need to invest in technology platforms that track investment performance, assist with cash management and financial planning, pay bills and compile financial statements. Staffing requirements are dictated by the breadth of services provided as well as the complexity and volume of the workload. Lastly, the family will likely need to secure office space. If the family enters into a long-term lease, they need to understand that they are making a commitment that may not be easily undone.

In addition to the start-up costs, families must consider the ongoing cost of maintaining the single family office, as well as operational challenges. In the current market climate, single family offices are evaluating their annual costs. Asset bases have decreased while expenses have remained the same. Family offices often face challenges with attracting and retaining talented professionals because the career paths are limited. Lastly, family offices struggle with remaining a cohesive family unit and transitioning to the next generation.

An alternative to forming a single family office is engaging a multifamily office. Multifamily offices offer integrated services without sacrificing confidentiality, advocacy and independence. Some multifamily offices are the result of a single family office opening its doors to other families to share expenses. Other multifamily offices have developed within financial institutions and wealth management practices. Benefits of the multifamily office include the ability to provide best practices to clients and providing those services more economically than a single family office.

There are many issues to consider in deciding whether a single family office provides the best fit for your family. While realizing that one size does not fit all, if you perform your due diligence while considering your family's goals, you will make the decision that best suits your family. ⓦ

TRENDS IN THE FAMILY OFFICE MARKET

Families are asking themselves whether their current asset base justifies the cost of opening and/or the cost of maintaining a family office. Consequently, we have seen a decline in new single family offices, a consolidation of established offices, and disbandment of some offices. The multifamily office market, on the other hand, has experienced growth in recent years. Even during the last few difficult years, client attrition was reported at less than 3 percent, according to a survey by the Family Wealth Alliance; that speaks volumes about the client satisfaction for families using multifamily offices. Each family's situation differs, but when making a decision about how to deal with your wealth management needs, doing due diligence on all of your available options will provide you with the best picture of what will work best for your family.

> # "Multifamily offices offer integrated services without sacrificing confiden-tiality, advocacy and independence."
> – Kristine M. Givens

How to reach Kristine M. Givens

Call me to schedule a convenient time to meet and discuss your personal situation. You can reach me at 312.461.5066.

WHAT'S ON MY DESK...

Pictures of my daughter

I NEVER LEAVE HOME WITHOUT...

My wallet, cell phone and BlackBerry

MY HOBBIES ARE...

Reading, golf and exercising

About Kristine M. Givens

Kristine M. Givens is a managing director and the head of the Chicago Family Office Services team for Harris myCFO, where she oversees the delivery of family office services to individuals and families with significant wealth. She has more than 20 years of tax experience with a focus on single family offices and multigenerational families. Ms. Givens, a CPA, received her undergraduate degree from Purdue University and obtained an MS in taxation from DePaul University. She is a member of the Chicago Finance Exchange and Illinois CPA Society. She also serves on the board of directors for Chicago-based Metropolitan Family Services.

Assets Under Management $16.4 billion	**Compensation Method** Asset-based, fixed and hourly fees
Minimum Fee for Initial Meeting None required	**Primary Custodian for Investor Assets** Multiple, please inquire
Minimum Net Worth Requirement $100 million	**Professional Services Provided** Planning and investment advisory services
Largest Client Net Worth $1 billion+	**Association Memberships** AICPA, Chicago Finance Exchange, Illinois CPA Society
Financial Services Experience 20 years	**Website** www.harrismycfo.com **Email** kristine.givens@harrismycfo.com

AUM figures are as of 6/30/10 and are applicable to Harris myCFO IAS LLC and certain divisions of Harris N.A. that do business under the brand name Harris myCFO™. All other information is combined for all entities and lines of business under the Harris myCFO™ brand.

Harris myCFO™ | 111 West Monroe Street, Suite 10E, Chicago, IL 60603 | 312.461.5066

San Francisco—Bay Area, CA | **Leading Wealth Advisor**

Harris myCFO™
Ron Gong, CPA, Managing Director

" How can I effectively coordinate advice from multiple advisors to ensure their strategies are aligned with my family's goals? "

By Ron Gong

When working with several advisors who specialize in different aspects of your financial picture, you may tend to view your wealth in separate compartments or silos. You rely on your CPA to provide tax compliance, consulting and financial reporting; your estate planning attorney to work on your family structure; your insurance agent to perform an annual checkup; and your portfolio managers to assist the family in determining your asset allocation and investment strategy. This silo approach may work when you dedicate the required time as the family's financial quarterback, but if you aspire to goals of efficiency, effective communication and excellent results, you might undertake a different, more integrated approach.

Employing an integrated approach in serving affluent families is becoming a trend in the wealth management industry. While you strive to work with best-of-class providers for every aspect of your wealth management strategy, you should not underestimate the importance of making sure these advisors understand how the other interdependent parts operate. This comprehensive approach should create a like-minded strategic vision across multiple generations for the family and foster coordinated advice based on knowledge of the entire situation.

The effectiveness of an integrated wealth management approach can be illustrated in our execution of an asset substitution during the annuity term of a grantor retained annuity trust (GRAT)—five months into the life of the GRAT. This action locked in significant appreciation for ultimate transfer to the trust's remainder beneficiaries. In this case, the trust's portfolio assets were closely monitored, the assets to be substituted were identified, valuations were completed, tax reporting was documented, and the transfer was completed within a few days. The client simply agreed to the idea and the work was performed. Having a multidisciplinary team thinking of the family's situation in a holistic manner made this successful transfer possible. It also highlights that unless constant close attention is paid to the planning put in place, opportunities can be easily overlooked.

Financial integration mandates that your trusted wealth management advisors work seamlessly as a unified team to collaborate and render advice with one voice. In this model, it is paramount that the family's goals and objectives come first. Ⓦ

TRUSTED ADVICE

Over the past several years, the challenging economy dramatically changed the role and expectations of a trusted advisor. More than ever, clients are seeking advice from individuals and companies that do not sell their own financial products and can therefore provide an objective viewpoint.

When families seek trusted advice, we encourage them to closely examine their advisor relationships and perform due diligence to ensure that fee structures are transparent and that no conflicts of interest exist.

"Employing an integrated approach in serving affluent families is becoming a trend in the wealth management industry."

– Ron Gong

How to reach Ron Gong

I prefer face-to-face meetings with prospective clients. Please feel free to call me at 650.210.5182.

WHAT'S ON MY DESK...

Tax returns for review, a client's house construction plans and project folders

I NEVER LEAVE HOME WITHOUT...

Saying good-bye to my two daughters

MY HOBBIES ARE...

Cars, tech gadgets and enjoying my salt-water reef tank

About Ron Gong

Ron Gong is a managing director with Harris myCFO Inc. for the Menlo Park, Calif., and San Francisco offices. He is responsible for the design and implementation of comprehensive family office solutions with a focus on multigenerational wealth planning. Mr. Gong advises clients on a broad range of tax and financial matters, including pre-liquidity transactions planning, technology-related merger and acquisitions, executive compensation, stock options and family succession planning. He joined Harris myCFO in 2000 and has more than 22 years of experience. He is a member of the organization's Executive Management Committee. Mr. Gong is a member of the American Institute of Certified Public Accountants and California Society of CPAs. He earned a bachelor's degree in accounting and business administration from Fresno State University in California.

Assets Under Management **$16.4 billion**	Compensation Method **Asset-based and fixed fees**
Minimum Fee for Initial Meeting **None required**	Primary Custodian for Investor Assets **Multiple, please inquire**
Minimum Net Worth Requirement **$100 million**	Professional Services Provided **Planning and investment advisory services**
Largest Client Net Worth **$1 billion+**	Association Memberships **AICPA, California Society of CPAs**
Financial Services Experience **22 years**	Website **www.harrismycfo.com** Email **ron.gong@harrismycfo.com**

AUM figures are as of 6/30/10 and are applicable to Harris myCFO IAS LLC and certain divisions of Harris N.A. that do business under the brand name Harris myCFO™. All other information is combined for all entities and lines of business under the Harris myCFO™ brand.

Harris myCFO™ | 1080 Marsh Road, Suite 100, Menlo Park, CA 94025 | 650.210.5000

New York, NY   Leading Wealth Advisor

The Mahoney Team at Morgan Stanley Smith Barney
Scott F. Mahoney, CPWA℠, Senior Vice President,
Senior Portfolio Manager, Family Wealth Director

" How do I know if my financial advisor is adding value to my portfolio? "

By Scott F. Mahoney

THE DIFFERENCE BETWEEN ALPHA AND BETA

Savvy investors know that alpha and beta are not only the first two letters in the Greek alphabet, they help distinguish between the returns generated on investments. When you fully understand the difference between the two you can more easily recognize if your financial advisor is adding value to your portfolio. And today, with so many prepackaged investments to choose from, seeking alpha can prove to be more important, and harder, than ever before.

Simply put, beta measures how much an asset moves in response to common, cyclical market risks and reflects the return achieved as a result of that movement. Alpha is additional return achieved as a result of security-selection skill—the extra value an active portfolio manager brings to your portfolio. This essay is not intended to make you an expert on alpha and beta; rather I hope it gives you enough information and confidence to ask the right questions of your advisor and to understand what you are paying for when you enlist financial assistance.

A Little History. Knowing the origin of alpha may help you get a clearer understanding of the difference between alpha and beta. Prior to the advent of capital-weighted equity indexes, all returns were viewed as alpha. A stockbroker would buy and sell stocks based on research. If a broker made you money, then you could say alpha was generated. The S&P 500 index would soon make it more difficult for this broker, because now returns would need to be in excess of the index. The return generated by the index would become known as beta.

Today you can find a comparable index for nearly every type of investment. There are indexes for growth and value stocks, corporate and government bonds, commodities, real estate and hedge funds to name a few. With so much beta available, it is no wonder why investors need to look closer and work harder to find alpha.

Finding Alpha. Finding alpha in your portfolio lies in understanding what is happening in the financial markets and how your portfolio will be impacted. For instance, advisors should actively seek out dislocations in the market and take advantage of them. An example of a dislocation occurred between the end of 2008 and the first quarter of 2009. During that period of time, high-quality corporate bonds were selling at 25 to 50 percent discounts. This created an opportunity for investors to buy low-risk investments at unusually high levels of potential returns. As a result, corporate bond managers who took advantage of this market dislocation provided alpha by showing returns in excess of 20 percent.

Given today's diverse investment resources, your advisor is probably using beta to help you at least keep up with the markets. How do you find out if the advisor is also seeking alpha? First discuss investment strategies for your personal financial situation. Then ask what potential market dislocation might create short-lived buying and selling opportunities. That will illustrate that your advisor is poised to make adjustments to your portfolio at the appropriate time. That will also help you justify paying higher fees for the extra value your advisor is providing.

The markets continue to change at an increasingly rapid pace, and your portfolio needs to change with the markets. With the right tools, good research and the opportunity to invest in different markets, an advisor can help you find alpha and capitalize on it. ⓦ

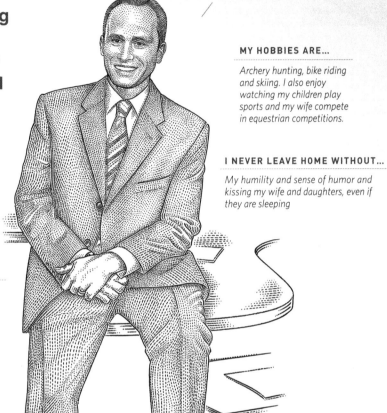

"Finding alpha in your portfolio lies in understanding what is happening in the financial markets and how your portfolio will be impacted."

– Scott F. Mahoney

How to reach Scott F. Mahoney

If you would like to learn more about alpha and beta, please give me a call at 866.932.3032. I have clients around the country and would be glad to talk over the phone or meet with you in person.

MY HOBBIES ARE...

Archery hunting, bike riding and skiing. I also enjoy watching my children play sports and my wife compete in equestrian competitions.

I NEVER LEAVE HOME WITHOUT...

My humility and sense of humor and kissing my wife and daughters, even if they are sleeping

WHAT'S ON MY DESK...

A thriving green plant my mom gave me when I got my first job—in 1991; a photo of my wife jumping over an oxer with her horse; and a notebook with my favorite quote on the cover: "Winners always want to have the ball in their hands when the game is on the line"

About Scott F. Mahoney

Raised in a working-class home with solid values, Mr. Mahoney was fortunate to get a great education and launch a career that lets him help people navigate through their life cycle of wealth. Determined to provide the highest level of service, he has assembled a team of professionals, each of whom shares his vision and passion for excellence. Together, they represent some of America's finest families, who inspire them by their life stories and philanthropic activities. Mr. Mahoney and his team have access to world-class intellectual capital and financial planning tools that enable them to customize every service they provide. Their clients are as close to them as family.

Assets Under Management
$240 million

Minimum Fee for Initial Meeting
None required

Minimum Net Worth Requirement
$2.5 million

Largest Client Net Worth
$100 million+

Financial Services Experience
18 years

Compensation Method **Asset-based fees**

Primary Custodian for Investor Assets **Morgan Stanley Smith Barney**

Professional Services Provided **Planning, investment advisory, money management and philanthropy services**

Association Memberships **IMCA, PMI**

Website
morganstanley.com/fa/themahoneyteam

Email
scott.mahoney@mssb.com

The Mahoney Team at Morgan Stanley Smith Barney | 1200 Mt. Kemble Avenue, 2nd Floor, Morristown, NJ 07962 | 866.932.3032